D1084873

DIRECTORY OF
CAMPUS-BUSINESS LINKAGES

DIRECTORY
OF
CAMPUS-BUSINESS
LINKAGES

Education and Business Prospering Together

Edited by

Dorothy C. Fenwick

AMERICAN COUNCIL ON EDUCATION/MACMILLAN
NEW YORK

Collier Macmillan Publishers
LONDON

Copyright © 1983 by Macmillan Publishing Company and American Council on Education

The American Council on Education/Macmillan Series in Higher Education

Macmillan Publishing Company
A Division of Macmillan, Inc.
866 Third Avenue
New York, NY 10022

Collier Macmillan Canada, Inc.

Library of Congress Catalog Card Number: 83-10018

Printed in the United States of America

printing number

1 2 3 4 5 6 7 8 9 10

Library of Congress Cataloging in Publication Data

Fenwick, Dorothy C.

   Directory of campus-business linkages.

   (The American Council on Education/Macmillan series in higher education)
   Includes indexes.
      1. Industry and education—United States—Directories. 2. Industry—United
States—Directories. 3. Business—United States—Directories. I. American
Council on Education. II. Title. III. Series.
L901.F418   1983   378'.103   83-10018
ISBN 0-02-910540-4 (Macmillan)

CONTENTS

v

PREFACE AND ACKNOWLEDGMENTS

In a system as vast and decentralized as American Education, productive ideas and useful examples, not mandate or fiat, are the impetus to progress and innovation. In his famous report on public high schools, James Conant, the distinguished scientist, statesman and university president singled out for special recognition a directory of innovative programs. He called on persons in education to be enterprising enough to adapt creative ideas to their own institutions.

This Directory of Campus-Business Linkages is similar to Conant's with its focus on college administrators, faculty and staff who are looking for ways to work with business and industry. With this use in mind, essential information is presented concisely and in a consistent format; the information should be sufficient to let a reader decide whether to write or call to learn more about the program or activity. In short, the standard for this volume is to have it meet Conant's test of sparking interest and action about educational possibilities.

The Directory contains examples of collaborative programs between post-secondary education and business, where they are located, who developed them and basic information about content, cost and participants. This Directory is not designed to be the definitive document on all that exists in the area of training and development and its relationship with post-secondary education. It is designed, however, to provide examples of creative interaction between two separate entities.

Taken as a whole, the Directory indicates programmatic trends nationally and presents a perspective on current linkage activities. It may serve as a reference on the activity of other institutions in nearby states or regions. It could establish benchmarks to be used by administrators to evaluate the status of their current programs.

The Directory can provide tangible evidence to local businesses or Boards of Trustees of programs outside the traditional academic arena which meet their needs efficiently and in a cost-effective manner.

There should be no doubt about the importance of joint ventures in education. Broad agreement exists that education and the workplace have too long been strangers to each other. It is becoming increasingly clear that the nation's economic vitality depends on the continued growth and learning of its citizens. Joint ventures contribute importantly to that purpose.

Acknowledgment is made to John Sullivan and Ann Lee for their special contributions to the Directory. Special recognition is made to Sylvia Lagerquist who supervised the development of the manuscript from concept to finished product.

The Directory of Campus-Business Linkages was funded, in part, by Mountain States Telephone and Telegraph Company. Our sincere appreciation goes to Fred Wells and his staff of the Mountain Bell Training and Education Center.

Dorothy C. Fenwick
January, 1983

HOW TO USE THIS DIRECTORY

The Directory is unique in that the data is self-reported; that is, each of the items reflects the objectives which both the institution and the company built into the activity; a self-reported perception of the collaborative program.

Each subsection of the program description provides, as concisely as possible, information which the reader can use to determine if further investigation would be worthwhile.

Institutional contacts include name, title, organization, mailing address and telephone number. This data was considered vital for the person who uses the Directory as a reference for new ideas and compensates for the limited space given to program description. Both contact persons are provided so that the reader may discuss the program with both the provider and the client for a thorough understanding of program potential. The point-of-contact information permits the reader to investigate more thoroughly those programs which appear to be of interest.

Program description/objectives gives limited information but provides an indication of the needs of the company and the institutional resources utilized.

The next five parts of the entry provide, as systematically as possible, elements which a reader interested in adopting or adapting similar programs would need. The date the program was initiated provides the immedia y of the program; time required of participant is of importance to the employee as well as employer. The length of the contract is information useful to an administrator developing contractual agreements while the location and number of participants are necessary data in light of the institutional concerns which must also be included in a planning cycle.

Program costs are given as percentages or in dollars. In some cases, true costs may be difficult to estimate given the intricacies of the institutional budget. The choice was given so that institutions would feel free to share the approximate costs and provide the reader with the financial implications as well as provide guidelines for establishing program costs.

The last part indicates the availability of additional information upon request. This is designed to encourage future investigation of those programs which may be of interest to the reader. The reader also needs to consider, in deciding on whether to investigate further a specific example, the following questions:

Do you have the resources within your institution that match the resources being utilized by a college in the Directory and/or do you have the adaptive capability?

Is there an identified need that is addressed by a Directory example?

Does your institutional mission encourage outreach to clientele which, heretofore, were not considered as likely collegiate participants?

What types of programs would appear to receive significant financial assistance from business? Is it possible to tap into that stream of income for your institution as you consider possible new directions?

What about your current cooperative education programs? Are there ideas here in the many examples of cooperative education you may be able to replicate or adapt to your institution?

These are representative of the types of questions which need to be asked as you read about the programs listed in the Directory.

The last section of the Directory contains indexes which categorize entries by state, by the name of the institution with which the company has an agreement, or by name of organization. Entries are also indexed by subject matter (Career Transition, Energy) and by the range and type (cooperative programs, use of facilities).

The last page of the Directory, the Self-Reporting Form, provides an opportunity for the readers to describe their own collaborative programs. Tear out the page, complete according to directions and mail to the address printed on the form. This information will be collected and published in the 2nd edition of the Directory, 1984.

CAMPUS-BUSINESS LINKAGES:

Education and Business Prospering Together

1. A-1 STONE AND MASONRY
        with
    CALIFORNIA BAPTIST COLLEGE

BS DEGREE FOR BUSINESS
EXECUTIVES

COMPANY CONTACT:
Bob Pentz
President
A-1 Stone and Masonry
9660 Arlington Avenue
Riverside, CA   92504

INSTITUTIONAL CONTACT:
Bob Jabs
Business Administration
California Baptist College
8432 Magnolia
Riverside, CA   92504
(714) 689-5771

PROGRAM DESCRIPTION/OBJECTIVES:
Opportunity for company employees to pursue coursework
towards an undergraduate degree
in business.

PROGRAM INITIATED: 1982

LENGTH OF STUDY FOR PARTICI-
PANT: 18 months

LENGTH OF CONTRACT: 18 months

LOCATION: On campus

PARTICIPANTS: 25 employees

PROGRAM COSTS PROVIDED BY:
Institution: $2500 per person
Company: $2500 per person

PRINTED MATERIALS AVAILABLE
FROM: Institution

2. ADAMS-RUSSELL, HEWLETT
    PACKARD AND MICROWAVE
    ASSOCIATES
        with
    TUFTS UNIVERSITY

MICROWAVE ENGINEERS

COMPANY CONTACT:
John Gillespie, Jr.
Bay State Skills Corporation
        representing
Adams-Russell, Hewlett Packard
and Microwave Associates
McCormack Office Building
One Ashburton Place
Room 2110
Boston, MA   02108
(617) 727-5431

INSTITUTIONAL CONTACT:
Arthur Uhlir
Department of Electrical
Engineering
Tufts University
Medford, MA   02155
(617) 628-5000

PROGRAM DESCRIPTION/OBJECTIVES:
A graduate level program in
microwave engineering specialist training.

PROGRAM INITIATED: 1982

LENGTH OF STUDY FOR PARTICI-
PANT: 1 academic year

LENGTH OF CONTRACT: 14 months

LOCATION: Tufts University

PARTICIPANTS: 16 engineers

PROGRAM COSTS PROVIDED BY:
Institution: $38,686
Company: $48,850
Other Source: $48,121 (Bay
State Skills Corporation)

PRINTED MATERIALS AVAILABLE
FROM: Company

3. ADVANCED TECHNOLOGY LABS
          with
      SEATTLE COMMUNITY COLLEGE
      DISTRICT

ELECTRONICS TRAINING PROGRAM

COMPANY CONTACT:
David Kinne
Advanced Technology Labs
13208 Northrup Way
Bellevue, WA   98905
(206) 641-5410

INSTITUTIONAL CONTACT:
Thomas F. Ris
Director
Contract Education Service
Seattle Community College
District
Seattle, WA   98119
(206) 587-4199

PROGRAM DESCRIPTION/OBJECTIVES:
To use resources at a time when
state funding was cut to train
entry level, CETA-eligible employees and upgrade women by
using district's expertise and
resources in the field of high
technology.

PROGRAM INITIATED: 1981

LENGTH OF STUDY FOR PARTICI-
PANT: 1 academic year

LENGTH OF CONTRACT: 2 years

LOCATION: North Seattle Community College

PARTICIPANTS: 70 pre- and on-
job trainees in high technology areas

PROGRAM COSTS PROVIDED BY:
Company: $23,500

PRINTED MATERIALS AVAILABLE
FROM: Not available

4. AKRON CITY HOSPITAL
          with
      KENT STATE UNIVERSITY

MANAGEMENT DEVELOPMENT PROGRAM

COMPANY CONTACT:
Ralph DeCristoforo
Akron City Hospital
525 East Market
Akron, OH   44309
(216) 375-3121

INSTITUTIONAL CONTACT:
Karen Rylander
Director, Continuing Education
Kent State University
327 Rockwell Hall
Kent, OH   44242
(216) 672-3100

PROGRAM DESCRIPTION/OBJECTIVES:
Pragmatic approach to the following management concepts:
planning and control, motivation, leadership and conflict
resolution, organizational
communications, decision making.

PROGRAM INITIATED: 1982

LENGTH OF STUDY FOR PARTICI-
PANT: 20 hours

LENGTH OF CONTRACT: 20 hours

LOCATION: Local hotel

PARTICIPANTS: 90 department
managers

PROGRAM COSTS PROVIDED BY:
Company: 100%

PRINTED MATERIALS AVAILABLE
FROM: Institution

5. AKRON CITY HOSPITAL
           with
    KENT STATE UNIVERSITY

SUPERVISORY DEVELOPMENT PROGRAM

COMPANY CONTACT:
Ralph DeCristoforo
Akron City Hospital
525 East Market
Akron, OH   44309
(216) 375-3121

INSTITUTIONAL CONTACT:
Karen Rylander
Director, Continuing Education
Kent State University
327 Rockwell Hall
Kent, OH   44242
(216) 672-3100

PROGRAM DESCRIPTION/OBJECTIVES:
Pragmatic approach to the following management concepts:
planning and control, motivation, leadership and conflict
resolution, organizational communications, decision making.

PROGRAM INITIATED: 1982

LENGTH OF STUDY FOR PARTICI-
PANT: 20 hours

LENGTH OF CONTRACT: 20 hours

LOCATION: Local hotel

PARTICIPANTS: 140 department
supervisors

PROGRAM COSTS PROVIDED BY:
Company: 100%

PRINTED MATERIALS AVAILABLE
FROM: Institution

6. ALABAMA DEPARTMENT OF
    MENTAL HEALTH
           with
    ALABAMA DEPARTMENT OF
    EDUCATION

ALABAMA MENTAL HEALTH TECHNOLOGY
LINKAGE PROGRAM

COMPANY CONTACT:
Helen Paulette Brignet
Human Resource Development
Specialist
Office of Planning and Staff
Development
Alabama Department of Mental
Health
Montgomery, AL   36130
(205) 834-4350

INSTITUTIONAL CONTACT:
Howard Gundy
Chancellor
Postsecondary Education
Alabama Department of Education
817 South Court Street
Montgomery, AL   36104
(205) 832-3340

PROGRAM DESCRIPTION/OBJECTIVES:
To upgrade work skills of incum-
bent human services workers in
the Alabama Department of
Mental Health.

PROGRAM INITIATED: 1978

LENGTH OF STUDY FOR PARTICI-
PANT: 2 academic years

LENGTH OF CONTRACT: 1 year
with renewal option

LOCATION: 5 community colleges
and 9 Department of Mental
Health facilities

PARTICIPANTS: Approximately
100 employees of the Alabama
Department of Mental Health

PROGRAM COSTS PROVIDED BY:
Institution: Employee release
time
Company: Record keeping,
facility supervision
Participant: Books

PRINTED MATERIALS AVAILABLE
FROM: Company

7. ALABAMA POWER COMPANY*
                with
    MISSISSIPPI STATE UNIVERSITY

COOPERATIVE EDUCATION PROGRAM

COMPANY CONTACT:
Jane Jackson
Cooperative Education
Coordinator
Alabama Power Company
P.O. Box 2641
Birmingham, AL   35291
(205) 250-1000, X3568

INSTITUTIONAL CONTACT:
Luther Epting
Director of Cooperative
Education
Mississippi State University
P.O. Box M
Mississippi State, MS   39762
(601) 325-3823

PROGRAM DESCRIPTION/OBJECTIVES:
To provide students an opportunity to receive relevant work
experience directly related to
the major field of study; to
provide employing organizations
a quality source of motivated
mature employees that may be
retained at graduation.

PROGRAM INITIATED: 1955

LENGTH OF STUDY FOR PARTICI-
PANT: Alternate semesters of
school and work, 5 years total

LENGTH OF CONTRACT: No formal
contract required

LOCATION: Throughout the
United States

PARTICIPANTS: 412 students of
various majors except architecture annually**

PROGRAM COSTS PROVIDED BY:
Institution: $187.67 per
student
Company: Pays students a
salary plus fringe benefits

PRINTED MATERIALS AVAILABLE
FROM: Institution

---

*Representative entry--complete
list available from institution.

**Figures given reflect the
entire program.

8. ALUMINUM COMPANY OF AMERICA
                with
        MARYVILLE COLLEGE

AFFILIATE ARTISTS

COMPANY CONTACT:
Elton R. Jones
Manager, Tennessee Public
Relations
Aluminum Company of America
P.O. Box 9128
Alcoa, TN   37701
(615) 977-3490

INSTITUTIONAL CONTACT:
Robert A. Ellis, Jr.
Vice President for Development
Maryville College
Maryville, TN   37801
(615) 982-6412

PROGRAM DESCRIPTION/OBJECTIVES:
To expand audiences for the performing arts, to support the
career development of young professional performers, and to offer American business the opportunity to invest in the cultural
life of the communities.

PROGRAM INITIATED: 1981

LENGTH OF STUDY FOR PARTICI-
PANT: 49 days

LENGTH OF CONTRACT: 7 months

LOCATION: Maryville College

PARTICIPANTS: 1 invited
lecturer

PROGRAM COSTS PROVIDED BY:
Institution: $5,739.47

PRINTED MATERIALS AVAILABLE
FROM: Institution

9. ALUMINUM COMPANY OF AMERICA
    ROCKDALE WORKS
            with
    TEXAS STATE TECHNICAL INSTITUTE

APPRENTICE TRAINING PROGRAM

COMPANY CONTACT:
Edwin E. Remaley
Works Mechanical Maintenance
Supervisor
ALCOA-Aluminum Company of America
P.O. Box 472
Rockdale, TX   76567
(512) 466-5811

INSTITUTIONAL CONTACT:
J. Don Pierson
Coordinator of Curriculum
Instructional Administration
Department
Texas State Technical Institute
Waco, TX   76705
(817) 799-3611, X293

PROGRAM DESCRIPTION/OBJECTIVES:
To provide ALCOA Rockdale Works
with an effective apprentice
training program that is
Rockdale Works job oriented
and emphasizes job performance.

PROGRAM INITIATED: 1981

LENGTH OF STUDY FOR PARTICI-
PANT: 6,000 hours

LENGTH OF CONTRACT: Quarterly
with renewal options

LOCATION: Rockdale, TX

PARTICIPANTS: 10-50 craft
apprentices in 11 craft areas

PROGRAM COSTS PROVIDED BY:
Company: 100%

PRINTED MATERIALS AVAILABLE
FROM: Institution and Company

10. AMERICAN ASSOCIATION OF
     RAILROADS
            with
     POLICE TRAINING INSTITUTE
     UNIVERSITY OF ILLINOIS

SPECIALIZED TRAINING FOR
RAILROAD POLICE OFFICERS

COMPANY CONTACT:
Jesse E. Williamson
Director of Training and
Project Development
Operations and Maintenance
Department
Association of American
Railroads
1920 I Street, NW
Washington, DC   20036
(202) 835-9288

INSTITUTIONAL CONTACT:
Clifford W. Van Meter
Director
Police Training Institute
University of Illinois
725 South Wright Street
Room 341
Champaign, IL   61820
(217) 333-2337

PROGRAM DESCRIPTION/OBJECTIVES:
Provide specialized police
training to meet various needs
of railroad police officers.

PROGRAM INITIATED: 1981

LENGTH OF STUDY FOR PARTICI-
PANT: Normally 1 week
(40 hours)

LENGTH OF CONTRACT: No ongoing
contract exists

LOCATION: Police Training
Institute

PARTICIPANTS: 100 police
officers

PROGRAM COSTS PROVIDED BY:
Company: 100%

PRINTED MATERIALS AVAILABLE
FROM: Institution

11. AMERICAN FLETCHER NATIONAL
     BANK
              with
     INDIANA VOCATIONAL
     TECHNICAL COLLEGE

CUSTOMER SERVICE/ASSISTANT CER-
TIFICATION PROGRAM, MANAGEMENT
TRAINING

COMPANY CONTACT:
Deanne Lane
Manager of Training
AFNB Training Center
American Fletcher National Bank
5704 West 86th Street
Indianapolis, IN   46278
(317) 639-7692

INSTITUTIONAL CONTACT:
Sue Beard
Director, Extended Services
Indiana Vocational Technical
College
1315 East Washington Street
Indianapolis, IN   46202
(317) 635-6100, X68

PROGRAM DESCRIPTION/OBJECTIVES:
To provide communication, human
relations, and management
skills for banking center managers and customer service
personnel.

PROGRAM INITIATED: 1981

LENGTH OF STUDY FOR PARTICI-
PANT: Not reported

LENGTH OF CONTRACT: 12 months
renewable

LOCATION: American Fletcher
National Bank

PARTICIPANTS: 550 managers
and customer service personnel

PROGRAM COSTS PROVIDED BY:
Company: 100%

PRINTED MATERIALS AVAILABLE
FROM: Not available

12. AMERICAN HEART ASSOCIATION
              with
     CENTRAL MICHIGAN
     UNIVERSITY*

TOWARD STRONG MANAGEMENT IN
THE VOLUNTARY SECTOR

COMPANY CONTACT:
Susan Calkin
Associate Project Director
Degree Program (Training)
American Heart Association
7320 Greenville Avenue
Dallas, TX   75231
(214) 750-5329

INSTITUTIONAL CONTACT:
Larry Murphy
Director, Institute for
Personal and Career Development
              and
John Schleede
Professor of Marketing
School of Business
Administration
Central Michigan University
Mt. Pleasant, MI   44859
(517) 774-3865

PROGRAM DESCRIPTION/OBJECTIVES:
To establish a behaviorally
based master's degree program
in voluntary agency management
designed to meet the needs of
the practitioner.

PROGRAM INITIATED: 1982

LENGTH OF STUDY FOR PARTICI-
PANT: 3 years

LENGTH OF CONTRACT: 3-year
FIPSE grant

LOCATION: Varies, all over
the country

PARTICIPANTS: 30 students per
year + managers and staff

PROGRAM COSTS PROVIDED BY:
Company: 50%
Participant: 50%

PRINTED MATERIALS AVAILABLE
FROM: Company

---

*Representative entry--complete
list available from institution.

13. AMERICAN INSTITUTE OF
    BANKING
            with
    MARSHALL UNIVERSITY

AMERICAN INSTITUTE OF BANKING

COMPANY CONTACT:
Ben Meredith
President, AIB Chapter
First Bank Cerido
P.O. Box 607
Cerido, WV   25507
(304) 453-1301

INSTITUTIONAL CONTACT:
Paul D. Hines
Vice President/Dean
Community College
Marshall University
16th Street and Hal Greer Blvd.
Huntington, WV   25701
(304) 696-3646

PROGRAM DESCRIPTION/OBJECTIVES:
To provide area bank employees
with the skills needed to function more effectively in their
positions.

PROGRAM INITIATED: 1976

LENGTH OF STUDY FOR PARTICI-
PANT: 1 semester at a time

LENGTH OF CONTRACT: 1 year,
renewable

LOCATION: Marshall University

PARTICIPANTS: 100 bank employees annually

PROGRAM COSTS PROVIDED BY:
Company: 100%

PRINTED MATERIALS AVAILABLE
FROM: Not available

14. AMERICAN INSTITUTE OF
    BANKING (WASHINGTON
    CHAPTER)
            with
    MONTGOMERY COLLEGE

BANKING AND FINANCIAL
MANAGEMENT

COMPANY CONTACT:
Jean Bathurst
Executive Director
American Institute of Banking
5010 Wisconsin Avenue
Suite B-8
Washington, DC   20016
(202) 362-5510

INSTITUTIONAL CONTACT:
Fred Saint
Instructional Dean
Department of Applied Sciences
Montgomery College
Takoma Park, MD   20012
(301) 587-4090

PROGRAM DESCRIPTION/OBJECTIVES:
To provide an opportunity for
people in banking to receive
college credit for evaluated
AIB courses toward an Associate
in Arts degree from Montgomery
College.

PROGRAM INITIATED: 1982

LENGTH OF STUDY FOR PARTICI-
PANT: Differs with each
individual

LENGTH OF CONTRACT: Ongoing

LOCATION: Takoma Park and
Germantown campuses

PARTICIPANTS: Unknown

PROGRAM COSTS PROVIDED BY:
Company: Tuition may be reimbursed by company
Participant: Tuition based on
student residence

PRINTED MATERIALS AVAILABLE
FROM: Institution

15. AMERICAN INTERNATIONAL
    GROUP, INC.
          with
    BOROUGH OF MANHATTAN
    COMMUNITY COLLEGE

SHORT TERM TRAINING FOR AMERICAN
INTERNATIONAL GROUP, INC.

COMPANY CONTACT:
Jannette Porta-Avalos
Training Specialist
American International Group, Inc.
70 Pine Street
New York, NY   10270
(212) 770-5107

INSTITUTIONAL CONTACT:
Sylvia Seidmann
Director of Company Training
Borough of Manhattan Community
College
1633 Broadway
New York, NY   10019
(212) 262-2675

PROGRAM DESCRIPTION/OBJECTIVES:
To upgrade the educational
level of employees in basic
studies and office skills.

PROGRAM INITIATED: 1981

LENGTH OF STUDY FOR PARTICI-
PANT: 1 semester

LENGTH OF CONTRACT: 12 months

LOCATION: American International
Group

PARTICIPANTS: 300 clerical and
secretarial employees annually

PROGRAM COSTS PROVIDED BY:
Other Source: $53,000 (voca-
tional education grant from
Albany)

PRINTED MATERIALS AVAILABLE
FROM: Institution

16. AT&T
          with
    MIDDLESEX COUNTY COLLEGE

CORPORATE COLLEGE

COMPANY CONTACT:
Diane Dorer
Personnel Department
Corporate Education Center
AT&T
P.O. Box 2016
New Brunswick, NJ   08903
(201) 699-2078

INSTITUTIONAL CONTACT:
Barbara L. Greene
Director of Extension Operations
Division of Continuing Education
Middlesex County College
Edison, NJ   08818
(201) 549-9898

PROGRAM DESCRIPTION/OBJECTIVES:
To provide college credit
courses that address job skills
for employees at work site.
Program generally addresses
management skills with supple-
mentary accounting and liberal
arts courses.

PROGRAM INITIATED: 1968

LENGTH OF STUDY FOR PARTICI-
PANT: 1 semester to duration
of program

LENGTH OF CONTRACT: Duration
of employee interest

LOCATION: Corporate premises

PARTICIPANTS: 50 management
and accounting personnel per
semester

PROGRAM COSTS PROVIDED BY:
Institution: Salaries and
administrative overhead
Company: Usually 100%
Participant: Usually reimbursed

PRINTED MATERIALS AVAILABLE
FROM: Institution

17. AMERICAN WATCHMAKERS
    INSTITUTE
    with
    OKLAHOMA STATE TECH

AMERICAN WATCHMAKERS INSTITUTE
SOLID STATE WATCH REPAIR SEMINAR
AND WORKSHOP SERIES

COMPANY CONTACT:
Milton Stevens
Executive Secretary
American Watchmakers Institute
P.O. Box 11011
Cincinnati, OH   45211
(513) 661-3838

INSTITUTIONAL CONTACT:
Gray Lawrence
Supervisor, Watch Micro-
Instrument and Jewelry
Small Business Trades Department
Oklahoma State Tech
4th and Mission
Okmulgee, OK   74447
(918) 756-6211, X271

PROGRAM DESCRIPTION/OBJECTIVES:
To upgrade skills and knowledge
of watchmakers and students in
repair of current styles of
watches and provide student opportunities for contact with
potential employer.

PROGRAM INITIATED: 1972

LENGTH OF STUDY FOR PARTICI-
PANT: Not reported

LENGTH OF CONTRACT: Not
reported

LOCATION: Not reported

PARTICIPANTS: 64

PROGRAM COSTS PROVIDED BY:
Company: 100%

PRINTED MATERIALS AVAILABLE
FROM: Institution

18. AMOCO PIPELINE COMPANY
    with
    OKLAHOMA STATE TECH

DIGITAL LOGIC

COMPANY CONTACT:
James R. Polston
Manager
AMOCO Pipeline Company
401 Eisenhower Lane
Lombard, IL   60148
(312) 932-5530

INSTITUTIONAL CONTACT:
Bill J. Lyons
Department Head
Electrical-Electronic
Technology
Oklahoma State Tech
4th and Mission
Okmulgee, OK   74447
(918) 756-6211, X252

PROGRAM DESCRIPTION/OBJECTIVES
Provide an educational background that enables AMOCO employees to be more receptive to
specialized training courses by
the company.

PROGRAM INITIATED: 1978

LENGTH OF STUDY FOR PARTICI-
PANT: Not reported

LENGTH OF CONTRACT: Not
reported

LOCATION: Not reported

PARTICIPANTS: 40-50

PROGRAM COSTS PROVIDED BY:
Company: 100%

PRINTED MATERIALS AVAILABLE
FROM: Not available

19. AMPEX CORPORATION
with
COLLEGE OF SAN MATEO

ELECTRONIC UPGRADE

COMPANY CONTACT:
Margaret Meyer
Personnel Training
Ampex Corporation
401 Broadway
Redwood City, CA   04063
(415) 367-2750

INSTITUTIONAL CONTACT:
James Petromilli
Project Director
Electronics Department
College of San Mateo
1700 West Hillsdale Blvd.
Building 19, Room 111
San Mateo, CA   94402
(415) 574-6228

PROGRAM DESCRIPTION/OBJECTIVES:
The upgrade program is provided
for electronic worker on site.
The Project attends to both the
need for higher tech skill
training as well as to providing job opportunities to
California's unemployed.

PROGRAM INITIATED: 1980

LENGTH OF STUDY FOR PARTICI-
PANT: Variable total approximately 540 hours

LENGTH OF CONTRACT: 12 months
with renewal option

LOCATION: Ampex Corporation

PARTICIPANTS: 20 employees
needing upgrading

PROGRAM COSTS PROVIDED BY:
Other Source: State of California

PRINTED MATERIALS AVAILABLE
FROM: Institution

20. AMSCO
with
JAMESTOWN COMMUNITY COLLEGE

METAL BRAKE OPERATION TRAINING

COMPANY CONTACT:
Bob Beckstrom
Plant Manager
Amsco
P.O. Box 549 Girts Road
Jamestown, NY   14701
(716) 484-1156

INSTITUTIONAL CONTACT:
Rose M. Scott
Continuing Education Assistant
Jamestown Community College
525 Falconer Street
Jamestown, NY   15701
(716) 665-5220

PROGRAM DESCRIPTION/OBJECTIVES:
To provide those individuals
participating in this course
with the necessary shop math and
blueprint reading skills as well
as safety techniques and hands-
on training to perform their
jobs as brake operators safely
and more efficiently.

PROGRAM INITIATED: Not reported

LENGTH OF STUDY FOR PARTICI-
PANT: 12 weeks

LENGTH OF CONTRACT: 12 months
with option to review

LOCATION: Amsco

PARTICIPANTS: 11 brake
operators

PROGRAM COSTS PROVIDED BY:
Institution: 40%
Company: 20%
Other Source: 20%

PRINTED MATERIALS AVAILABLE
FROM: Not available

21. THE ANSUL COMPANY
    with
    UNIVERSITY OF WISCONSIN
    EXTENSION

RETIREMENT PLANNING SEMINAR

COMPANY CONTACT:
Carol Rickaby
Benefits Officer
Personnel Department
The Ansul Company
1 Stanton Street
Marinette, WI   54143
(715) 735-7411

INSTITUTIONAL CONTACT:
Mary S. Blazer
Continuing Education
Coordinator
University of Wisconsin
Extension
U.W. Center - Marinette
Bay Shore, Marinette, WI
54143
(715) 735-7477

PROGRAM DESCRIPTION/OBJECTIVES:
Preparing employees for retirement; reviewing company plan,
psychology of retirement, health
and safety, financial planning
and best use of leisure time/
educational opportunities.

PROGRAM INITIATED: 1981

LENGTH OF STUDY FOR PARTICI-
PANT: 8 hours

LENGTH OF CONTRACT: 4 months

LOCATION: Ansul Company

PARTICIPANTS: 50 company employees (management and hourly
employees)

PROGRAM COSTS PROVIDED BY:
Institution: $100 (administra-
tive)
Company: $800

PRINTED MATERIALS AVAILABLE
FROM: Institution and Company

22. APPLE COMPUTER
    with
    EVERGREEN VALLEY COLLEGE

DRAFTING TO INTERNATIONAL
STANDARDS

COMPANY CONTACT:
Rose Gardner
Manager
Engineering Services
Apple Computer
10240 Bubb
Cupertino, CA   95014

INSTITUTIONAL CONTACT:
Andrew McFarlin
Engineering Instructor and
Coordinator
Evergreen Valley College
3095 Yerba Buena Road
San Jose, CA   95135
(408) 274-7900, X6570

PROGRAM DESCRIPTION/OBJECTIVES:
Designed to upgrade the technical skills of personnel
through a non-credit experience.

PROGRAM INITIATED: 1982

LENGTH OF STUDY FOR PARTICI-
PANT: 1 course, 24 hours in
6-8 week period

LENGTH OF CONTRACT: 1 course
per contract

LOCATION: On-site

PARTICIPANTS: Estimated 30
drafters and designers

PROGRAM COSTS PROVIDED BY:
Institution: 100% (formative
stage)

PRINTED MATERIALS AVAILABLE
FROM: Not yet available

23. ARMSTRONG INTERNATIONAL
    CORPORATION*
         with
    WESTERN MICHIGAN UNIVERSITY

WESTERN MICHIGAN UNIVERSITY
OFFICE OF PUBLIC SERVICE

COMPANY CONTACT:
Douglas Bloss
Armstrong International
Corporation
900 Maple Street
P.O. Box 381
Three Rivers, MI   49093

INSTITUTIONAL CONTACT:
Jack S. Wood
Director
WESTOPS
Western Michigan University
Kalamazoo, MI   49008
(616) 383-0077

PROGRAM DESCRIPTION/OBJECTIVES:
Provide up-to-date technical
information as requested by
business and industries in
southwest Michigan.

PROGRAM INITIATED: 1981

LENGTH OF STUDY FOR PARTICI-
PANT: 9 months to date

LENGTH OF CONTRACT: On-going

LOCATION: Western Michigan
University

PARTICIPANTS: Indeterminate

PROGRAM COSTS PROVIDED BY:
Institution: 100%

PRINTED MATERIALS AVAILABLE
FROM: Institution

----

*Representative entry--complete
list available from institution.

24. ASHLAND OIL*
         with
    MARSHALL UNIVERSITY

INFORMATION SERVICE TO BUSINESS,
INDUSTRY, AND GOVERNMENT
AGENCIES

COMPANY CONTACT:
Sharon Payne
Reference Librarian
Ashland Oil
Russell, KY   41169
(606) 329-3333

INSTITUTIONAL CONTACT:
Kenneth T. Slack
Director of University
Libraries
Marshall University
Huntington, WV   25705
(304) 696-3120

PROGRAM DESCRIPTION/OBJECTIVES:
Access to reference materials
is provided to local businesses
and governmental agencies
through requests.

PROGRAM INITIATED: 1972

LENGTH OF STUDY FOR PARTICI-
PANT: Not available

LENGTH OF CONTRACT: Informal
verbal agreement

LOCATION: Marshall University

PARTICIPANTS: Approximately
20-25 industries, agencies, etc.

PROGRAM COSTS PROVIDED BY:
Institution: 100% (with
business support through
charitable gifts)

PRINTED MATERIALS AVAILABLE
FROM: Not reported

----

*Representative entry--complete
list available from institution.

25. ASSOCIATION OF SCHOOL
     BUSINESS OFFICIALS OF THE
     U.S. AND CANADA
             with
     MICHIGAN TECHNOLOGICAL
     UNIVERSITY

FINANCIAL AND MANAGERIAL
ACCOUNTING AND REPORTING FOR
SCHOOL SYSTEMS

COMPANY CONTACT:
Charles Stolberg
Director of Research
Association of School Business
Officials
720 Garden Street
Park Ridge, IL   60068
(312) 823-9320

INSTITUTIONAL CONTACT:
Sam B. Tidwell
Professor of Accounting
School of Business and
Engineering Administration
Michigan Technological
University
Houghton, MI   49931
(906) 487-2668

PROGRAM DESCRIPTION/OBJECTIVES:
Provide educational opportunity
for school business officials to
study generally accepted accounting and financial reporting standards as they apply
specifically to elementary and
secondary school systems.

PROGRAM INITIATED: 1959

LENGTH OF STUDY FOR PARTICI-
PANT: 1-4 weeks (6 hours daily)

LENGTH OF CONTRACT: As programs
develop

LOCATION: Michigan Technological University

PARTICIPANTS: School business
officials

PROGRAM COSTS PROVIDED BY:
Participant: 100%

PRINTED MATERIALS AVAILABLE
FROM: Company

26. ATEC INDUSTRIAL
     TRAINING, INC.
             with
     MT. WACHUSETT COMMUNITY
     COLLEGE

ATEC-MT. WACHUSETT HYDRAULICS

COMPANY CONTACT:
Alex Tremblay
President
Atec Industrial Training, Inc.
P.O. Box 512
Westford, MA   01886
(617) 692-8344

INSTITUTIONAL CONTACT:
Richard F. Fox
Dean, Continuing Education
Mt. Wachusett Community College
444 Greem Street
Gardner, MA   01440
(617) 632-8261

PROGRAM DESCRIPTION/OBJECTIVES:
To train in locating and repair-
ing problems in a hydraulic
system.

PROGRAM INITIATED: 1982

LENGTH OF STUDY FOR PARTICI-
PANT: 7 weeks at 2-1/2 hours
per week

LENGTH OF CONTRACT: 3 months
with renewal option

LOCATION: Mt. Wachusett Community College

PARTICIPANTS: 17 various
applicants

PROGRAM COSTS PROVIDED BY:
Participant: $150 per

PRINTED MATERIALS AVAILABLE
FROM: Institution

27. ATLANTIC RICHFIELD COMPANY
with
OKLAHOMA STATE TECH

ELECTRICAL PRINCIPLES

COMPANY CONTACT:
Marcus O. Durham
Senior Analytical Engineer
Atlantic Richfield Company
P.O. Box 521
Tulsa, OK   74102
(918) 588-8200

INSTITUTIONAL CONTACT:
Bill J. Lyons
Department Head
Electrical-Electronic
Technology
Oklahoma State Tech
4th and Mission
Okmulgee, OK   74447
(918) 756-6211, X252

PROGRAM DESCRIPTION/OBJECTIVES:
To provide maintenance technicians with basic technical
knowledge and skills with emphasis on motors and controls.
Also an introduction to catho-
dic protection of pipeline
systems.

PROGRAM INITIATED: 1978

LENGTH OF STUDY FOR PARTICI-
PANT: Not reported

LENGTH OF CONTRACT: Not
reported

LOCATION: Not reported

PARTICIPANTS: 30-36

PROGRAM COSTS PROVIDED BY:
Company: 100%

PRINTED MATERIALS AVAILABLE
FROM: Not available

28. ATLAS ENERGY GROUP
with
KENT STATE UNIVERSITY

GEOLOGY SHORT COURSE

COMPANY CONTACT:
John McNally
Atlas Energy Group
5201 Mahoning Road, NW
Warren, OH   44483
(216) 847-7202

INSTITUTIONAL CONTACT:
Karen Rylander
Director, Continuing Education
Kent State University
327 Rockwell Hall
Kent, OH   44242
(216) 672-3100

PROGRAM DESCRIPTION/OBJECTIVES:
Topics covered included: basic
concepts of geology, geological
history of northeastern Ohio,
and petroleum.

PROGRAM INITIATED: 1981

LENGTH OF STUDY FOR PARTICI-
PANT: 9 hours

LENGTH OF CONTRACT: 9 hours

LOCATION: Kent State
University

PARTICIPANTS: 30 employees

PROGRAM COSTS PROVIDED BY:
Company: 100%

PRINTED MATERIALS AVAILABLE
FROM: Institution

29. AULTMAN HOSPITAL
           with
     KENT STATE UNIVERSITY

EFFECTIVE BUSINESS WRITING

COMPANY CONTACT:
Ronald Lamb
Aultman Hospital
2600 6th Street, SW
Canton, OH   44710
(216) 438-6352

INSTITUTIONAL CONTACT:
Karen Rylander
Director, Continuing Education
Kent State University
327 Rockwell Hall
Kent, OH   44242
(216) 672-3100

PROGRAM DESCRIPTION/OBJECTIVES:
Provides a practical review of
the fundamentals of written communication for professions in
business and industry. It emphasizes the application of
successful strategies for
writing persuasive and efficient prose in the various
business forms.

PROGRAM INITIATED: 1982

LENGTH OF STUDY FOR PARTICI-
PANT: 10 hours + 1 hour individual follow-up

LENGTH OF CONTRACT: 10 hours
+ 1 hour individual follow-up

LOCATION: Aultman Hospital

PARTICIPANTS: 12 upper
managers

PROGRAM COSTS PROVIDED BY:
Company: 100%

PRINTED MATERIALS AVAILABLE
FROM: Institution

30. AULTMAN HOSPITAL
           with
     KENT STATE UNIVERSITY

LISTENING SKILLS

COMPANY CONTACT:
Ronald Lam
Aultman Hospital
2600 6th Street, SW
Canton, OH   44710
(216) 438-6352

INSTITUTIONAL CONTACT:
Karen Rylander
Director, Continuing Education
Kent State University
327 Rockwell Hall
Kent, OH   44242
(216) 672-3100

PROGRAM DESCRIPTION/OBJECTIVES:
An overview of communication
and active listening skills
from both one-to-one and small
group perspectives.

PROGRAM INITIATED: 1981

LENGTH OF STUDY FOR PARTICI-
PANT: 2 hours

LENGTH OF CONTRACT: 2 hours

LOCATION: Aultman Hospital

PARTICIPANTS: 180 first-line
supervisors

PROGRAM COSTS PROVIDED BY:
Company: 100%

PRINTED MATERIALS AVAILABLE
FROM: Institution

31. NOT REPORTED*
          with
     AURORA COLLEGE

MANAGEMENT APPLICATION
PROJECT CLASS

COMPANY CONTACT:
Specific company not identified

INSTITUTIONAL CONTACT:
Donald M. Cassiday, Jr.
Dean of Graduate Studies
Aurora College
347 South Gladstone
Aurora, IL   60506
(312) 892-6844

PROGRAM DESCRIPTION/OBJECTIVES:
To provide practical on-the-job
management experience to graduate students enabling them to
apply academic theory to real
life while accomplishing real-
life tasks for their employers.

PROGRAM INITITATED: 1980

LENGTH OF STUDY FOR PARTICI-
PANT: 2 years

LENGTH OF CONTRACT: 2 years

LOCATION: Aurora College

PARTICIPANTS: 90 junior to
middle level managers annually

PROGRAM COSTS PROVIDED BY:
Institution: $15,000
Company: highly varied
Participant: $390/term or
$1170/year

PRINTED MATERIALS AVAILABLE
FROM: Institution

————————

*Representative entry--complete
list available from institution.

32. BERING STRAITS NATIVE
     CORPORATION
          with
     NORTHWEST COMMUNITY COLLEGE

FINANCIAL AND MANAGERIAL
PLANNING FOR VILLAGE
CORPORATION

COMPANY CONTACT:
John Tetpin
Director
Village Services
Bering Straits Native
Corporation
Nome, AK   99762
(907) 443-5252

INSTITUTIONAL CONTACT:
Nancy Mendenahll
Director, Community Services
Northwest Community College
Pouch 400
Nome, AK   99762
(907) 443-2201

PROGRAM DESCRIPTION/OBJECTIVES:
Training for Village Corporation
managers and board members.

PROGRAM INITIATED: 1982

LENGTH OF STUDY FOR PARTICI-
PANT: 1 week

LENGTH OF CONTRACT: 30 months

LOCATION: Brevig Mission,
Shaktoolik, AK

PARTICIPANTS: 8-10 corporate
officers and board members

PROGRAM COSTS PROVIDED BY:
Institution: $7,000
Company: $4,000

PRINTED MATERIALS AVAILABLE
FROM: Not available

33. BESSER COMPANY
with
ALPENA COMMUNITY COLLEGE

BLOCKMAKERS' WORKSHOP

COMPANY CONTACT:
Lucas Pfeiffenberger
Manager, Research and Training
Center
Besser Company
Johnson Street
Alpena, MI   49707
(517) 354-4111

INSTITUTIONAL CONTACT:
Alan Reed
Dean, Occupational Education
Applied Arts and Science
Alpena Community College
666 Johnson Street
Alpena, MI   49707
(517) 356-9021

PROGRAM DESCRIPTION/OBJECTIVES:
To provide training to various
levels of personnel involved in
the blockmaking process.
Courses have included concrete
masonry technology, block production vibrapac, product
handling, equipment control,
preventive maintenance and
block production bescopac.

PROGRAM INITIATED: 1964

LENGTH OF STUDY FOR PARTICI-
PANT: 1 to 6 weeks

LENGTH OF CONTRACT: Ongoing

LOCATION: Alpena Community
College

PARTICIPANTS; 225 mechanical
and electrical machine operators

PROGRAM COSTS PROVIDED BY:
Company: $210/student
Participant: $196-260/sess-
ion (amount based on residency)

PRINTED MATERIALS AVAILABLE
FROM: Institution

34. BETHLEHEM STEEL CORPORATION
with
DUNDALK COMMUNITY COLLEGE

RESCUE TRAINING FROM CONFINED
SPACES

COMPANY CONTACT:
Martin Mossa
Division of Safety Engineering
Bethlehem Steel Corporation
Sparrows Point, MD   21219
(301) 388-4408

INSTITUTIONAL CONTACT:
Norma S. Tucker
Director of Continuing Education
Dundalk Community College
7200 Sollers Point Road
Baltimore, MD   21222
(301) 282-6700

PROGRAM DESCRIPTION/OBJECTIVES:
This program was designed to
offer rescue training techniques
for employees in an industrial
setting who face the potential
hazard of being trapped in a
confined space during the conduct of their work.

PROGRAM INITIATED: 1982

LENGTH OF STUDY FOR PARTICI-
PANT: 16 hours

LENGTH OF CONTRACT: 2,000
workers (10 per class)

LOCATION: Bethlehem Steel
Plant

PARTICIPANTS: 40 workers
per month

PROGRAM COSTS PROVIDED BY:
Institution: $272 per 16 hours
Company: $1.50 per hour
Other Source: State aid

PRINTED MATERIALS AVAILABLE
FROM: Institution

35. BIRMINGHAM BUSINESS
     COMMUNITY*
          with
     BIRMINGHAM-SOUTHERN
     COLLEGE

DIVISION OF ADULT STUDIES AND
SPECIAL PROGRAMS

COMPANY CONTACT:
Specific company not identified

INSTITUTIONAL CONTACT:
Jim Watson
Director of Adult Studies
Birmingham-Southern College
Birmingham, AL   35254
(205) 328-5250, X386

PROGRAM DESCRIPTION/OBJECTIVES:
To provide an evening degree
granting program and special
programs to strengthen Birmingham-Southern College's relationship with the Birmingham business community. Program offers
majors in 7 disciplines,
special programs for women and
retirees and courses at 2
local hospitals.

PROGRAM INITIATED: 1978

LENGTH OF STUDY FOR PARTICI-
PANT: Miniterms

LENGTH OF CONTRACT: Ongoing

LOCATION: Birmingham-Southern
College campus

PARTICIPANTS: 277

PROGRAM COSTS PROVIDED BY:
Participant: 100%

PRINTED MATERIALS AVAILABLE
FROM: Institution

---

*Representative entry--complete
list available from institution.

36. BIRMINGHAM CITY GOVERNMENT
          with
     BIRMINGHAM-SOUTHERN
     COLLEGE

PROJECT WORK-LEARN/EDUCATION
WORK RETREATS

COMPANY CONTACT:
Birmingham City Government
800 8th Avenue West
Box A-10
Birmingham, AL   35254

INSTITUTIONAL CONTACT:
Ned Moomaw
Dean
Birmingham-Southern College
Birmingham, AL   35254
(205) 328-5250, X200

PROGRAM DESCRIPTION/OBJECTIVES:
Education/Work Retreats are
designed to bring together faculty from the College and
executives from various firms,
agencies or organizations to
address topics of mutual interest and to plan future collaborative activities.

PROGRAM INITIATED: 1977

LENGTH OF STUDY FOR PARTICI-
PANT: 2-day retreat

LENGTH OF CONTRACT: 2 days

LOCATION: Held in resort area
to insure relaxed exchange of
ideas

PARTICIPANTS: 44 Birmingham
City Council members, Major of
Birmingham and Birmingham-
Southern Faculty members

PROGRAM COSTS PROVIDED BY:
Institution: 100%

PRINTED MATERIALS AVAILABLE
FROM: Institution

37. BIRMINGHAM EXECUTIVES*
       with
    BIRMINGHAM-SOUTHERN
    COLLEGE

PROJECT WORK-LEARN/EXECUTIVES
IN RESIDENCE

COMPANY CONTACT:
Specific company not identified

INSTITUTIONAL CONTACT:
Jim Watson
Director of Adult Studies
Birmingham-Southern College
Birmingham, AL   35254
(205) 328-5250

PROGRAM DESCRIPTION/OBJECTIVES:
Birmingham executives attend
regular academic classes,
special seminars, and contribute their expertise to the
College. Personal and professional growth is emphasized.

PROGRAM INITIATED: 1977

LENGTH OF STUDY FOR PARTICI-
PANT: 2 weeks

LENGTH OF CONTRACT: 2 weeks

LOCATION: Birmingham-Southern
College campus

PARTICIPANTS: 45 Birmingham
area business executives

PROGRAM COSTS PROVIDED BY:
Institution: 100%

PRINTED MATERIALS AVAILABLE
FROM: Institution

---

*Representative entry--complete
list available from institution.

38. EMPLOYEES FROM AREA
    BUSINESSES*
       with
    BIRMINGHAM-SOUTHERN
    COLLEGE

PROJECT WORK-LEARN/THE
SOUTHERN EXPOSURE-LISTENER
PROGRAM

COMPANY CONTACT:
Specific company not identified

INSTITUTIONAL CONTACT:
Ned Moomaw
Dean
Birmingham-Southern College
Birmingham, AL   35254
(205) 328-5250, X200

PROGRAM DESCRIPTION/OBJECTIVES:
Program was designed to provide
employees of Birmingham business an opportunity to attend
Birmingham-Southern College as
"listeners." For a nominal fee,
these employers are permitted
to attend as many class sessions as they desire.

PROGRAM INITIATED: 1977

LENGTH OF STUDY FOR PARTICI-
PANT: Ongoing each semester

LENGTH OF CONTRACT: Ongoing

LOCATION: Birmingham-Southern
College

PARTICIPANTS: Over 75 up to
1981 of various Birmingham
area employees and community
persons

PROGRAM COSTS PROVIDED BY:
Participant: $10.00

PRINTED MATERIALS AVAILABLE
FROM: Institution

---

*Representative entry--complete
list available from institution.

39. LOCAL BUSINESS, INDUSTRIES
AND GOVERNMENT*
with
BIRMINGHAM-SOUTHERN
COLLEGE

PROJECT WORK-LEARN/VISITING
PROFESSORS

COMPANY CONTACT:
Varies
800 8th Avenue West
Birmingham, AL 35254

INSTITUTIONAL CONTACT:
Ned Moomaw
Dean
Birmingham-Southern College
Birmingham, AL   35254
(205) 328-5250, X200

PROGRAM DESCRIPTION/OJBECTIVES:
To provide opportunities for
Birmingham-Southern College
faculty members to spend time
working in a local business,
industry, labor, governmental
or professional positions.

PROGRAM INITIATED: 1977

LENGTH OF STUDY FOR PARTICI-
PANT: 4-6 weeks

LENGTH OF CONTRACT: 4-6 weeks

LOCATION: On-the-job sites,
Birmingham, AL

PARTICIPANTS: 45 full-time
faculty representing departments such as English, Marketing, etc.

PROGRAM COSTS PROVIDED BY:
Institution: 100%

PRINTED MATERIALS AVAILABLE
FROM: Institution

---

*Representative entry--complete
list available from institution.

40. BROOKWOOD MEDICAL CENTER*
with
BIRMINGHAM-SOUTHERN
COLLEGE

PROJECT WORK-LEARN/CAREER
CONSULTANT PROGRAM

COMPANY CONTACT:
Carol Gillespie Grizzle
Psychologist
Brookwood Medical Center
Birmingham, AL   35209
(205) 879-7953

INSTITUTIONAL CONTACT:
Penny Goodwin
Coordinator of Career
Counseling and Placement
Birmingham-Southern College
Birmingham, AL   35254
(205) 328-5250, X403

PROGRAM DESCRIPTION/OBJECTIVES:
The Career Consultant Program
is designed to put college students in direct contact with
people in local business, industrial, labor, governmental,
educational, religious, and professional organizations. The
contact may be through an individualized career information interview or as a campus
speaker.

PROGRAM INITIATED: 1977

LENGTH OF STUDY FOR PARTICI-
PANT: Ongoing; contacts
scheduled as needed

LENGTH OF CONTRACT: Ongoing

LOCATION: Work site or campus

PARTICIPANTS: Approximately
400 consultants from all areas
of the work world

PROGRAM COSTS PROVIDED BY:
Institution: 100%

---

*Representative entry--complete
list available from institution.

41. BROWARD COUNTY HOSPITALS
with
BROWARD COMMUNITY COLLEGE

NURSING SPONSORSHIP PROGRAM*

COMPANY CONTACT:
Several hospitals

INSTITUTIONAL CONTACT:
Wanda Thomas
Director, Division of Allied
Health Technologies
Broward Community College
3501 S.W. Davie Road
Ft. Lauderdale, FL   33314
(305) 475-6767

PROGRAM DESCRIPTION/OBJECTIVES:
To provide hospital employees
and other persons the financial
means to become an R.N.   To
increase the number of available R.N.'s in the county and
specifically sponsoring
hospitals.

PROGRAM INITIATED: 1979

LENGTH OF STUDY FOR PARTICI-
PANT: 2 years

LENGTH OF CONTRACT: Continuous agreement

LOCATION: Broward Community
College Sponsorship Hospitals

PARTICIPANTS: 7 hospitals
and 450 students per year

PROGRAM COSTS PROVIDED BY:
Institution: 50%
Company: 50%

PRINTED MATERIALS AVAILABLE
FROM: Institution

---

*Representative entry--complete
list available from institution.

42. BROWN AND ROOT CORPORATION
with
NORTHLAND PIONEER COLLEGE

POWER PLANT CONSTRUCTION
TECHNOLOGY

COMPANY CONTACT:
Ben May
Project Director
Brown and Root Corporation
Springerville, AZ   85938
(602) 337-2977

INSTITUTIONAL CONTACT:
Ronald E. Glenn
Director of Vocational
Education
Northland Pioneer College
1200 Nermose Drive
Holbrook, AZ   86025
(602) 536-7871

PROGRAM DESCRIPTION/OBJECTIVES:
To provide training for employees of Brown and Root as they
move from one phase of construction to the next.

PROGRAM INITIATED: 1981

LENGTH OF STUDY FOR PARTICI-
PANT: Continuing

LENGTH OF CONTRACT: Until
project is completed in 1985

LOCATION: Springerville, AZ

PARTICIPANTS: 260 construction workers yearly

PROGRAM COSTS PROVIDED BY:
Institution: $60,000 per year
Company: $50,000 per year
which includes supplies, supervision, facilities and equipment; Tucson Electric also provides facilities not included
in $50,000

PRINTED MATERIALS AVAILABLE
FROM: Institution and Company

43. BULOVA WATCH COMPANY
         with
     OKLAHOMA STATE TECH

BULOVA WATCH COMPANY SERIES OF
ADVANCED REPAIR WORKSHOPS

COMPANY CONTACT:
Leo Helmprecht, Manager
Field Training Services
Bulova Watch Company
75-20 Astoria Blvd.
Jackson Heights, NY   11370
(212) 335-6000

INSTITUTIONAL CONTACT:
Gray Lawrence
Supervisor, Watch Micro-
Instrument and Jewelry
Small Business Trades
Department
Oklahoma State Tech
4th and Mission
Okmulgee, OK   74447
(918) 756-6211, X271

PROGRAM DESCRIPTION/OBJECTIVES:
To foster closer relations
within the industry and upgrade
skills and knowledge of current
watchmakers in the field.   To
expose students to the latest
types and styles of watches
produced in the industry as
well as provide them opportunities for contact with potential employers.

PROGAM INITIATED: 1965

LENGTH OF STUDY FOR PARTICI-
PANT: Not reported

LENGTH OF CONTRACT: Not
reported

LOCATION: Not reported

PARTICIPANTS: 64

PROGRAM COSTS PROVIDED BY:
Institution: 35%
Company: 65%

PRINTED MATERIALS AVAILABLE
FROM: Not available

44. BURROUGHS CORPORATION
         with
     ASSOCIATION OF AMERICAN
     COLLEGES

BUILDING BRIDGES BETWEEN
BUSINESS ON CAMPUS

COMPANY CONTACT:
Bill Faught
Former Area Recruiting Manager
Burroughs Corporation
701 Columbia Drive
Sacramento, CA   95825
(916) 971-3458

INSTITUTIONAL CONTACT:
Kathryn Mohrman
Director, Office of National
Affairs
Association of American Colleges
1818 R Street, NW
Washington, DC   20009
(202) 387-3760

PROGRAM DESCRIPTION/OBJECTIVES:
Program designed to acquaint
middle-management personnel
with liberal arts faculty in an
effort to increase awareness of
job opportunities and educational experiences for the benefit of future graduates.

PROGRAM INITIATED: 1981

LENGTH OF STUDY FOR PARTICI-
PANT: 1-day conference; informal networking continuing
afterwards

LENGTH OF CONTRACT: 1 year

LOCATION: Retreat settings

PARTICIPANTS: 30 faculty members from liberal arts disciplines, human resource managers
and corporation trainers per
meeting

PROGRAM COSTS PROVIDED BY:
Other Source: 100% (small
grants from local business)

PRINTED MATERIALS AVAILABLE
FROM: Institution

45. BUTLER COUNTY HISTORICAL
     SOCIETY
            with
     BUTLER COUNTY COMMUNITY
     COLLEGE

EXCURSION INTO HISTORY "CIVIL
WARFARE"

COMPANY CONTACT:
Charles Heilmann
President
Butler County Historical
Society
409 Houser Drive
El Dorado, KS   67042
(316) 321-4196

INSTITUTIONAL CONTACT:
Larry DeVane
Dean of Liberal Arts and
Sciences
Walborn Administration
Building
Butler County Community
College
El Dorado, KS   67042
(316) 321-5083, X110

PROGRAM DESCRIPTION/OBJECTIVES:
Opportunity for college and
community to provide an educational experience for local
citizens.

PROGRAM INITIATED: Not
reported

LENGTH OF STUDY FOR PARTICI-
PANT: 1 day

LENGTH OF CONTRACT: Informal

LOCATION: Butler County Community College

PARTICIPANTS: 1,000 local
citizens

PROGRAM COSTS PROVIDED BY:
Institution: $3,000
Company: $3,000
Other Source: $300 (El
Dorado Art Association)

PRINTED MATERIALS AVAILABLE
FROM: Institution

46. CAMPBELL AND DARBY METALS*
            with
     TRI-COUNTY TECHNICAL
     COLLEGE

SHEET METAL FABRICATION

COMPANY CONTACT:
Barney Darby
Vice President
Campbell and Darby Metals
P.O. Box 73
Anderson, SC   29622
(803) 225-6906

INSTITUTIONAL CONTACT:
Ronald N. Talley
Director, Comprehensive
Manpower Training
Tri-County Technical College
P.O. Box 587
Pendleton, SC   29670
(803) 646-8361

PROGRAM DESCRIPTION/OBJECTIVES:
To train persons in the layout
and fabrication of products
manufactured from sheet metal.

PROGRAM INITIATED: 1982

LENGTH OF STUDY FOR PARTICI-
PANT: 9 months

LENGTH OF CONTRACT: 9 months

LOCATION: Tri-County Technical College

PARTICIPANTS: 20 sheet metal
workers

PROGRAM COSTS PROVIDED BY:
Institution: Indirect
Company: Indirect
Other Source: $42,800 (fed-
eral CETA funds)

PRINTED MATERIALS AVAILABLE
FROM: Institution

---

*Representative entry--complete
list available from institution.

47. CANADORE COLLEGE AND
    ST. CLAIR COLLEGE
        with
    CENTRAL MICHIGAN UNIVERSITY

CANADIAN COMMUNITY COLLEGE
PROGRAM

COMPANY CONTACT:
Neil Cornthwaite
Applied Arts and Technology
Canadore College
P.O. Box 5001
North Bay, Ontario
Canada P1B 8K9
        and
Joyce McInerney
1001 Grand Avenue West
Thames Campus
St. Clair College
Chatham Ontario
Canada N7M 5E4

INSTITUTIONAL CONTACT:
Lawrence R. Murphy
Director
Institute for Personal and
Career Development
Central Michigan University
Mt. Pleasant, MI   48859
(517) 774-3865

PROGRAM DESCRIPTION/OBJECTIVES:
To provide graduate level education program to Subject Matter Specialists currently
teaching in Canadian community
colleges.

PROGRAM INITIATED: Not
reported

LENGTH OF STUDY FOR PARTICI-
PANT: 22 months average

LENGTH OF CONTRACT: Ongoing

LOCATION: North Bay and
Sudbury, Ontario

PARTICIPANTS: 70 faculty of
Canadian Community College
and public school teachers

PROGRAM COSTS PROVIDED BY:
Participant: 100%

PRINTED MATERIALS AVAILABLE
FROM: Institution

48. CAPE COD BANK AND TRUST
    COMPANY
        with
    CAPE COD COMMUNITY COLLEGE*

MANAGEMENT DEVELOPMENT PROGRAM

COMPANY CONTACT:
Irene Charles
Director of Personnel
Cape Cod Bank and Trust Company
Off Station Avenue
South Yarmouth, MA   02664
(617) 775-3500

INSTITUTIONAL CONTACT:
Jean L. Souther
Chairman, Management Program
Business Technologies
Cape Cod Community College
West Barnstable, MA   20668
(617) 362-2131, X361

PROGRAM DESCRIPTION/OBJECTIVES:
To provide seminars, workshops
and programs to meet the continual management training
needs of local organizations.

PROGRAM INITIATED: 1981

LENGTH OF STUDY FOR PARTICI-
PANT: Varies 4 hour; 8 hour
workshops and seminars 6 week
(15 hour) programs

LENGTH OF CONTRACT: 12 months

LOCATION: Cape Cod Community
College Campus

PARTICIPANTS: 10-15 per program of first line and middle
level supervisors and managers

PROGRAM COSTS PROVIDED BY:
Institution: 10%
Company: 90%

PRINTED MATERIALS AVAILABLE
FROM: Institution

---

*Representative entry--complete
list available from institution.

49. CAREER HORIZONS BOARD OF
CONSULTANTS
with
EASTERN MICHIGAN
UNIVERSITY

CAREER HORIZONS BOARD OF
CONSULTANTS

COMPANY CONTACT:
Eugene R. Karrer
Chairman, Career Horizons Board
of Consultants
300 Knobby View Drive
Holly, MI   48442
(313) 887-8417

INSTITUTIONAL CONTACT:
Laurence N. Smith
Vice-President for Student
Affairs
Eastern Michigan University
101 Pierce Hall
Ypsilanti, MI   48197
(313) 487-2390

PROGRAM DESCRIPTION/OBJECTIVES:
A comprehensive program to keep
faculty and students in the
university attuned to the
changing nature of the world of
work through the use of business leaders as consultants in
short courses and seminars.

PROGRAM INITIATED: 1978

LENGTH OF STUDY FOR PARTICI-
PANT: Not available

LENGTH OF CONTRACT: Ongoing

LOCATION: On campus

PARTICIPANTS: 40-50 consultants annually

PROGRAM COSTS PROVIDED BY:
Institution: $2,000
Company: In-kind
Participant: In-kind

PRINTED MATERIALS AVAILABLE
FROM: Institution

50. CENTER FOR INDUSTRIAL
RESEARCH AND SERVICES
with
IOWA STATE UNIVERSITY

SMALL BUSINESS DEVELOPMENT
CENTER

COMPANY CONTACT:
Lloyd E. Anderson
Coordinator, SBDC
Center For Industrial Research
and Services
Iowa State University
205 Engineering Annex
Ames, IA   50011
(515) 294-3420

INSTITUTIONAL CONTACT:
Jan A. DeYoung
Assistant Director, SBDC
Department of Economics
Iowa State University
East Hall
Ames, IA   50011
(515) 294-8069

PROGRAM DESCRIPTION/OBJECTIVES:
Major thrust of the program is
to provide business counseling
to all types of small businesses.
Also there are workshops for
those planning to go into business, along with management
courses and conferences to interest those already operating
small businesses. Each center
houses a management information
library and is involved in developing and disseminating publications aimed at solving specific business problems. Assistance is provided on most
any phase of management, production or marketing. Selected
topics include: developing business strategies for individual
firms and towns, trade area
analysis, improving management
and profit structures, and
training and motivating employees.

PROGRAM INITIATED: 1981

LENGTH OF STUDY FOR PARTICI-
PANT: Varies with topic and
participant

LENGTH OF CONTRACT: 12 month
renewable

(Cont.)

27

50. (Cont.)

LOCATION: Community based

PARTICIPANTS: Approximately
5,000 members of the local
business community

PROGRAM COSTS RPOVIDED BY:
Other Source: Small Business
Administration with % state
institution match

PRINTED MATERIALS AVAILABLE
FROM: Institution

PARTICIPANTS: Varies, an average of 170 business leaders,
professionals, civic leaders
and representatives of the
college community

PROGRAM COSTS PROVIDED BY:
Institution: 100%

PRINTED MATERIALS AVAILABLE
FROM: Institution

*Representative entry--complete
list available from institution.

51. CENTRAL BANK AND TRUST*
          with
     BIRMINGHAM-SOUTHERN
     COLLEGE

PROJECT WORK-LEARN/THE WORK
AND CULTURE SEMINARS

COMPANY CONTACT:
Philip C. Jackson, Jr.
Chief Executive Officer
Central Bank and Trust
Birmingham, AL   35203
(205) 933-3000

INSTITUTIONAL CONTACT:
Bob Wingard
Director of Church Relations
Birmingham-Southern College
Birmingham, AL   35254
(205) 328-5250, X206

PROGRAM DESCRIPTION/OBJECTIVES:
The purpose of the Work and
Culture Seminar is to bring together the college community
with business-professional-
governmental leaders, to discuss areas where culture makes
an impact on the working world.

PROGRAM INITIATED: 1978

LENGTH OF STUDY FOR PARTICI-
PANT: Series of luncheons,
usually 5 in 1 year

LENGTH OF CONTRACT: Ongoing

LOCATION: Birmingham-Southern
College

52.   CENTRAL ILLINOIS LIGHT
      COMPANY*
            with
      BRADLEY-BUSINESS TASK FORCE

BRADLEY-BUSINESS TASK FORCE

COMPANY CONTACT:
Bill Vogelsang
Executive Vice President
Central Illinois Light Company
300 Liberty Street
Peoria, IL   61602
(309) 676-5271

INSTITUTIONAL CONTACT:
James Ballowe
Dean of the Graduate School
and Associate Provost
Bradley University
Peoria, IL   61625
(309) 676-7611, X388, 389

PROGRAM DESCRIPTION/OBJECTIVES:
To develop joint programs between business and Bradley for
the mutual benefit of both.

PROGRAM INITIATED: 1982

LENGTH OF STUDY FOR PARTICI-
PANT: Not available

LENGTH OF CONTRACT: Not
reported

PARTICIPANTS: 30 business
executives and university
administrators

PROGRAM COSTS PROVIDED BY:
Not reported

PRINTED MATERIALS AVAILABLE
FROM: Institution

---

*Representative entry--complete
list available from institution.

53.   CENTRAL STATES CONFERENCE
      OF BANKERS ASSOCIATIONS
            with
      UNIVERSITY OF WISCONSIN -
      MADISON

PROCHNOW GRADUATE SCHOOL OF
BANKING AT THE UNIVERSITY OF
WISCONSIN - MADISON

COMPANY CONTACT:
Richard I. Doolittle
Executive Vice President
Prochnow Graduate School of
Banking
122 West Washington Avenue
Madison, WI   53703
(608) 256-7021

INSTITUTIONAL CONTACT:
Robert H. Bock
Dean
School of Business and
Graduate School of Business
University of Wisconsin -
Madison
1155 Observatory Drive
Madison, WI   53706
(608) 262-1553

PROGRAM DESCRIPTION/OBJECTIVES:
To provide bankers with a broad
and fundamental understanding
of significant banking, economic and monetary problems.

PROGRAM INITIATED: 1945

LENGTH OF STUDY FOR PARTICI-
PANT: 3 years

LENGTH OF CONTRACT: Perpetual

LOCATION: University of
Wisconsin - Madison

PARTICIPANTS: 1,500 bank officers and officers of bank
regulatory agencies

PROGRAM COSTS PROVIDED BY:
Institution: 5%
Company: 95%

PRINTED MATERIALS AVAILABLE
FROM: Company

54. CHAMPION INTERNATIONAL
             with
       FAIRFIELD UNIVERSITY

LUNCHTIME LECTURE SERIES

COMPANY CONTACT:
James Donohue
Associate Director
Champion International
1 Champion Plaza
Stamford, CT   06921
(203) 358-7000

INSTITUTIONAL CONTACT:
Alan Katz
Associate Professor
Politics Department
Fairfield University
North Benson Road
Fairfield, CT   06430
(203) 255-5411

PROGRAM DESCRIPTION/OBJECTIVES:
To make available intellectu-
ally stimulating ideas to a
bright, interested adult audi-
ence. Presentations are ar-
ranged in series, i.e., four
lectures on "America in the
'80's" or eight lectures on
the Renaissance.

PROGRAM INITIATED: 1981

LENGTH OF STUDY FOR PARTICI-
PANT: Ranges from 25 lectures
over a year to 1 or 2

LENGTH OF CONTRACT: 2
13-15 week semesters

LOCATION: Corporate headquarters in Stamford, CT

PARTICIPANTS: Approximately
50 ranging from clerical
staff through corporate
executives

PROGRAM COSTS PROVIDED BY:
Company: $4500.00

PRINTED MATERIALS AVAILABLE
FROM: Not reported

55. CHEN SCHOOL
             with
       RUTGERS, THE STATE UNI-
       VERSITY OF NEW JERSEY

PRIMARY AFFILIATION

COMPANY CONTACT:
Regina Harris
Executive Director
Chen School
51 Rector Street
Newark, NJ   07102
(201) 624-1681

INSTITUTIONAL CONTACT:
Lucille Joel
Associate Dean for Clinical
Affairs
College of Nursing
Rutgers, The State University
of New Jersey
University Avenue
Newark, NJ   07102
(201) 648-5298

PROGRAM DESCRIPTION/OBJECTIVES:
Manpower sharing; student
placement.

PROGRAM INITIATED: 1981

LENGTH OF STUDY FOR PARTICI-
PANT: Academic year

LENGTH OF CONTRACT: 10 months

LOCATION: Chen School and
Rutgers

PARTICIPANTS: 1

PROGRAM COSTS PROVIDED BY:
Shared equally by exchange of
time between company and
institution

PRINTED MATERIALS AVAILABLE
FROM: Institution

56. CHEVROLET MOTOR DIVISION
              with
      STATE UNIVERSITY COLLEGE
      AT BUFFALO

L-4 TRAINING PROJECT (Training
for the Future)

COMPANY CONTACT:
Richard Kujawa
Production Superintendent
Chevrolet Motor Division
General Motors
River Road
Tonawanda, NY   14150
(716) 879-5305

INSTITUTIONAL CONTACT:
William T. Ganley
Director, Center for Applied
Research
State University College at
Buffalo
1300 Elmwood Avenue, G.C. 409
Buffalo, NY   14222
(716) 878-4110

PROGRAM DESCRIPTION/OBJECTIVES:
Quality of work life training,
technical skills, instructional
materials development, training
skills.

PROGRAM INITIATED: 1981

LENGTH OF STUDY FOR PARTICI-
PANT: 40 hours instruction
each

LENGTH OF CONTRACT: 9 months

LOCATION: Chevy-Tonawanda
plant, in-house

PARTICIPANTS: 3,000 hourly and
salary employees

PROGRAM COSTS PROVIDED BY:
Institution: $74,500
Company: $1,000,000
Other Source: Private
Industry Council, New York
Education Departments

PRINTED MATERIALS AVAILABLE
FROM: Not reported

57. CHEVRON, USA, INC.
              with
      EL PASO COMMUNITY COLLEGE

MACHINING PROCESSES TRAINING
PROGRAM

COMPANY CONTACT:
L.A. Wilson
Chief Engineer
Chevron, USA, Inc.
P.O. Box 20002
El Paso, TX   79998
(915) 722-1411

INSTITUTIONAL CONTACT:
Gregory F. Linden
Associate Dean
Community Services/Continuing
Education
El Paso Community College
P.O. Box 20500
El Paso, TX   79998
(915) 594-2597

PROGRAM DESCRIPTION/OBJECTIVES:
To provide machining processes
skills development training.

PROGRAM INITIATED: 1980

LENGTH OF STUDY FOR PARTICI-
PANT: 180 hours in half day
increments

LENGTH OF CONTRACT: 12 month
renewed annually

LOCATION: Chevron, USA, Inc.

PARTICIPANTS: 16 plant maintenance personnel annually

PROGRAM COSTS PROVIDED BY:
Company: $15,200

PRINTED MATERIALS AVAILABLE
FROM: Institution

58. CHRYSLER LEARNING, INC.
              with
     CENTRAL MICHIGAN UNIVERSITY

CHRYSLER CENTER

COMPANY CONTACT:
Walter Hempel
Academic Affairs
Chrysler Learning, Inc.
1200 East McNichols
Highland Park, MI   48203
(313) 956-1578

INSTITUTIONAL CONTACT:
Lawrence R. Murphy
Director
Institute for Personal and
Career Development
Central Michigan University
Mt. Pleasant, MI   48859
(517) 774-3865

PROGRAM DESCRIPTION/OBJECTIVES:
Bachelor's Program in Management and Supervision building
on Chrysler's 2-year certificate program.

PROGRAM INITIATED: Not
reported

LENGTH OF STUDY FOR PARTICI-
PANT: 2-4 years

LENGTH OF CONTRACT: Ongoing

LOCATION: On site and in
nearby classrooms

PARTICIPANTS: Not reported

PROGRAM COSTS PROVIDED BY:
Company: 100%

PRINTED MATERIALS AVAILABLE
FROM: Institution

59. CITIBANK*
              with
     THE COLLEGE OF STATEN
     ISLAND

OUTREACH PROGRAMS

COMPANY CONTACT:
Eileen Sini
Citibank
399 Park Avenue
New York, NY   10022
(212) 559-0037

INSTITUTIONAL CONTACT:
Michael J. Pefrides
Associate Dean of Faculty
Outreach Centers
College of Staten Island
130 Stuyvesant Place
Staten Island, NY   10301
(212) 390-7551

PROGRAM DESCRIPTION/OBJECTIVES:
Off campus credit courses appli-
cable to AAS degrees with management emphasis. Non-credit
occupational training programs.

PROGRAM INITIATED: 1974

LENGTH OF STUDY FOR PARTICI-
PANT: Varies

LENGTH OF CONTRACT: Varies

LOCATION: In-plant

PARTICIPANTS: Varies

PROGRAM COSTS PROVIDED BY:
Institution: 40%
Company: 40%
Participant: 20%

PRINTED MATERIALS AVAILABLE
FROM: Institution and Company

---

*Representative entry--complete
list available from institution.

60. CLEVELAND CLIFFS IRON
     COMPANY*
                with
     MICHIGAN TECHNOLOGICAL
     UNIVERSITY

COOPERATIVE FOR RESEARCH ON
FOREST SOILS (CROFS)

COMPANY CONTACT:
Ray Haskings
Woodlands Manager
Forest Products Division
Cleveland Cliffs Iron Company
P.O. Box 338
Munifing, MI   49862
(906) 452-6221

INSTITUTIONAL CONTACT:
F.H. Erbisch
Acting Director of Research
Michigan Technological
University
Houghton, MI   49931
(906) 487-2225

PROGRAM DESCRIPTION/OBJECTIVES:
The primary objective of the
Cooperative for Research on
Forest Soils (CROFS) is to encourage the development of
technologies and resources necessary to increase forest productivity. This objective is
to be acoomplished through
funding research and technology transfer activities. These
functions will be performed in
a cooperative venture between
industry, university and public agency members.

PROGRAM INITIATED: 1977

LENGTH OF STUDY FOR PARTICI-
PANT: 1 month to several
years

LENGTH OF CONTRACT: Renewed
annually by payment of dues

LOCATION: Michigan Technological University

PARTICIPANTS: Various numbers
of forest research personnel
annually

PROGRAM COSTS PROVIDED BY:
Institution: 25% of direct
Company: $2,000 per year (can
be changed)

PRINTED MATERIALS AVAILABLE
FROM: Institution

---

*Representative entry--complete
list available from institution.

61. CLEVELAND CLINIC FOUNDATION
                with
          KENT STATE UNIVERSITY

CAREER DEVELOPMENT PROGRAM

COMPANY CONTACT:
Fred Buck
Cleveland Clinic Foundation
9500 Euclid Avenue
Cleveland, OH   44106
(216) 444-2380

INSTITUTIONAL CONTACT:
Karen Rylander
Director, Continuing Education
Kent State University
327 Rockwell Hall
Kent, OH   44242
(216) 672-3100

PROGRAM DESCRIPTION/OBJECTIVES:
Assists in identifying employees potential; provides information about options, career
paths, and retraining; teaches
a decision-making process to
employees.

PROGRAM INITIATED: 1981

LENGTH OF STUDY FOR PARTICI-
PANT: 15 hours + 1 hour individual counseling

LENGTH OF CONTRACT: 15 hours
+ 1 hour individual counseling

LOCATION: Cleveland Clinic
Foundation

PARTICIPANTS: 63 clerical
staff members

PROGRAM COSTS PROVIDED BY:
Company: 100%

PRINTED MATERIALS AVAILABLE
FROM: Institution

62. CLEVELAND STATE UNIVERSITY

MASTER OF EDUCATION IN POST-
SECONDARY EDUCATION

COMPANY CONTACT:
Numerous placements*

INSTITUTIONAL CONTACT:
Laura A. Wilson
Coordinator
Postsecondary Education Program
Cleveland State University
Department of Educational
Specialists
1419 Rhodes Tower
Cleveland, OH   44115
(216) 687-3704

PROGRAM DESCRIPTION/OBJECTIVES:
Master's degree program designed for students planning to
enter the field of training in
the business sector.

PROGRAM INITIATED: 1981

LENGTH OF STUDY FOR PARTICI-
PANT: Academic program with
6 month internship in business
education

LENGTH OF CONTRACT: Not
available

LOCATION: Varies

PARTICIPANTS: 100

PROGRAM COSTS PROVIDED BY:
Not reported

PRINTED MATERIALS AVAILABLE
FROM: Institution

_____

*Representative entry--complete
list available from institution.

63. COLLEGE AND UNIVERSITY
PERSONNEL ASSOCIATION
with
CENTRAL MICHIGAN UNIVERSITY

CUPA/CMU DEGREE PROGRAM

COMPANY CONTACT:
Steve Miller
Executive Director
College and University Personnel
Association
Suite 120
11 Dupont Circle
Washington, DC   20036
(202) 462-1038

INSTITUTIONAL CONTACT:
Lawrence R. Murphy
Director
Institute for Personal and
Career Development
Central Michigan University
Mt. Pleasant, MI   48859
(517) 774-3865

PROGRAM DESCRIPTION/OBJECTIVES:
To provide a graduate level program in Management and Supervision with a concentration in
Personnel Administration.

PROGRAM INITIATED: Not reported

LENGTH OF STUDY FOR PARTICI-
PANT: 36 months average

LENGTH OF CONTRACT: Ongoing

LOCATION: Varies in conjunction with national and regional
meetings

PARTICIPANTS: 25 college and
university personnel officers

PROGRAM COSTS PROVIDED BY:
Participant: 100%

PRINTED MATERIALS AVAILABLE
FROM: Institution

64. COLLEGE HOSPITAL OF THE
UNIVERSITY OF MEDICINE AND
DENTISTRY OF NEW JERSEY
with
RUTGERS, THE STATE UNIVER-
SITY OF NEW JERSEY

PRIMARY AFFILIATION

COMPANY CONTACT:
Hazel Williams
Director of Nursing
College Hospital
100 Bergen Street
Newark, NJ   07101
(201) 456-5669

INSTITUTIONAL CONTACT:
Lucille Joel
Associate Dean for Clinical
Affairs
College of Nursing
Rutgers, The State University
of New Jersey
University Avenue
Newark, NJ   07102
(201) 648-5298

PROGRAM DESCRIPTION/OBJECTIVES:
Manpower sharing; continuing
education institute; student
placement.

PROGRAM INITIATED: 1980

LENGTH OF STUDY FOR PARTICI-
PANT: Academic year

LENGTH OF CONTRACT: 10 months

LOCATION: College Hospital
and Rutgers

PARTICIPANTS: 9 clinical
specialists and college
faculty

PROGRAM COSTS PROVIDED BY:
Shared equally by exchange of
time between company and
institution

PRINTED MATERIALS AVAILABLE
FROM: Institution

65. COMPANIES IN NEW YORK AREA
EMPLOYING 50+ WORKERS
with
THE COLLEGE OF NEW ROCHELLE

TUITION-AID BENEFITS SURVEY IN
GREATER NEW YORK (part of
"Workers as Students")

COMPANY CONTACT:
Not available

INSTITUTIONAL CONTACT:
Ronald W. Pollack
Director, Financial Aid
College of New Rochelle
New Rochelle, NY   10801
(914) 632-5300

PROGRAM DESC PTION/OBJECTIVES:
To compile a comprehensive directory of the tuition aid programs available to employees in
New York, to help adults obtain financial aid.

PROGRAM INITIATED: 1980

LENGTH OF STUDY FOR PARTICI-
PANT: 2 years

LENGTH OF CONTRACT: Not
available

LOCATION: College of New
Rochelle

PARTICIPANTS: No individual
participants

PROGRAM COSTS PROVIDED BY:
Institution: $114,060
Other Source: $172,835 (grant
from FIPSE)

PRINTED MATERIALS AVAILABLE
FROM: Institution

66. VARIOUS FIRMS AND
     GOVERNMENT AGENCIES*
          with
     COLUMBIA COLLEGE

BUSINESS INTERNSHIPS

COMPANY CONTACT:
Specific company not identified

INSTITUTIONAL CONTACT:
James G. Bouknight
Chairman, Department of
Business and Economics
Columbia College
Columbia, SC   29203
(803) 786-3724

PROGRAM DESCRIPTION/OBJECTIVES:
To provide senior business administration majors with the
types of hands-on experiences
necessary to apply their
training to work situations.

PROGRAM INITIATED: 1982

LENGTH OF STUDY FOR PARTICI-
PANT: 7½ weeks

LENGTH OF CONTRACT: 7½ weeks

LOCATION: Usually in the
Columbia, SC area

PARTICIPANTS: 30 senior business administration and
accounting majors

PROGRAM COSTS PROVIDED BY:
Institution: No direct
Company: Varies
Participant: Little

PRINTED MATERIALS AVAILABLE
FROM: Institution

----

*Representative entry--complete
list available from institution.

67. COMMUNITY CAREERS COUNCIL
          with
     MERRITT COLLEGE

INFORMATIONAL INTERVIEW
REFERRAL

COMPANY CONTACT:
Frankie Arrington
Director, Clearinghouse
Community Careers Council
1730 Franklin Street
Oakland, CA   94612
(415) 763-4234

INSTITUTIONAL CONTACT:
Thressa Herzfeld
Student Services Specialist
Career Center
Merritt College
12500 Campus Drive
Oakland, CA   94519
(415) 436-2444

PROGRAM DESCRIPTION/OBJECTIVES:
Local business and professional
representatives volunteer to be
interviewed by students interested in their occupation. Students request through college
Career Center and are matched
by Clearinghouse.

PROGRAM INITIATED: 1980

LENGTH OF STUDY FOR PARTICI-
PANT: No prerequisite length

LENGTH OF CONTRACT: Ongoing

LOCATION: Merritt College

PARTICIPANTS: 150 students
investigating a variety of
occupations per semester

PROGRAM COSTS PROVIDED BY:
Costs of Clearinghouse shared
by Peralta College and District
and New Oakland Committee

PRINTED MATERIALS AVAILABLE
FROM: Institution and Company

68. COMMUNITY NURSING SERVICE
    OF ESSEX AND WEST HUDSON
           with
    RUTGERS, THE STATE UNI-
    VERSITY OF NEW JERSEY

PRIMARY AFFILIATION

COMPANY CONTACT:
Carolyn Smith
Associate Director
Community Nursing Service
of Essex and West Hudson
451 Lincoln Avenue
Orange, NJ   07050
(201) 673-0158

INSTITUTIONAL CONTACT:
Lucille Joel
Associate Dean for Clinical
Affairs
College of Nursing
Rutgers, The State University
of New Jersey
University Avenue
Newark, NJ   07102
(201) 648-5298

PROGRAM DESCRIPTION/OBJECTIVES:
Manpower sharing; student
placement.

PROGRAM INITIATED: 1981

LENGTH OF STUDY FOR PARTICI-
PANT: Academic year

LENGTH OF CONTRACT: 10 months

LOCATION: Community Nursing
Service and Rutgers

PARTICIPANTS: 2

PROGRAM COSTS PROVIDED BY:
Shared equally by exchange of
time between company and
institution

PRINTED MATERIALS AVAILABLE
FROM: Institution

69. COMPUTER SCIENCE
    CORPORATION
         with
    UNIVERSITY OF SOUTHERN
    CALIFORNIA

MS IN SYSTEMS MANAGEMENT

COMPANY CONTACT:
Cinda Semisch
Manager of Human Resources
Computer Science Corporation
8727 Colesville Road
Silver- Spring, MD   20910
(301) 589-1545, X425

INSTITUTIONAL CONTACT:
Jon W. Whitton
Field Representative
Eastern Region
University of Southern
California
5510 Columbia Pike #200
Arlington, VA   22204
(703) 521-5025

PROGRAM DESCRIPTION/OBJECTIVES:
The MS in Systems Management is
designed to meet the graduate
education needs of modern managers who seek competence in
the systems approach and its
use in formulation of strategy
and policy decisions.

PROGRAM INITIATED: 1980

LENGTH OF STUDY FOR PARTICI-
PANT: 2 years

LENGTH OF CONTRACT: 2 years

LOCATION: Silver Spring, MD

PARTICIPANTS: 20 management
level personnel

PROGRAM COSTS PROVIDED BY:
Company: $615 per course per
student

PRINTED MATERIALS AVAILABLE
FROM: Institution

70. COMPUTERVISION
with
WORCESTER POLYTECHNIC
INSTITUTE

ENGINEERING WITH EMPHASES ON
CAD/CAM

COMPANY CONTACT:
Computervision
through
John Gillespie, Jr.
Bay State Skills Corporation
McCormack Office Building
One Ashburton Place
Room 2110
Boston, MA   02108
(617) 727-5431

INSTITUTIONAL CONTACT:
Donald N. Zwiep
Head, Mechanical Engineering
Worcester Polytechnic Institute
Institute Road
Worcester, MA   01609
(617) 753-1411

PROGRAM DESCRIPTION/OBJECTIVES:
Training will focus on "pilot"
courses, utilizing the robotics
laboratory. It will be offered
to familiarize community leaders, business executives and
friends of the school with this
new CAD/CAM technology.

PROGRAM INITIATED: 1982

LENGTH OF STUDY FOR PARTICI-
PANT: Open house activity 1-3
hours long and introductory
courses

LENGTH OF CONTRACT: 2 years

LOCATIONS: Worcester Polytechnic Institute

PARTICIPANTS: 200 community
residents

PROGRAM COSTS PROVIDED BY:
Institution: $62,777
Company: $75,395
Other Source: $67,875 (Bay
State Skills Corporation)

PRINTED MATERIALS AVAILABLE
FROM: Company

71. CON EDISON*
with
THE COLLEGE OF STATEN
ISLAND

OUTREACH PROGRAMS

COMPANY CONTACT:
Judith Warner
Con Edison
708 1st Avenue
New York, NY   10017
(212) 576-3186

INSTITUTIONAL CONTACT:
Michael J. Pefrides
Associate Dean of Faculty
Outreach Centers
College of Staten Island
130 Stuyvesant Place
Staten Island, NY   10301
(212) 390-7551

PROGRAM DESCRIPTION/OBJECTIVES:
Off campus credit courses appli-
cable to AAS degrees with a technical emphasis. Non-credit occupational training programs.

PROGRAM INITIATED: 1974

LENGTH OF STUDY FOR PARTICI-
PANT: Varies

LENGTH OF CONTRACT: Varies

LOCATION: In-plant

PARTICIPANTS: Varies

PROGRAM COSTS PROVIDED BY:
Institution: 40%
Company: 40%
Participant: 20%

PRINTED MATERIALS AVAILABLE
FROM: Institution and Company

_____

*Representative entry--complete
list available from institution.

72. CONNECTICUT NATURAL GAS
            with
     UNIVERSITY OF HARTFORD

ON-SITE UNDERGRADUATE CREDIT

COMPANY CONTACT:
Michael J. Keppler
Industrial Relations
Administrator
Connecticut Natural Gas Company
P.O. Box 1500
Hartford, CT   06144
(203) 727-3000

INSTITUTIONAL CONTACT:
William T. George
Program Development Consultant
Division of Adult Educational
Services
University of Hartford
200 Bloomfield Avenue
West Hartford, CT   06117
(203) 243-4507/4381

PROGRAM DESCRIPTION/OBJECTIVES:
Undergraduate business courses.

PROGRAM INITIATED: 1981

LENGTH OF STUDY FOR PARTICI-
PANT: 1 semester

LENGTH OF CONTRACT: Indefinite

LOCATION: Connecticut Natural
Gas

PARTICIPANTS: 7 qualified employees per semester

PROGRAM COSTS PROVIDED BY:
Company: 100%

PRINTED MATERIALS AVAILABLE
FROM: Not available

73. CONTINENTAL PIPELINE
     COMPANY
            with
     OKLAHOMA STATE TECH

DIGITAL PRINCIPLES, INTRO-
DUCTION TO MICROPROCESSORS

COMPANY CONTACT:
R.C. Ashlock
Superintendent of Terminals
Continental Pipeline Company
3025 East Skelly Drive
Suite 420
Tulsa, OK   74105
(918) 743-8803

INSTITUTIONAL CONTACT:
Bill J. Lyons
Department Head
Electrical-Electronics
Technology
Oklahoma State Tech
4th and Mission
Okmulgee, OK   74447
(918) 765-6211, X252

PROGRAM DESCRIPTION/OBJECTIVES:
To provide instrumentation technicians with current state-of-
the-art with increased awareness of microprocessor capabilities.

PROGRAM INITIATED: 1982

LENGTH OF STUDY FOR PARTICI-
PANT: Not reported

LENGTH OF CONTRACT: Not
reported

LOCATION: Not reported

PARTICIPANTS: 24 employees
annually

PROGRAM COSTS PROVIDED BY:
Company: 100%

PRINTED MATERIALS AVAILABLE
FROM: Not available

74. COORS
                  with
        COLORADO SCHOOL OF MINES

WELLNESS PROGRAM

COMPANY CONTACT:
Ben Mason
Consultant
Coors Company
Golden, CO   80401
(303) 988-6462

INSTITUTIONAL CONTACT:
Kathryn Jens, Ph.D.
Director of Student Development
Colorado School of Mines
Golden, CO   80401
(303) 273-3377

PROGRAM DESCRIPTION/OBJECTIVES
Increase C.S.M. students' and
Coors employees' knowledge of
wellness, health and mental
health prevention, decrease al-
cohol abuse.

PROGRAM INITIATED: 1981

LENGTH OF STUDY FOR PARTICI-
PANT: Variable

LENGTH OF CONTRACT: 2 years

LOCATION: On campus

PARTICIPANTS: 200 initially,
increasing

PROGRAM COSTS PROVIDED BY:
Company: $15,000

PRINTED MATERIALS AVAILABLE
FROM: Institution

75. COPELAND CORPORATION
                  with
        EDISON STATE COMMUNITY
        COLLEGE

SUPERVISORY TRAINING: SMALL
GROUP COMMUNICATION

COMPANY CONTACT:
Susan Way
Corporate Manager
Employee Relations
Copeland Corporation
Campbell Road
Sidney, OH   45365
(513) 498-3353

INSTITUTIONAL CONTACT:
Gary W. Wilson
Assistant Dean for Continuing
Education
Edison State Community College
1973 Edison Drive
Piqua, OH   45356
(513) 778-8600

PROGRAM DESCRIPTION/OBJECTIVES:
Improve employee relations,
better trained workers, more
efficient work performance and
decrease in the frequency of
misunderstandings between
employees.

PROGRAM INITIATED: 1981

LENGTH OF STUDY FOR PARTICI-
PANT: 26 hours

LENGTH OF CONTRACT: 1 month
with renewal options

LOCATION: Hueston Woods State
Park

PARTICIPANTS: 10 first-line
supervisors

PROGRAM COSTS PROVIDED BY:
Institution: $913.00
Company: $2,414.80
Other Source: $273.00

PRINTED MATERIALS AVAILABLE
FROM: Institution

76. CRANE NAVAL WEAPON SUPPORT
     CENTER*
              with
     UNIVERSITY OF EVANSVILLE

COOPERATIVE EDUCATION

COMPANY CONTACT:
Mary Swarn
Personnel Department
Crane Naval Weapons Support
Center
Crane, IN   47522
(812) 854-1606

INSTITUTIONAL CONTACT:
John D. Small
Director of Cooperative
Education
University of Evansville
P.O. Box 329
Evansville, IN   47711
(812) 479-2652

PROGRAM DESCRIPTION/OBJECTIVES:
Combine classroom education
with work experience in
industry.

PROGRAM INITIATED: 1947

LENGTH OF STUDY FOR PARTICI-
PANT: 5 to 7 quarterly work
periods.

LENGTH OF CONTRACT: Not
reported

LOCATION: Industrial work
site

PARTICIPANTS: 120 electrical,
mechanical, civil and computer
engineering and computer
science students

PROGRAM COSTS PROVIDED BY:
Participant: 100%

PRINTED MATERIALS AVAILABLE
FROM: Institution and
Company

_____

*Representative entry--complete
list available from institution.

77. DAN RIVER, INC.
              with
     DANVILLE COMMUNITY COLLEGE

SUPERVISION FOR DAN RIVER, INC.

COMPANY CONTACT:
Ed Carroll
Director, Industrial Relations
Dan River, Inc.
West Main Street
Danville, VA   24541
(804) 799-7368

INSTITUTIONAL CONTACT:
Max R. Glass
Director, Continuing Education
Danville Community College
1008 South Main Street
Danville, VA   24541
(804) 797-3553

PROGRAM DESCRIPTION/OBJECTIVES:
To train hourly employees to
assume positions in supervision.

PROGRAM INITIATED: 1978

LENGTH OF STUDY FOR PARTICI-
PANT: 3 quarters on a part-
time basis

LENGTH OF CONTRACT: 9 months
with continual option

LOCATION: Danville Community
College

PARTICIPANTS: 20 hourly employees per class

PROGRAM COSTS PROVIDED BY:
Institution: $3,000 per class
Company: $5,350 per class

PRINTED MATERIALS AVAILABLE FROM:
FROM: Institution

78. DATA GENERAL*
with
WORCESTER STATE COLLEGE

EDUCATION AT YOUR DOORSTEP

COMPANY CONTACT:
Steven Widen
Training Specialist
Data General
4400 Computer Drive
Westboro, MA   01581
(617) 366-8911

INSTITUTIONAL CONTACT:
William O'Neill
Dean, Division of Graduate and
Continuing Education
Worcester State College
486 Chandler Street
Worcester, MA   01602
(617) 793-8100

PROGRAM DESCRIPTION/OBJECTIVES:
To meet the educational needs
of Westboro area company employees, to facilitate employee
training and development in
areas of high need, high quality credit-bearing training at
a convenient time and location.

PROGRAM INITIATED: 1981

LENGTH OF STUDY FOR PARTICI-
PANT: Not reported

LENGTH OF CONTRACT: None

LOCATION: Westboro High School

PARTICIPANTS: 90 employees
per semester

PROGRAM COSTS PROVIDED BY:
Institution: $130 per course
Company: $130 per course

PRINTED MATERIALS AVAILABLE
FROM: Institution

---

*Representative entry--complete
list available from institution.

79. DAVEY LANDSCAPE
with
KENT STATE UNIVERSITY

MANAGEMENT DEVELOPMENT SEMINAR

COMPANY CONTACT:
Gordon Ober
Davey Landscape
117 South Water Street
Kent, OH   44240
(216) 673-9511

INSTITUTIONAL CONTACT:
Karen Rylander
Director, Continuing Education
Kent State University
327 Rockwell Hall
Kent, OH   44242
(216) 672-3100

PROGRAM DESCRIPTION/OBJECTIVSS:
Designed to develop an understanding of leadership activities that build individual motivation, group support, improve
quality of decisions and their
implementation.

PROGRAM INITIATED: 1980

LENGTH OF STUDY FOR PARTICI-
PANT: 4 hours

LENGTH OF CONTRACT: 4 hours

LOCATION: Kent State University

PARTICIPANTS: 16 district
managers

PROGRAM COSTS PROVIDED BY:
Company: 100%

PRINTED MATERIALS AVAILABLE
FROM: Institution

80. DAVEY TREE EXPERT COMPANY
with
KENT STATE UNIVERSITY

LEADERSHIP, EMPLOYEE BEHAVIOR
AND PRODUCTIVITY

COMPANY CONTACT:
Harry Taylor
Davey Tree Expert Company
117 South Water Street
Kent, OH   44240
(216) 673-9511

INSTITUTIONAL CONTACT:
Karen Rylander
Director, Continuing Education
Kent State University
327 Rockwell Hall
Kent, OH   44242
(216) 672-3100

PROGRAM DESCRIPTION/OBJECTIVES:
Designed to explore the supervisor's leadership role and to
identify and develop activities
and skills in communication,
motivation, problem solving and
decision making that build productive units. Related skills,
such as performance evaluation,
training and development are
also covered.

PROGRAM INITIATED: 1981

LENGTH OF STUDY FOR PARTICI-
PANT: 16 hours + 2 hour follow-
up session

LENGTH OF CONTRACT: 16 hours
+ 2 hour follow-up session

LOCATION: Davey Tree Expert
Company

PARTICIPANTS: 25 first-line
supervisors

PROGRAM COSTS PROVIDED BY:
Company: 100%

PRINTED MATERIALS AVAILABLE
FROM: Institution

81. DAYTONA BEACH AREA BUSINESS
COMMUNITY
with
BETHUNE-COOKMAN COLLEGE

PARTNERS-IN-PROGRESS

COMPANY CONTACT:
R.G. Mulligan
Former Visiting Professor at
Bethune-Cookman College
NASA Headquarters
Code NS
Washington, DC   20546
(202) 755-3140

INSTITUTIONAL CONTACT:
Shirley Lee
Director of Planning and
Development
Business Division
Bethune-Cookman College
640 Second Avenue
Daytona Beach, FL   32015
(904) 255-1401, X355

PROGRAM DESCRIPTION/OBJECTIVES:
To develop closer links with
the community through seminars
on contemporary business management topics designed by campus faculty in an effort to
create more intern or cooperative experiences for students.

PROGRAM INITIATED: 1981

LENGTH OF STUDY FOR PARTICI-
PANT: Varied

LENGTH OF CONTRACT: 1 year

LOCATION: Campus and community

PARTICIPANTS: 50-100 local
businessmen

PROGRAM COSTS PROVIDED BY:
Institution: $5,000
(administrative)
Company: NASA - salary

PRINTED MATERIALS AVAILABLE
FROM: Institution

82. DEARBORN CHEMICAL
with
COLLEGE OF LAKE COUNTY

IMPROVING SUPERVISORY SKILLS

COMPANY CONTACT:
Neil Everett
Plant Manager
Dearborn Chemical
300 Genesee
Lake Zurich, IL   60047
(312) 438-8241

INSTITUTIONAL CONTACT:
Keri Thiessen
Business/Industry Training
Coordinator
Open Campus
College of Lake County
Grayslake, IL   60030
(312) 223-3616

PROGRAM DESCRIPTION/OBJECTIVES:
To improve, develop, and introduce skills and techniques
necessary for effective
supervision.

PROGRAM INITIATED: 1981

LENGTH OF STUDY FOR PARTICI-
PANT: 11 weeks

LENGTH OF CONTRACT: 11 weeks

LOCATION: Dearborn Chemical

PARTICIPANTS: 14 supervisors
of various departments

PROGRAM COSTS PROVIDED BY:
Company: $1,683

PRINTED MATERIALS AVAILABLE
FROM: Institution

83. DEFENSE CONTRACT AUDIT
AGENCY
with
CENTRAL MICHIGAN UNIVERSITY

DCAA EXECUTIVE DEVELOPMENT
PROGRAM

COMPANY CONTACT:
Chuck Starrett, Jr.
Deputy Director
Defense Contract Audit Agency
130 Cameron Station
Alexandria, VA   22314
(202) 274-6785

INSTITUTIONAL CONTACT:
Lawrence R. Murphy
Director
Institute for Personal and
Career Development
Central Michigan University
Mt. Pleasant, MI   48859
(517) 774-3865

PROGRAM DESCRIPTION/OBJECTIVES:
To provide an 8-course graduate
level professional development
program for selected employees
of the DCAA. Participants may
apply the courses toward a
graduate program with CMU.

PROGRAM INITIATED: Not
reported

LENGTH OF STUDY FOR PARTICI-
PANT: 18 months

LENGTH OF CONTRACT: Ongoing

LOCATION: Courses are offered
at several locations around the
U.S.

PARTICIPANTS: 28 DCAA employees, grade GS 13 and above

PROGRAM COSTS PROVIDED BY:
Company: 100%

PRINTED MATERIALS AVAILABLE
FROM: Institution

84. DEFENSE MAPPING AGENCY
with
PANAMA CANAL COLLEGE

ASSOCIATE DEGREE IN EARTH
SCIENCES

COMPANY CONTACT:
Jack E. Staples
Director
Defense Mapping Agency
InterAmerican Geodetic Survey
Cartographic School
Drawer 936
APO Miami, FL   34004

INSTITUTIONAL CONTACT:
Jack E. Staples
Dean
Panama Canal College
DODDS, Panama Region
APO Miami, FL   34002

PROGRAM DESCRIPTION/OBJECTIVES:
Provide academic degree program
for military and governmental
employees in Earth Sciences
area.

PROGRAM INITIATED: 1982

LENGTH OF STUDY FOR PARTICI-
PANT: 4 semesters

LENGTH OF CONTRACT: Memoran-
dum of understanding

LOCATION: Panama Canal College

PARTICIPANTS: 40 Panama Canal
employees annually

PROGRAM COSTS PROVIDED BY:
Institution: 40%
Company: 20%
Participant: 40%

PRINTED MATERIALS AVAILABLE
FROM: Not reported

85. DELCO REMY DIVISION OF
GENERAL MOTORS
with
MERIDIAN JUNIOR COLLEGE

APPRENTICESHIP TRAINING PROGRAM
FOR MAINTENANCE PERSONNEL

COMPANY CONTACT:
Leroy Johnston
Personnel Manager
Delco Remy
Highway 11 South
P.O. Box 4396
Meridian, MS   39301
(601) 485-5122

INSTITUTIONAL CONTACT:
Jack Shank
Dean, Continuing Education
Meridian Junior College
5500 Highway 19 North
Meridian, MS   39301
(601) 483-8241, X112

PROGRAM DESCRIPTION/OBJECTIVES:
To provide classroom training
to accompany apprenticeship program for Delco Remy for personnel training as maintenance
mechanics and/or electricians.

PROGRAM INITIATED: 1978

LENGTH OF STUDY FOR PARTICI-
PANT: 4 years, part-time

LENGTH OF CONTRACT: Ongoing

LOCATION: Meridian Junior
College

PARTICIPANTS: 15 mechanics
and electricians annually

PROGRAM COSTS PROVIDED BY:
Institution: $5,000
Company: $24,000 (participants
receive hourly wage rate paid
for regular work while attending classes)

PRINTED MATERIALS AVAILABLE
FROM: Not available

86. DELOITTE, HASKINS AND SELLS
with
CENTENARY COLLEGE

ACCOUNTING DEGREE DESIGNED BY ACCOUNTANTS

COMPANY CONTACT:
Guy Budinsack
Manager, Accounting
Deloitte, Haskins & Sells
111 Madison Avenue
Morristown, NJ   07960
(201) 540-0940

INSTITUTIONAL CONTACT:
Dan Sherwood
Dean of External Affairs
Development
Centenary College
400 Jefferson Street
Hackettstown, NJ   07840
(201) 852-1400

PROGRAM DESCRIPTION/OBJECTIVES:
Design an Accounting degree
with total input from the accounting representatives.
Skill tests given to measure
value of program. All text
books reviewed and chapters
eliminated that are unneces-
sary. Supply instructors also.

PROGRAM INITIATED: 1980

LENGTH OF STUDY FOR PARTICI-
PANT: 4 year degree program

LENGTH OF CONTRACT: 4 years

LOCATION: Centenary College

PARTICIPANTS: 25 business
majors/accounting majors
annually

PROGRAM COSTS PROVIDED BY:
Institution: Total
Company: In-kind

PRINTED MATERIALS AVAILABLE
FROM: Institution

87. DIGITAL CORPORATION
with
JOHNSON STATE COLLEGE

AB/BA DEGREE AT DIGITAL CORPORATION

COMPANY CONTACT:
Jack Burnham
Training and Development Manager
Digital Corporation
Burlington, VT   05401
(802) 863-1611

INSTITUTIONAL CONTACT:
William A. Cook
Academic Dean
Johnson State College
Johnson, VT   05656
(802) 635-2356, X220

PROGRAM DESCRIPTION/OBJECTIVES:
Associate of Science and Bachelor of Arts degree program in
general business offered on location for employees at Digital
Corporation. Objectives: provide convenient and complete
degree program related to employee needs and business needs.

PROGRAM INITIATED: 1981

LENGTH OF STUDY FOR PARTICI-
PANT: 5 years

LENGTH OF CONTRACT: 5 years

LOCATION: Burlington, VT

PARTICIPANTS: 70+ Digital
employees per semester

PROGRAM COSTS PROVIDED BY:
Company: 100%
Participant: (If a student
drops out or makes less than
C, student must pay back
company)

PRINTED MATERIALS AVAILABLE
FROM: Institution

88. DIGITAL EQUIPMENT
     CORPORATION
          with
     PRINCE GEORGE'S COMMUNITY
     COLLEGE

PRE-SUPERVISORY TRAINING

COMPANY CONTACT:
Phil Pons
Director of Training
Digital Equipment Corporation
8301 Professional Place
Landover, MD   20785
(301) 459-7900

INSTITUTIONAL CONTACT:
Veronica Norwood
Director, Contract Services
Prince George's Community
College
301 Largo Road
Largo, MD   20772
(301) 322-0726

PROGRAM DESCRIPTION/OBJECTIVES:
To provide training in effective communication skills, individual and group dynamics, decision-making techniques, and
fundamentals of management to
employees designated for promotion to a supervisory position.

PROGRAM INITIATED: 1981

LENGTH OF STUDY FOR PARTICI-
PANT: 53 hours

LENGTH OF CONTRACT: 1 month

LOCATION: The Sheraton Hotel,
Lanham, MD

PARTICIPANTS: 15 employees
designated for promotion to a
supervisory position

PROGRAM COSTS PROVIDED BY:
Company: 58%
Other Source: 42% (state
funding)

PRINTED MATERIALS AVAILABLE
FROM: Institution

89. DOVER TEXTILES, INC.
          with
     GARDNER-WEBB COLLEGE

MANAGEMENT EDUCATION

COMPANY CONTACT:
Dean Garver
Assistant Director of
Industrial Relations
Dover Textiles, Inc.
P.O. Drawer 208
Shelby, NC   28150
(704) 487-2361

INSTITUTIONAL CONTACT:
Larry L. Sale
Dean of Continuing Education
and Summer School
Gardner-Webb College
Boiling Springs, NC   28017
(704) 434-2361

PROGRAM DESCRIPTION/OBJECTIVES:
Bachelor of Science degree program in business management for
Dover Textiles employees and
their spouses on-site during
the evening hours.

PROGRAM INITIATED: 1981

LENGTH OF STUDY FOR PARTICI-
PANT: 4 years

LENGTH OF CONTRACT: Indefinite

LOCATION: Dover Training
Center

PARTICIPANTS: 20 variety of
employees per semester

PROGRAM COSTS PROVIDED BY:
Institution: 37.5%
Participant: 27.5%
Other Source: 25% (North
Carolina legislative grant)

PRINTED MATERIALS AVAILABLE
FROM: Institution

90. DUKE POWER COMPANY
       with
    GARDNER-WEBB COLLEGE

MANAGEMENT EDUCATION

COMPANY CONTACT:
Robert Via
Training Supervisor
McGuire Nuclear Plant of Duke
Power Company
P.O. Box 33189
Charlotte, NC   28242
(704) 875-1361

INSTITUTIONAL CONTACT:
Larry L. Sale
Dean of Continuing Education
and Summer School
Gardner-Webb College
Boiling Springs, NC   28017
(704) 434-2361

PROGRAM DESCRIPTION/OBJECTIVES:
Bachelor of Science degree program in business management for
employees and spouses, Construction and Production Divi-
sions, McGuire Nuclear Plant,
Duke Power Company, on-site
during the evening hours.

PROGRAM INITIATED: 1982

LENGTH OF STUDY FOR PARTICI-
PANT: 4 years

LENGTH OF CONTRACT: Ongoing

LOCATION: Training Room A

PARTICIPANTS: 30 variety of
employees

PROGRAM COSTS PROVIDED BY:
Institution: 24%
Company: 47.5%
Other Source: 28.5% (North
Caroline legislative grant)

PRINTED MATERIALS AVAILABLE
FROM: Institution

91. DUPONT
       with
    UNIVERSITY OF MARYLAND -
    BALTIMORE COUNTY

DUPONT-UMBC PROJECT TO EXPRESS
INTERFERON

COMPANY CONTACT:
Bruce Korant
Research Supervisor of
Molecular Genetics
Dupont Experimental Station
Building 328
Wilmington, DE   19898
(302) 772-4823

INSTITUTIONAL CONTACT:
P. Lovett
Professor of Biological Sciences
University of Maryland -
Baltimore County
Catonsville, MD   21228
(301) 455-2249

PROGRAM DESCRIPTION/OBJECTIVES:
Production of human interferon
in B. subtilis.

PROGRAM INITIATED: 1981

LENGTH OF STUDY FOR PARTICI-
PANT: 2 years

LENGTH OF CONTRACT: 2 years

LOCATION: On campus

PARTICIPANTS: 5 Ph.D. level
special research assistants

PROGRAM COSTS PROVIDED BY:
Company: $500,000

PRINTED MATEIRALS AVAILABLE
FROM: Not reported

92. E.I. DUPONT DE NEMOURS,
     COMPANY
               with
     PATRICK HENRY COMMUNITY
     COLLEGE

COMPUTER LANGUAGE TRAINING FOR
MANAGEMENT

COMPANY CONTACT:
Wayne Watson
Chairman of Management Training
E.I. DuPont De Nemours, Company
Martinsville, VA   24112
(703) 632-9761

INSTITUTIONAL CONTACT:
Steve Maradian
Director
Continuing Education -
Community Service
Patrick Henry Community College
P.O. Drawer 5311
Martinsville, VA   24115
(705) 635-8777

PROGRAM DESCRIPTION/OBJECTIVES:
Provide language training in
"fortran" and "basic" for
management personnel.

PROGRAM INITIATED: 1982

LENGTH OF STUDY FOR PARTICI-
PANT: 12 weeks

LENGTH OF CONTRACT: 12 weeks
with renewal and/or new
training options

LOCATION: DuPont, Martinsville

PARTICIPANTS: 60 mid and upper
management personnel

PROGRAM COSTS PROVIDED BY:
Company: $16,000

PRINTED MATERIALS AVAILABLE
FROM: Institution

93. EL PASO ELECTRIC COMPANY
               with
     EL PASO COMMUNITY COLLEGE
     DISTRICT

MID-MANAGEMENT DEVELOPMENT
PROGRAM

COMPANY CONTACT:
Jack Duffey
Director of Training
El Paso Electric Company
P.O. Box 982
El Paso, TX   79960
(915) 543-5711

INSTITUTIONAL CONTACT:
Gregory F. Linden
Associate Dean
Community Services/Continuing
Education
El Paso Community College
P.O. Box 20500
El Paso, TX   79998
(915) 594-2597

PROGRAM DESCRIPTION/OBJECTIVES:
To provide mid-management
skills development training.

PROGRAM INITIATED: 1976

LENGTH OF STUDY FOR PARTICI-
PANT: 64 hours in half or
full day increments

LENGTH OF CONTRACT: 12 months
renewed annually

LOCATION: El Paso Electric
Company

PARTICIPANTS: 120 mid-management personnel annually

PROGRAM COSTS PROVIDED BY:
Company: $5,500

PRINTED MATERIALS AVAILABLE
FROM: Institution

94. ELECTRICAL PRODUCTS
    CORPORATION*
        with
    MERRITT COLLEGE

COOPERATIVE EDUCATION

COMPANY CONTACT:
Harry Inn
Electrical Products Corporation
P.O. Box 23444
Oakland, CA   94623
(415) 655-9300

INSTITUTIONAL CONTACT:
Carolyn Schuetz
Coordinator, Cooperative and
Occupational Education
Career Center
Merritt College
12500 Campus Drive
Oakland, CA   94619
(415) 436-2446

PROGRAM DESCRIPTION/OBJECTIVES:
Provides students with learning
in a work situation, generally
relating work to college studies. Provides opportunity for
career exploration or upgrading
on the job. Provides employer
with back-up services/training
for employee.

PROGRAM INITIATED: 1970

LENGTH OF STUDY FOR PARTICI-
PANT: Usually at least 2
semesters

LENGTH OF CONTRACT: At least
1 semester

LOCATION: Merritt College

PARTICIPANTS: 400 students in
all college disciplines per
semester

PROGRAM COSTS PROVIDED BY:
Institution: Staff salaries
Company: Student salaries
Other Source: $10,000 (federal
and state grants)

PRINTED MATERIALS AVAILABLE FROM
FROM: Institution

---

*Representative entry--complete
list available from institution.

95. EPISCOPAL HOSPITAL
        with
    WIDENER UNIVERSITY

ASSOCIATE IN SCIENCE DEGREE ON-
SITE FOR RADIOLOGIC
TECHNOLOGISTS

COMPANY CONTACT:
Jane Leggieri
Program Director
School of Radiography
Episcopal Hospital
Front Street and Lehigh Avenue
Philadelphia, PA   19125
(215) 427-7000

INSTITUTIONAL CONTACT:
Michael P. Murphy
Associate Dean
University College
Widener University
P.O. Box 7139, Concord Pike
Wilmington, DE   19803
(302) 478-3000, X332

PROGRAM DESCRIPTION/OBJECTIVES:
To provide the requirements on-
site for completing an Associate's degree in radiologic technology at University College.

PROGRAM INITIATED: 1982

LENGTH OF STUDY FOR PARTICI-
PANT: 3-5 semesters of part-
time study

LENGTH OF CONTRACT: 12 months
with renewal option

LOCATION: Episcopal Hospital

PARTICIPANTS: 15-25 students
in radiologic technology programs, or technicians already
in the field

PROGRAM COSTS PROVIDED BY:
Participant: $95 per credit
hour

PRINTED MATERIALS AVAILABLE
FROM: Institution

96. EQUITABLE LIFE ASSURANCE
SOCIETY OF THE UNITED
STATES
with
MANHATTAN COLLEGE

EQUITABLE/MANHATTAN COLLEGE
MIDTOWN PROGRAM IN HIGHER
EDUCATION

COMPANY CONTACT:
Peter A. Lipuma
Vice President
General Studies
Equitable Life Assurance Society
1285 Avenue of the Americas
New York, NY   10019
(212) 554-3476

INSTITUTIONAL CONTACT:
Thomas E. Chambers
Dean
School of General Studies
Manhattan College
Manhattan College Parkway
Riverdale, NY   10471
(212) 920-0341

PROGRAM DESCRIPTION/OBJECTIVES:
A cooperative higher education
program which coordinates the
financial and the physical facility resources of a major international insurance carrier
with the academic and teaching
resources of a private independent college.

PROGRAM INITIATED: Not reported

LENGTH OF STUDY FOR PARTICI-
PANT: 1 semester

LENGTH OF CONTRACT: 12 months
continuous program for classrooms, yearly lease for office

LOCATION: Conference Center
at the Equitable Headquarters
Building

PARTICIPANTS: Approximately
90 high school, college and
graduate students per year

PROGRAM COSTS PROVIDED BY:
Institution: $20,000
Company: $32,000
Participant: $90

PRINTED MATERIALS AVAILABLE
FROM: Institution and Company

97. ERIE INSURANCE GROUP
with
VILLA MARIA COLLEGE

BUSINESS INTERNSHIP

COMPANY CONTACT:
Martin P. Eisert
Director, Human Resources
Erie Insurance Group
144 East 6th Street
Erie, PA   16530
(814) 452-6831

INSTITUTIONAL CONTACT:
Ruth F. Hahn
Chairperson, Business Department
Villa Maria College
2551 West Lake Road
Erie, PA   16505
(814) 838-1966, X242

PROGRAM DESCRIPTION/OBJECTIVES:
Educationally directed internship in an institution in which
the student learns by observa-
tion and participation in the
functioning of a particular department within a business or
industry.

PROGRAM INITIATED: 1978

LENGTH OF STUDY FOR PARTICI-
PANT: 1 semester usually;
can be up to 4 months during
summer

LENGTH OF CONTRACT: Dependent
on student availability

LOCATION: Villa Maria College

PARTICIPANTS: 1 senior business major

PROGRAM COSTS PROVIDED BY:
Company: Approximately $850
Participant: Travel costs

PRINTED MATERIALS AVAILABLE
FROM: Institution

98. ERNST AND WHINNEY*
with
CASE WESTERN RESERVE
UNIVERSITY

INDUSTRIAL SOCIAL WORK

COMPANY CONTACT:
Kenneth Macjen
National Director
Personnel Assistance Program
Ernst and Whinney
2000 National City Center
Cleveland, OH   44115
(216) 566-7333

INSTITUTIONAL CONTACT:
Holly Krailo
Director
Industrial Social Work Program
School of Applied Social
Sciences
Case Western Reserve University
2035 Abington Road
Cleveland, OH   44106
(216) 368-2135

PROGRAM DESCRIPTION/OBJECTIVES:
To demonstrate the scope and
potential of social work practice in business and labor settings through the use of
graduate internships.

PROGRAM INITIATED: 1981

LENGTH OF CONTRACT: 1 academic year

LOCATION: Ernst and Whinney

PARTICIPANTS: 1 graduate
social work student**

PROGRAM COSTS PROVIDED BY:
Institution: 50%
Company: 50%

PRINTED MATERIALS AVAILABLE
FROM: Institution

---

*Representative entry--complete
list available from institution.

**Figures given reflect the en-
tire program.

99. ESCAN
with
BAY DE NOC COMMUNITY
COLLEGE

CONTRACTING WITH BUSINESS AND
INDUSTRY (CWB&I)

COMPANY CONTACT:
Paul Parker
Escan Corporation
Danforth Road
Escanaba, MI   49829
(906) 786-3997

INSTITUTIONAL CONTACT:
Chuck Gold
Program Director
Bay de Noc Community College
College Avenue
Escanaba, MI   49829
(906) 786-5802

PROGRAM DESCRIPTION/OBJECTIVES:
CWB&I is a method of specialized individual career orienta-
tion, training, and opportunities. It utilizes the local
business and industrial complex of the community as a
training laboratory. Students
can acquire job skills in interests and capabilities under
realistic settings.

PROGRAM INITIATED: 1976

LENGTH OF STUDY FOR PARTICI-
PANT: 2 semesters

LENGTH OF CONTRACT: 2 semesters

LOCATION: Bay College/local
businesses

PARTICIPANTS: 90 annually

PROGRAM COSTS PROVIDED BY:
Participant: $560.00

PRINTED MATERIALS AVAILABLE
FROM: Institution

100. EXOLON COMPANY
with
STATE UNIVERSITY COLLEGE
AT BUFFALO

EVALUATION STUDY OF WORKER
ATTITUDES

COMPANY CONTACT:
Robert F. Taylor
Works Manager
Personnel Department
Exolon Company
1000 East Niagara Street
Tonowanda, NY   14150
(716) 693-4550

INSTITUTIONAL CONTACT:
William T. Ganley
Director, Center for Applied
Research
State University College at
Buffalo
1300 Elmwood Avenue, GC 409
Buffalo, NY   14222
(716) 878-4110

PROGRAM DESCRIPTION/OBJECTIVES:
Tabulate raw data, analyze data,
 etermine for similar and dis-
similar reaction, submit a
written report identifying the
implications.

PROGRAM INITIATED: 1981

LENGTH OF STUDY FOR PARTICI-
PANT: 4 months

LENGTH OF CONTRACT: 4 months

LOCATION: Exolon in-house

PARTICIPANTS: 29 managers-
supervisors, employees

PROGRAM COSTS PROVIDED BY:
Institution: $1,900
Company: $3,400

PRINTED MATERIALS AVAILABLE
FROM: Not reported

101. EXXON*
with
DREW UNIVERSITY

COOPERATIVE EDUCATION IN
CHEMISTRY

COMPANY CONTACT:
Paul Smith
Public Affairs Department
Exxon
P.O. Box 101
Florham Park, NJ   07932
(201) 765-6622

INSTITUTIONAL CONTACT:
James M. Miller
Chairman
Department of Chemistry
Drew University
Madison, NJ   07940
(201) 377-3000

PROGRAM DESCRIPTION/OBJECTIVES:
An optional co-op program for
chemistry majors with non-alter-
nating work periods. Some college credit given for work; program completed in 4 years.

PROGRAM INITIATED: 1980

LENGTH OF STUDY FOR PARTICI-
PANT: 2 work periods: 1 of
3 months and 1 of 8 months

LENGTH OF CONTRACT: 2 years

LOCATION: Various chemical and
pharmaceutical companies

PARTICIPANTS: Approximately 2
junior and senior chemistry
majors annually

PROGRAM COSTS PROVIDED BY:
Company: Salary

PRINTED MATERIALS AVAILABLE
FROM: Institution

---

*Representative entry--complete
list available from institution.

53

102. EXXON*
with
DREW UNIVERSITY

RESEARCH INSTITUTE FOR
SCIENTISTS EMERITII (RISE)

COMPANY CONTACT:
Paul Smith
Public Affairs Department
Exxon
P.O. Box 101
Florham Park, NJ   07932
(201) 765-6622

INSTITUTIONAL CONTACT:
George deStevens
Director, RISE
Chemistry Department
Drew University
Madison, NJ   07940
(201) 377-3000

PROGRAM DESCRIPTION/OBJECTIVES:
Retirees (including early retirees) from industry are provided space and facilities at
the university in return for
their help in directing the research of undergraduate students. Students receive better
education and an improved image
of industry.

PROGRAM INITIATED: 1977

LENGTH OF STUDY FOR PARTICI-
PANT: 2 to 3 years renewable

LENGTH OF CONTRACT: 2 years,
renewable

LOCATION: Drew University

PARTICIPANTS: 2 expanding to
12; currently chemistry retirees but expanding to all sciences and math

PROGRAM COSTS PROVIDED BY:
Institution: minimal

PRINTED MATERIALS AVAILABLE
FROM: Institution

---

*Representative entry--complete
list available from institution.

103. FAIRCHILD INDUSTRIES
with
UNIVERSITY OF MARYLAND

FAIRCHILD SCHOLARS AND DOCTORA
FELLOWS PROGRAM

COMPANY CONTACT:
Frank Schmidt
Vice President
Employee Relations and
Administrative Services
Fairchild Industries
Fairchild Space and Electric
Company
20301 Century Blvd.
Germantown, MD   20767
(301) 428-6495

INSTITUTIONAL CONTACT:
Anthony Ephremides
Professor and Program Director
Electrical Engineering
Department
University of Maryland
College Park, MD 20742
(301) 454-6871

PROGRAM DESCRIPTION/OBJECTIVES
To provide MS or Ph.D. trainin
at full salary to outstanding
electrical engineering graduates at a time of great need
for postgraduate engineers.
Students work 3 days per week,
and study 2 days per week work
ing on their degree. They spe
cialize in communication and
computer engineering.

PROGRAM INITIATED: 1980

LENGTH OF STUDY FOR PARTICI-
PANT: 2 years for MS, 3 additional years for Ph.D. at 2
full days per week

LENGTH OF CONTRACT: Minimum 3
years, renewable

LOCATION: University of Maryland

PARTICIPANTS: 30 MS candidate
and 9 Ph.D. candidates in elec
trical engineering annually

PROGRAM COSTS PROVIDED BY:
Company: $240,000 per year

PRINTED MATERIALS AVAILABLE
FROM: Institution

104. FEDERAL LAW ENFORCEMENT
TRAINING CENTER
with
ALABAMA STATE UNIVERSITY*

CRIMINAL JUSTICE INTERN PROGRAM

COMPANY CONTACT:
Peter W. Phillips
Education Advisor
Office of the Director
Federal Law Enforcement
Training Center
Glynco, GA   31524
(912) 267-2336

INSTITUTIONAL CONTACT:
Nicholas Astone
Criminal Justice Director
Alabama State University
P.O. Box 271
Montgomery, AL   36101
(205) 832-6072

PROGRAM DESCRIPTION/OBJECTIVES:
To provide quality internship
experiences for graduate and
undergraduate criminal justice
majors.

PROGRAM INITIATED: 1978

LENGTH OF STUDY FOR PARTICI-
PANT: 1 academic quarter or
semester

LENGTH OF CONTRACT: Not
available

LOCATION: Federal Law Enforcement Training Center

PARTICIPANTS: Usually 4 graduates and undergraduates per
term

PROGRAM COSTS PROVIDED BY:
Company: Provides lodging at
nominal cost
Participant: 100%

PRINTED MATERIALS AVAILABLE
FROM: Company

---

*Representative entry--complete
list available from institution.

105. FIREMAN'S FUND INSURANCE
COMPANIES
with
DOMINICAN COLLEGE OF SAN
RAFAEL

DOMINICAN COLLEGE/FIREMAN'S
FUND JOINT DATA PROCESSING
PROGRAM

COMPANY CONTACT:
Mike Dowling
Vice President
Corporate Training and
Development
Fireman's Fund Insurance
Companies
3333 California Street
San Francisco, CA   94119

INSTITUTIONAL CONTACT:
Edward T. Engle, Jr.
Chairman
Department of Business
Administration
Dominican College
San Rafael, CA   94901
(415) 457-4440

PROGRAM DESCRIPTION/OBJECTIVES:
To provide hands-on COBOL data
processing training in an intensive three-course sequence,
with curriculum, hardware and
facilities provided by company.

PROGRAM INITIATED: 1982

LENGTH OF STUDY FOR PARTICI-
PANT: 3 15-week semesters

LENGTH OF CONTRACT: Open

LOCATION: Fireman's Fund, 1600
Los Gamos Drive, San Rafael,
CA   94911

PARTICIPANTS: 100 full- and
part-time students who have
passed a qualifying exam
annually

PROGRAM COSTS PROVIDED BY:
Participant: Tuition $660/
semester

PRINTED MATERIALS AVAILABLE
FROM: Institution

106. FIRST NATIONAL BANK OF
      CHICAGO*
            with
      VANDERBILT UNIVERSITY

THE VANDERBILT INSTITUTE FOR
THE ADVANCED STUDY OF CORPORATE
LEARNING ENVIRONMENTS

COMPANY CONTACT:
Richard Wood
Senior Vice President
First National Bank of Chicago
Chicago, IL   60670
(312) 732-4000

INSTITUTIONAL CONTACT:
John C. Glidewell
Director, Vanderbilt Institute
for the Advanced Study of Cor-
porate Learning Environments
Peabody College
Vanderbilt University
Box 321
Nashville, TN   37203
(615) 322-8414

PROGRAM DESCRIPTION/OBJECTIVES:
Established by Peabody College,
Vanderbilt's school of education and human development, the
Institute seeks to contribute
to the enhancement of learning
in corporations through research, program evaluation and
the conduct of various types of
educational activities. The Institute offers joint research
programs on a contractual basis
to corporations interested in
assessing the impact of corporate learning environments on
the development of productivity
in the corporation. Specific
information about each joint
venture is available on request.

PROGRAM INITIATED: 1982

LENGTH OF STUDY FOR PARTICI-
PANT: 6 months to 6 years

LENGTH OF CONTRACT: 6 months
to 6 years

LOCATION: On campus, at corporate site, or both

PARTICIPANTS: 12 research associates who are faculty members who represent several colleges within the university.

PROGRAM COSTS PROVIDED BY:
Institution: Varies with contract but usually less than 40%
Company: Varies with contract
but usually exceeds 60%

PRINTED MATERIALS AVAILABLE
FROM: Institution

---

*Representative entry--complete
list available from institution

107. FISHER-SCIENTIFIC
            with
      INDIANA UNIVERSITY OF
      PENNSYLVANIA

PLANNING FOR PROSPERITY

COMPANY CONTACT:
James Cename
Plant Manager
Fisher Scientific
Indiana, PA   15701
(412) 463-0253

INSTITUTIONAL CONTACT:
C.A. Altimus, Jr.
Dean, School of Business
Indiana University of
Pennsylvania
109 McElhany Hall
Indiana, PA   15705
(412) 357-2520

PROGRAM DESCRIPTION/OBJECTIVES:
Provide a positive atmosphere
in plant for upgrading of
worker skills and equipment.

PROGRAM INITIATED: 1981

LENGTH OF STUDY FOR PARTICI-
PANT: 1/2 year

LENGTH OF CONTRACT: 1 year

LOCATION: Indiana, PA

PARTICIPANTS: 300 employees

PROGRAM COSTS PROVIDED BY:
Com ny: 75%
Participant: 25%
Other Source: Union funds for
members

PRINTED MATERIALS AVAILABLE
FROM: Institution

108. FORT LOGAN MENTAL HEALTH
      CENTER
              with
      ARAPAHOE CETA

CAREER EMPLOYMENT EXPERIENCE
AND WORK EXPERIENCE

COMPANY CONTACT:
Boris Gertz
Coordinator of Training
Fort Logan Mental Health
Center
3920 West Oxford Avenue
Denver, CO   80237
(303) 761-0220

INSTITUTIONAL CONTACT:
Arlla Schildmeier
Counselor
Arapahoe CETA
311 South Broadway
Englewood, CO   80110
(303) 761-7673

PROGRAM DESCRIPTION/OBJECTIVES:
To provide trainees with job
and/or work experience; opportunities to "shadow" hospital
staff as part of career-
explorations

PROGRAM INITIATED: 1977

LENGTH OF STUDY FOR PARTICI-
PANT: Variable, 3 months,
6 months, 1 year

LENGTH OF CONTRACT: 12 months
renewable

LOCATION: Fort Logan Mental
Health Center

PARTICIPANTS: Approximately 14-
18 year olds

PROGRAM COSTS PROVIDED BY:
Institution: $3.50 per hour to
trainees

PRINTED MATERIALS AVAILABLE
FROM: Institution

109. GALLAUDET COLLEGE
              with
      PRINCE GEORGE'S COMMUNITY
      COLLEGE

CERTIFIED PROFESSIONAL
SECRETARIAL PROGRAM

COMPANY CONTACT:
Irene Pruitt
Manager, Personnel
Gallaudet College
Kendall Green
Washington, DC   20002
(202) 651-5517

INSTITUTIONAL CONTACT:
Veronica S. Norwood
Director, Contract Services
Prince George's Community
College
301 Largo Road
Largo, MD   20772
(301) 322-0726

PROGRAM DESCRIPTION/OBJECTIVES:
To prepare participants to successfully complete the Certified Professional Secretary Examination and to enhance present skills and abilities, leading to positions of greater
responsibility.

PROGRAM INITIATED: 1980

LENGTH OF STUDY FOR PARTICI-
PANT: 5 1-semester credit
classes and 3 18-30 hour non-
credit classes offered over a
24-month period

LENGTH OF CONTRACT: Renewable
each semester

LOCATION: Gallaudet College

PARTICIPANTS: 16 clerk-typists
and secretaries

PROGRAM COSTS PROVIDED BY:
Company: 50%
Other Source: 50% (state
funding)

PRINTED MATERIALS AVAILABLE
FROM: Institution

110. GENERAL BUSINESS
      SERVICES, INC.
            with
      MONTGOMERY COMMUNITY
      COLLEGE

TAX PREPARATIONS CERTIFICATION

COMPANY CONTACT:
Andy Rains
Vice President
Tax Services
General Business Services, Inc.
51 Monroe Street
Rockville, MD   20850
(301) 424-1040

INSTITUTIONAL CONTACT:
Thomas W. Fuhr
Coordinator
Off-Campus Credit Program
Montgomery Community College
51 Mannakee Street
Rockville, MD   20850
(301) 279-5254

PROGRAM DESCRIPTION/OBJECTIVES:
To meet need of prospective tax
preparers to pass an IRS
special enrollment exam.

PROGRAM INITIATED: 1981

LENGTH OF STUDY FOR PARTICI-
PANT: 1 semester

LENGTH OF CONTRACT: Open-ended

LOCATION: GBS facility

PARTICIPANTS: 44 adult
students

PROGRAM COSTS PROVIDED BY:
Company: $5,227

PRINTED MATERIALS AVAILABLE
FROM: Company

111. GENERAL MOTORS CORPORATION
            with
      COLLEGE OF ALAMEDA

GENERAL MOTORS TRAINING
CENTER PROGRAM

COMPANY CONTACT:
A.H. Warner
Manager
Training Department
General Motors
1444 Marina Blvd.
San Francisco, CA   94577
(415) 357-7200

INSTITUTIONAL CONTACT:
John Price
Division Chairperson
Business Transportation
Department
College of Alameda
555 Atlantic Avenue
Alameda, CA   94501
(415) 522-7221

PROGRAM DESCRIPTION/OBJECTIVES:
Provide product service training for General Motors Dealer
technicians under the auspices
of the General Motors Training
Center.

PROGRAM INITIATED: 1981

LENGTH OF STUDY FOR PARTICI-
PANT: 185 total days of
training plus 10 instructor
training days in Michigan

LENGTH OF CONTRACT: 1 academic year

LOCATION: General Motors
Training Center, San Leandro,
CA

PARTICIPANTS: 3 instructors
in Auto Mechanics

PROGRAM COSTS PROVIDED BY:
Company: $51,747.53

PRINTED MATERIALS AVAILABLE
FROM: Company

112. GENERAL MOTORS CORPORATION
with
GOLDEN WEST COLLEGE

GMC/GWC AUTOMOTIVE--DIESEL CON-
TRACT INSTRUCTION

COMPANY CONTACT:
Ed Banett
Region Training Supervisor
General Motors Corporation
1105 Riverside Drive
Burbank, CA   91506
(213) 849-5544

INSTITUTIONAL CONTACT:
Gene L. Tardy
Director of Community and
Corporate Relations
Public Information Department
Golden West College
15744 Golden West Street
Huntington Beach, CA   92647
(714) 892-7711

PROGRAM DESCRIPTION/OBJECTIVES:
To provide "state-of-the-art"
instruction to dealer/agency
employees of General Motors
Corporation.

PROGRAM INITIATED: 1981

LENGTH OF STUDY FOR PARTICI-
PANT: 8-16 hours

LENGTH OF CONTRACT: 12 months,
170 teaching days

LOCATION: Gold West College

PARTICIPANTS: 12-20 dealership
employees per class

PROGRAM COSTS PROVIDED BY:
Institution: 5%
Company: 95%

PRINTED MATERIALS AVAILABLE
FROM: Institution

113. GENERAL MOTORS CORPORATION
with
MACOMB COMMUNITY COLLEGE

COOPERATIVE TRAINING PROGRAM

COMPANY CONTACT:
Calvin H. Cook
Manager
General Motors Training Center
General Motors Corporation
30901 Van Dyke
Warren, MI   48090
(313) 575-0246

INSTITUTIONAL CONTACT:
Edward J. Lynch
Dean
Occupational Education
Technology
Macomb Community College
14500 Twelve Mile Road
Warren, MI   48093
(313) 445-7432

PROGRAM DESCRIPTION/OBJECTIVES:
To provide product service
training for General Motors
dealer technicians under the
auspices of the General Motors
Training Center.

PROGRAM INITIATED: 1981

LENGTH OF STUDY FOR PARTICI-
PANT: Varies

LENGTH OF CONTRACT: 7/27/81 -
6/22/82; to be renewed for
period of 8/2/82 to 7/31/83

LOCATION: General Motors
Training Center

PARTICIPANTS: Varying number of
G.M. dealer technicians

PROGRAM COSTS PROVIDED BY:
Not reported

PRINTED MATERIALS AVAILABLE
FROM: Not reported

114. GENERAL MOTORS CORPORATION
with
OKLAHOMA STATE TECH

OKLAHOMA STATE TECH/GENERAL
MOTORS CORPORATION COOPERATIVE
EDUCATION PROGRAM

COMPANY CONTACT:
Jim Collier
Manager
General Motors Corporation
12101 N.E. Expressway, RR #1
Oklahoma City, OK   73131
(405) 733-6011

INSTITUTIONAL CONTACT:
W.E. Bailey
Automotive Center Coordinator
Oklahoma State Tech
4th and Mission
Okmulgee, OK   74447
(918) 756-6211, X279

PROGRAM DESCRIPTION/OBJECTIVES:
Provide technical instruction
for General Motors dealer technicians to service and repair
components and systems of new
model vehicles with particular
emphasis on computerized control and diesel engines.

PROGRAM INITIATED: 1981

LENGTH OF STUDY FOR PARTICI-
PANT: Not reported

LENGTH OF CONTRACT: Not
reported

LOCATION: Not reported

PARTICIPANTS: 1,450 dealer
technicians

PROGRAM COSTS PROVIDED BY:
Company: 100%

PRINTED MATERIALS AVAILABLE
FROM: Institution

115. INDUSTRIAL MANUFACTURING
COMPANY
with
GEORGIA INSTITUTE OF
TECHNOLOGY

MOTIVATION FOR SUPERVISORS

COMPANY CONTACT:
H. Ben Roberson
Director, Industrial Education
Department
Georgia Institute of
Technology
Atlanta, GA   30332
(404) 894-3950

INSTITUTIONAL CONTACT:
H. Ben Roberson
Director, Industrial Education
Department
Georgia Institute of
Technology
Atlanta, GA   30332
(404) 894-3950

PROGRAM DESCRIPTION/OBJECTIVES:
To provide supervisors with motivational tools they can use
with employees and to train
them in the use of motivational
tools and implementation in the
work place.

PROGRAM INITIATED: Not
reported

LENGTH OF STUDY FOR PARTICI-
PANT: 16 hours

LENGTH OF CONTRACT: 2 weeks

LOCATION: In-plant

PARTICIPANTS: 50 supervisors

PROGRAM COSTS PROVIDED BY:
Institution: 50%
Company: 50%

PRINTED MATERIALS AVAILABLE
FROM: Institution

116. PUBLIC UTILITY COMPANY
            with
      GEORGIA INSTITUTE OF
      TECHNOLOGY

EVERY SUPERVISOR A TRAINER

COMPANY CONTACT:
H. Ben Roberson
Director, Industrial Education
Department
Georgia Institute of
Technology
Atlanta, GA   30332
(404) 894-3950

INSTITUTIONAL CONTACT:
H. Ben Roberson
Director, Industrial Education
Department
Georgia Institute of
Technology
Atlanta, GA   30332
(404) 894-3950

PROGRAM DESCRIPTION/OBJECTIVES:
The program is a train-the-
trainer program dealing with
objectives, lesson plans,
teaching techniques. The objective is for the participants
to plan and deliver a 10-minute
lesson using skills and knowledge gained in the course.

PROGRAM INITIATED: Not
reported

LENGTH OF STUDY FOR PARTICI-
PANT: 24 hours

LENGTH OF CONTRACT: 4 weeks

LOCATION: In-plant

PARTICIPANTS: 12 foremen

PROGRAM COSTS PROVIDED BY:
Institution: 25%
Company: 75%

PRINTED MATERIALS AVAILABLE
FROM: Institution

117. STEEL SPECIALTY COMPANY
            with
      GEORGIA INSTITUTE OF
      TECHNOLOGY

MANAGEMENT COMMUNICATION
PROCESS TRAINING

COMPANY CONTACT:
H. Ben Roberson
Director, Industrial Education
Department
Georgia Institute of
Technology
Atlanta, GA   30332
(404) 894-3950

INSTITUTIONAL CONTACT:
H. Ben Roberson
Director, Industrial Education
Department
Georgia Institute of
Technology
Atlanta, GA   30332
(404) 894-3950

PROGRAM DESCRIPTION/OBJECTIVES:
To train managers in the steps
of communication process and in
the use of the process.

PROGRAM INITIATED: Not
reported

LENGTH OF STUDY FOR PARTICI-
PANT: 8 hours

LENGTH OF CONTRACT: 4 weeks

LOCATION: In-plant

PARTICIPANTS: 65 foremen, area
managers, managers and plant
managers

PROGRAM COSTS PROVIDED BY:
Institution: 50%
Company: 50%

PRINTED MATERIALS AVAILABLE
FROM: Institution

118. GIANT FOOD, INC.
with
PRINCE GEORGE'S COMMUNITY
COLLEGE

BASIC INSTRUMENT REPAIR

COMPANY CONTACT:
Chuck Moon
Manager, Maintenance
Giant Food, Inc.
6300 Sheriff Road
Landover, MD   20785
(301) 386-0525

INSTITUTIONAL CONTACT:
Veronica Norwood
Director, Contract Services
Prince George's Community
College
301 Largo Road
Largo, MD   20772
(301) 322-0726

PROGRAM DESCRIPTION/OBJECTIVES:
To provide instruction in basic
analog and digital electronics
to anable participants to
troubleshoot computerized store
equipment.

PROGRAM INITIATED: 1982

LENGTH OF STUDY FOR PARTICI-
PANT: 32 hours (1 2-hour class
per week)

LENGTH OF CONTRACT: 32 weeks
with renewal

LOCATION: Prince George's
Community College

PARTICIPANTS: 11 first-level
technicians per session

PROGRAM COSTS PROVIDED BY:
Company: 61%
Other Source: 39% (state
funding)

PRINTED MATERIALS AVAILABLE
FROM: Institution

119. GODDARD SPACE FLIGHT
CENTER
with
PRINCE GEORGE'S COMMUNIT
COLLEGE

CERTIFIED PROFESSIONAL
SECRETARIAL PROGRAM

COMPANY CONTACT:
Bonnie Kaiser
Employee Development
Specialist
Goddard Space Flight Center
Greenbelt Road
Greenbelt, MD   20770
(301) 344-8930

INSTITUTIONAL CONTACT:
Veronica Norwood
Director, Contract Services
Prince George's Community
College
301 Largo Road
Largo, MD   20772
(301) 322-0726

PROGRAM DESCRIPTION/OBJECTIVES
To prepare participants to successfully complete the Certified Professional Secretary Examination and to enhance present skills and abilities, leading to positions of greater
responsibility.

PROGRAM INITIATED: 1978

LENGTH OF STUDY FOR PARTICI-
PANT: 5 1-semester credit
classes and 3 18-30 hour non-
credit classes offered over a
24-month period

LENGTH OF CONTRACT: Renewable
each semester

LOCATION: Goddard Space Flight
Center

PARTICIPANTS: 16 clerks-
typists and secretaries

PROGRAM COSTS PROVIDED BY:
Company: 50%
Other Source: 50% (state
funding)

PRINTED MATERIALS AVAILABLE
FROM: Institution

120. GOMBERT VOLKSWAGON-MAZDA*
                with
        SPARTANBURG TECHNICAL
        COLLEGE

RETURN-TO-INDUSTRY PROGRAM

COMPANY CONTACT:
Howard Gombert
Gombert Volkswagon-Mazda
402 McCrary Drive
Spartanburg, SC   29303
(803) 585-2492

INSTITUTIONAL CONTACT:
Jane Reece
Director of Grants and
Staff Development
Spartanburg Technical College
P.O. Drawer 4386
Spartanburg, SC   29303
(803) 576-5770

PROGRAM DESCRIPTION/OBJECTIVES:
Program provides faculty with
information on rapidly changing
technology and procedures by
placing instructors in business,
industry, or health care facilities for "hands-on" experience in new trends and technology. For periods of 2-15 weeks,
instructors have worked in 50
industries in the past 3 years.
The current information is in-
serted immediately into classrooms and labs resulting in 72
curriculum revisions and the development of 8 custom-designed
courses. Benefits are obvious
to students, instructors, the
company involved and the industrial community as a whole.

PROGRAM INITIATED: 1978

LENGTH OF STUDY FOR PARTICI-
PANT: 2-15 weeks

LENGTH OF CONTRACT: Ongoing

LOCATION: Spartanburg County
businesses

PARTICIPANTS: Approximately 30
faculty members

PROGRAM COSTS PROVIDED BY:
Institution: $3,000

PRINTED MATERIALS AVAILABLE
FROM: Institution

*Representative entry--complete
list available from institution.

121. GOODYEAR AEROSPACE
                with
        KENT STATE UNIVERSITY

PRINCIPLES OF MANAGEMENT

COMPANY CONTACT:
Rod Harris
Goodyear Aerospace
1210 Massilon Road
Akron, OH   44315
(216) 794-3270

INSTITUTIONAL CONTACT:
Karen Rylander
Director, Continuing Education
Kent State University
327 Rockwell Hall
Kent, OH   44242
(216) 672-3100

PROGRAM DESCRIPTION/OBJECTIVES:
Principles covered include motivation, problem-solving, leadership, communications, and disci-
pline. Subordinates are sur-
veyed to obtain information on
the general work environment.
Program culminates in development of an action plan.

PROGRAM INITIATED: 1980

LENGTH OF STUDY FOR PARTICI-
PANT: 16 hours + 4-hour
follow-up sessions

LENGTH OF CONTRACT: 16 hours
+ 4-hour follow-up sessions

LOCATION: Local hotel

PARTICIPANTS: 96 persons with
technical and engineering
backgrounds

PROGRAM COSTS PROVIDED BY:
Company: 100%

PRINTED MATERIALS AVAILABLE
FROM: Institution

122. GOODYEAR TIRE AND
RUBBER COMPANY
with
KENT STATE UNIVERSITY

MANAGEMENT SEMINAR

COMPANY CONTACT:
Dan Lyons
and
Jack Hathaway
Goodyear Tire and Rubber
Company
1144 East Market
Akron, OH   44310
(216) 796-2837
(216) 796-6332

INSTITUTIONAL CONTACT:
Karen Rylander
Director, Continuing Education
Kent State University
327 Rockwell Hall
Kent, OH   44242
(216) 672-3100

PROGRAM DESCRIPTION/OBJECTIVES:
Designed to develop understanding of concepts and skills in
the areas of cost effectiveness,
profit control, fiscal disci-
pline, return on investment,
and managing a business in an
inflationary environment. An
exploration of corporate strategy is also conducted.

PROGRAM INITIATED: 1980

LENGTH OF STUDY FOR PARTICI-
PANT: 84 hours

LENGTH OF CONTRACT: 84 hours

LOCATION: Kent State University

PARTICIPANTS: 60 upper and
middle managers

PROGRAM COSTS PROVIDED BY:
Company: 100%

PRINTED MATERIALS AVAILABLE
FROM: Institution

123. GRAPHIC CENTER
with
UNIVERSITY OF HARTFORD

MANAGEMENT AND SALES TRAINING

COMPANY CONTACT:
Robert Charbeneau
President
The Graphic Center
26 Tobey Road
Bloomfield, CT   06002
(203) 522-2223

INSTITUTIONAL CONTACT:
William T. George
Program Development Consultant
Division of Adult Educational
Services
University of Hartford
200 Bloomfield Avenue
West Hartford, CT   06117
(203) 243-4507/4381

PROGRAM DESCRIPTION/OBJECTIVES:
First and second line management programs and sale skills.

PROGRAM INITIATED: 1979

LENGTH OF STUDY FOR PARTICI-
PANT: 5 to 6 weeks (12.5
hours per program)

LENGTH OF CONTRACT: 4 programs

LOCATION: The Graphic Center

PARTICIPANTS: 12 first and
second line managers

PROGRAM COSTS PROVIDED BY:
Company: 100%

PRINTED MATERIALS AVAILABLE
FROM: Institution

124. GREENEVILLE/GREENE COMPANY
     CHAMBER OF COMMERCE
          with
     TUSCULUM COLLEGE

MANAGEMENT DEVELOPMENT PROGRAM

COMPANY CONTACT:
Ruth Reynolds
Executive Director
Greeneville/Greene Company
Chamber of Commerce
Greeneville, TN 37743
(615) 638-4111

INSTITUTIONAL CONTACT:
John Reiners
Director of Planning and Budget
Tusculum College
Tusculum Station
Greeneville, TN 37743
(615) 639-9471

PROGRAM DESCRIPTION/OBJECTIVES:
To provide working personnel
with a training program in basic skills of management;
course work in management principles, accounting, human re-
actions, computer usage, communications and economics. Offered in the evenings; upon
completion of the 6 one-credit
courses participants receive
certificate.

PROGRAM INITIATED: 1981

LENGTH OF STUDY FOR PARTICI-
PANT: Completion of 6 courses
each lasting 6 weeks

LENGTH OF CONTRACT: Ongoing

LOCATION: Tusculum College

PARTICIPANTS: 20 ranging
from unemployed to senior engineers in first cycle

PROGRAM COSTS PROVIDED BY:
Institution: $5,000
Company: Option to reimburse
employee
Participant: $30 per course

PRINTED MATERIALS AVAILABLE
FROM: Institution

125. H&R BLOCK, INC.
          with
     PIONEER COMMUNITY COLLEGE

H&R BLOCK TAX PREPARATION

COMPANY CONTACT:
Bernie Smith
Regional Director
H&R Block, Inc.
3600 South Noland Road
Independence, MO   64055
(816) 461-6345

INSTITUTIONAL CONTACT:
Roland A. Morreale
Program Coordinator
Adult Distributive Education
Pioneer Community College
560 Westport Road
Kansas City, MO   64111
(816) 753-4949

PROGRAM DESCRIPTION/OBJECTIVES:
To provide cooperative program-
ming and accreditation for tax
preparation courses offered by
H&R Block to the public and to
its employees.

PROGRAM INITIATED: 1979

LENGTH OF STUDY FOR PARTICI-
PANT: Varies--13 weeks to 2
days

LENGTH OF CONTRACT: Open-
ended

LOCATION: H&R Block offices

PARTICIPANTS: Approximately
400 general public and Block
employees annually

PROGRAM COSTS PROVIDED BY:
Institution: 25%
Company: 24%
Other Source: 51% (state aid
and vocational reimbursement)

PRINTED MATERIALS AVAILABLE
FROM: Company

126. HANCOCK MUTUAL LIFE
      INSURANCE COMPANY
           with
      SIMMONS COLLEGE

SIMMONS/HANCOCK PROGRAM

COMPANY CONTACT:
Les Hemmings
Manager
Corporate Personnel Operations
John Hancock Mutual Life
Insurance
John Hancock Place
Boston, MA   02117
(617) 421-2263

INSTITUTIONAL CONTACT:
Isabelle Pound
Program Director
Continuing Education
Simmons College
300 The Fenway
Boston, MA   02115
(617) 738-2141

PROGRAM DESCRIPTION/OBJECTIVES:
A series of three management
courses offered to John Hancock
employees, grades 7 to 16, to
assist in professional development and encourage further
education.

PROGRAM INITIATED: 1981

LENGTH OF STUDY FOR PARTICI-
PANT: 12 months

LENGTH OF CONTRACT: 15 months

LOCATION: The Hancock Tower,
Boston, MA

PARTICIPANTS: 180 senior secretarial and first-line
supervisors

PROGRAM COSTS PROVIDED BY:
Company: Absorbs all costs

PRINTED MATERIALS AVAILABLE
FROM: Institution and Company

127. HARTFORD HOSPITAL
           with
      UNIVERSITY OF HARTFORD

CAREER FATIGUE AND BURNOUT

COMPANY CONTACT:
Jack Lylis
Director of Education
Hartford Hospital
Hartford, CT   06115
(203) 524-3011

INSTITUTIONAL CONTACT:
Gilbert J. Maffeo
Program Development Consultant
Division of Adult Educational
Services
University of Hartford
200 Bloomfield Avenue
West Hartford, CT   06117
(203) 243-4350/4381

PROGRAM DESCRIPTION/OBJECTIVES
To provide information and
skills training concerning the
prevention of burnout.

PROGRAM INITIATED: 1981

LENGTH OF STUDY FOR PARTICI-
PANT: 1-3 days

LENGTH OF CONTRACT: 1-3 days
ongoing

LOCATION: On-site

PARTICIPANTS: 15-25 employees

PROGRAM COSTS PROVIDED BY:
Company: 100%

PRINTED MATERIALS AVAILABLE
FROM: Institution and Company

128. HARTFORD HOSPITAL
            with
      UNIVERSITY OF HARTFORD

SEMINAR IN GROUP DECISION
MAKING

COMPANY CONTACT:
Jack Lylis
Director of Education
Hartford Hospital
Hartford, CT   06115
(203) 524-3011

INSTITUTIONAL CONTACT:
Gilbert J. Maffeo
Program Development Consultant
Division of Adult Educational
Services
University of Hartford
200 Bloomfield Avenue
West Hartford, CT   06117
(203) 243-4350/4381

PROGRAM DESCRIPTION/OBJECTIVES:
To provide skills training in
decision making, conflict resolution and small group
processes.

PROGRAM INITIATED: 1981

LENGTH OF STUDY FOR PARTICI-
PANT: 1-3 days

LENGTH OF CONTRACT: 1-3 days
ongoing

LOCATION: On-site

PARTICIPANTS: 15-25 employees
per program

PROGRAM COSTS PROVIDED BY:
Company: 100%

PRINTED MATERIALS AVAILABLE
FROM: Institution and Company

129. HERCULES, INC.
            with
      BRIGHAM YOUNG UNIVERSITY

MANAGEMENT TRAINING FOR
SUPERVISORS

COMPANY CONTACT:
Weldon Daines
Training Coordinator
Product Engineering
Hercules, Inc. Bacchus Works
Magna, UT   84044
(801) 250-5911, X3205

INSTITUTIONAL CONTACT:
Richard L. White
Coordinator of Management
Programs, Conferences and
Workshops
Brigham Young University
156 HCEB
Provo, UT   84602

PROGRAM DESCRIPTION/OBJECTIVES:
To teach management skills to
engineers who have been promot-
ed to be supervisors.

PROGRAM INITIATED: 1982

LENGTH OF STUDY FOR PARTICI-
PANT: 2 full days of training

LENGTH OF CONTRACT: Trained 3
groups within 2-month time
period

LOCATION: Hercules plant

PARTICIPANTS: 75 engineering
supervisors and their department managers

PROGRAM COSTS PROVIDED BY:
Company: 100%

PRINTED MATERIALS AVAILABLE
FROM: Institution

130. HEWLETT-PACKARD*
with
EVERGREEN VALLEY COLLEGE

TRANSITION TO TECHNOLOGY

COMPANY CONTACT:
Sylvia Gerst
Affirmative Action Officer
Hewlett-Packard
3000 Hanover Street
Palo Alto, CA   94304
(415) 857-1501, X3716

INSTITUTIONAL CONTACT:
Andrew McFarlin
Engineering Instructor
and Coordinator
Evergreen Valley College
3095 Yerba Buena Road
San Jose, CA   95135
(408) 274-7900, X6570

PROGRAM DESCRIPTION/OBJECTIVES:
To provide those with no prior
understanding of technical
fields of employment with a realistic exposure to several
such fields so that an intelligent approach might be made in
determining a suitable training
program.

PROGRAM INITIATED: 1977

LENGTH OF STUDY FOR PARTICI-
PANT: 135 hours during semester (9 hours per week)

LENGTH OF CONTRACT: Agreements
with individual company personnel to teach

LOCATION: Evergreen Valley
College

PARTICIPANTS: 80-100 unemployed
women

PROGRAM COSTS PROVIDED BY:
Institution: 100% subsequent
years

Other Source: 100% first year
from Women's Equity Grant

PRINTED MATERIALS AVAILABLE
FROM: Institution

---

*Representative entry--complete
list available from institution.

131. HEWLETT-PACKARD
with
MERRITT COLLEGE

ELECTRONICS INSTRUCTOR/
ENGINEER EXCHANGE

COMPANY CONTACT:
Edward Butts
Engineer
Hewlett-Packard
c/o Merritt College
12500 Campus Drive
Oakland, CA   95619
(415) 436-2427

INSTITUTIONAL CONTACT:
Jim Albritton
Chair, Electronics Department
Merritt College
12500 Campus Drive
Oakland, CA   95619
(415) 436-2427

PROGRAM DESCRIPTION/OBJECTIVES:
Instructors are exchanged with
engineers from firm for 1 year
to maintain currency with
industry.

PROGRAM INITIATED: 1980

LENGTH OF STUDY FOR PARTICI-
PANT: 1 year

LENGTH OF CONTRACT: Open-ended

LOCATION: Merritt College

PARTICIPANTS: 1 electronics
engineer per year

PROGRAM COSTS PROVIDED BY:
Institution: None (exchange
program)
Company: None (exchange
program)

PRINTED MATERIALS AVAILABLE
FROM: Institution

132. HEWLETT PACKARD*
            with
      PALOMAR COMMUNITY COLLEGE

WORKSITE TRAINING/ELECTRONICS TECHNOLOGY

COMPANY CONTACT:
Robert E. Schultz
Technical Training Manager
Hewlett-Packard
16399 West Bernardo Drive
San Diego, CA   92128
(714) 487-4100, X239

INSTITUTIONAL CONTACT:
Thomas C. Dolan
Director
or Linda M. Repsher
Coordinator
Worksite Training/Vocational
Education
Palomar Community College
1140 West Mission Road
San Marcos, CA   92069
(714) 744-1150, X2567

PROGRAM DESCRIPTION/OBJECTIVES:
Provide an electronics training
program to employees with inade-
quate or obsolete skills at
their worksite. This enables
employees to upgrade their
skills/knowledge in a highly
technical and rapidly changing
field.

PROGRAM INITIATED: 1979

LENGTH OF STUDY FOR PARTICI-
PANT: General electronics technology, 18 months; microelec-
tronics technology, 12 months

LENGTH OF CONTRACT: Ongoing

LOCATION: Palomar Community
College

PARTICIPANTS: 400 entry-level
technicians annually

PROGRAM COSTS PROVIDED BY:
Institution: $27,390 per pro-
gram annually
Company: $150,000 annually

PRINTED MATERIALS AVAILABLE
FROM: Institution and Company

---

*Representative entry--complete
list available from institution.

133. HONEYWELL INFORMATION
      SYSTEMS, INC.
            with
      REGIS COLLEGE

REGIS COLLEGE/HONEYWELL BAY STATE SKILLS TRAINING PROGRAM IN COMPUTER PROGRAMMING

C MPANY CONTACT:
Timothy W. Kilduff
Manager
Community Relations and
Public Affairs
Honeywell Information
Systems, Inc.
200 Smith Street
Waltham, MA   02154
(617) 895-3201

INSTITUTIONAL CONTACT:
Edward Mulholland
Academic Dean
Regis College
235 Wellesley Street
Weston, MA   02193
(617) 893-1820, X293

PROGRAM DESCRIPTION/OBJECTIVES:
To retrain professional adults
to be computer programmers
(entry level skills).

PROGRAM INITIATED: 1981

LENGTH OF STUDY FOR PARTICI-
PANT: Pilot: 20 weeks; expanded program, 30 weeks

LENGTH OF CONTRACT: Pilot:
6 months; expanded program,
9 months

LOCATION: Regis College,
Weston, MA, and Honeywell,
Waltham, MA

PARTICIPANTS: Pilot, 30; expanded program: 35 adult
professionals

PROGRAM COSTS PROVIDED BY:
Institution: $11,967
Company: $120,764
Participant: $8,250
Other Source: $50,165 (state
funds)

PRINTED MATERIALS AVAILABLE
FROM: Not reported

134. HOSPITAL COUNCIL
UNILATERAL COMMITTEE
with
SAN DIEGO COMMUNITY
COLLEGE

LVN TO RN APPRENTICESHIP
PROGRAM

COMPANY CONTACT:
Marlene Ruiz
Staff Development Director
Chairperson, Unilateral
Committee
Kaiser Foundation Hospital
4647 Zion
San Diego, CA   92120
(714) 563-2554

INSTITUTIONAL CONTACT:
Maryann Gellis
Program Dean
Nursing
San Diego Community College
1313 Twelfth Avenue
San Diego, CA   92101
(714) 230-2439

PROGRAM DESCRIPTION/OBJECTIVES:
Upgrade licensed LVN to RN;
assist personal development;
financial support while continuing education.

PROGRAM INITIATED: 1981

LENGTH OF STUDY FOR PARTICI-
PANT: 1 year

LENGTH OF CONTRACT: Ongoing;
optional with some area
hospitals

LOCATION: Supporting hospital

PARTICIPANTS: 40 LVN

PROGRAM COSTS PROVIDED BY:
Company: 10 hours/week
Participant: 6 hours/week
Other Source: CWETA 6 hours/
week

PRINTED MATERIALS AVAILABLE
FROM: Institution

135. IMB WORLD TRADE
ORGANIZATION*
with
AMERICAN UNIVERSITY

COOPERATIVE EDUCATION PROGRAM

COMPANY CONTACT:
William Kushner
Manager of Export Regulation
Special License Country
IMB World Trade Organization
1801 K Street, NW
Washington, DC   20006
(202) 833-6356

INSTITUTIONAL CONTACT:
April K. Nichols
Cooperative Education Program
Career Center
American University
Washington, DC   20016
(202) 686-6800

PROGRAM DESCRIPTION/OBJECTIVES:
To provide opportunities for
liberal arts undergraduate and
graduate students to test career goals and earn academic
credit by working in preprofes-
sional positions in private business, non-profit or government
organization.

PROGRAM INITIATED: 1974

LENGTH OF STUDY FOR PARTICI-
PANT: 4 or 6 months

LENGTH OF CONTRACT: 4 or 6
months

LOCATION: The majority of the
placement, although not restricted to, are in the metropolitan Washington, DC, area.

PARTICIPANTS: 400 degree-seek-
ing undergraduate and graduate
students from all academic programs per year

PROGRAM COSTS PROVIDED BY:
Company: 100% of student
salaries
Participant: Tuition for academic credit earned through
this program

PRINTED MATERIALS AVAILABLE
FROM: Institution

(Cont.)

135. (Cont.)

---

136. INSTITUTE FOR MOTOR FLEET TRAINING
with
UNIVERSITY OF HARTFORD

MAINTENANCE OF COMMERCIAL VEHICLES - PHASE I

COMPANY CONTACT:
Mr. William Simons
Fleet Training Specialist
Institute for Motor Fleet
Training
The Pennsylvania State
University
University Park, PA   16802
(814) 865-2581

INSTITUTIONAL CONTACT:
M. Brady
Director, Continuing Education
Division of Adult Educational
Services
University of Hartford
200 Bloomfield Avenue
West Hartford, CT   06117
(203) 243-4387

PROGRAM DESCRIPTION/OBJECTIVES:
Technical training in motor
fleet maintenance designed for
maintenance supervisors of com-
mon carriers, etc. Curriculum
developed by the Institute for
Motor Fleet Training at Pennsylvania State University.

PROGRAM INITIATED: 1981

LENGTH OF STUDY FOR PARTICI-
PANT: 3 days (18 contact hours)

LENGTH OF CONTRACT: This will
be an annual offering

LOCATION: Hartford, CT

PARTICIPANTS: 18 supervisors,
fleet owners

PROGRAM COSTS PROVIDED BY:
Company: 100%

PRINTED MATERIALS AVAILABLE
FROM: Institution

137. INSURANCE COMPANY OF NORTH AMERICA
with
UNIVERSITY OF PENNSYLVANIA

PENN/INA PROGRAM

COMPANY CONTACT:
John Hurley
Director of Training, Education
and Development
Insurance Company of North
America
1600 Arch Street
Philadelphia, PA   19101
(215) 241-1000

INSTITUTIONAL CONTACT:
Katherine Pollak
Vice Dean
College of General Studies
University of Pennsylvania
210 Logan Hall
Philadelphia, PA   19104
(215) 243-4847

PROGRAM DESCRIPTION/OBJECTIVES:
To provide a liberal arts education at the work site for
qualified employees of a major
corporation.

PROGRAM INITIATED: 1981

LENGTH OF STUDY FOR PARTICI-
PANT: Students may take
courses as long as they like
for enrichment only or towards
a BA degree

LENGTH OF CONTRACT: 4 years
plus

LOCATION: INA Headquarters

PARTICIPANTS: 150 currently
accepted, no current limit on
admissions for any permanent
INA employee

PROGRAM COSTS PROVIDED BY:
Institution: $10,500 + pro-
fessors' salaries
Company: $28,000 + individual
tuition
Participant: Books

PRINTED MATERIALS AVAILABLE
FROM: Institution and Company

138. INTERNAL REVENUE SERVICE*
                with
      UNIVERSITY OF NORTH
      FLORIDA

COOPERATIVE EDUCATION

COMPANY CONTACT:
Diane Holifield
Recruiting Coordinator
P.O. Box 35045
Internal Revenue Service
Jacksonville, FL   32202
(904) 791-2966

INSTITUTIONAL CONTACT:
Carol Ann Boyles
Director, Career Planning
Student Affairs
University of North Florida
4567 St. Johns Bluff Road South
Jacksonville, FL   32216
(904) 646-2955

PROGRAM DESCRIPTION/OBJECTIVES:
To provide students with opportunities to blend academic
theory with real life work experiences.

PROGRAM INITIATED: 1977

LENGTH OF STUDY FOR PARTICI-
PANT: 2 semesters minimum

LENGTH OF CONTRACT: 2 semesters minimum

LOCATION: Jacksonville, FL

PARTICIPANTS: 40 juniors,
seniors and graduate students
per semester

PROGRAM COSTS PROVIDED BY:
Institution: 100% of staff
salaries
Company: 100% of student
salaries

PRINTED MATERIALS AVAILABLE
FROM: Institution

---

*Representative entry--complete
list available from institution.

139. INTERNATIONAL BROTHERHOOD
      OF ELECTRICAL WORKERS
                with
      FLORIDA JUNIOR COLLEGE

ADVANCED MOTOR CONTROLS CLASS
JOURNEYMEN ELECTRICIANS

COMPANY CONTACT:
Thomas Gilmore
Director
Electrical Local
I.B.E.W.
2941 Dawn Road
Jacksonville, FL   32216
(904) 737-7533

INSTITUTIONAL CONTACT:
James R. Myers
Dean, Occupational Education
Florida Junior College
101 West State Street
Jacksonville, FL   32202
(904) 633-8284

PROGRAM DESCRIPTION/OBJECTIVES:
To update/upgrade Journeymen
Electricians to optimize their
effectiveness in maintaining
the state of the art of electri-
cal/electronic systems.

PROGRAM INITIATED: 1982

LENGTH OF STUDY FOR PARTICI-
PANT: 1 semester

LENGTH OF CONTRACT: Continuing

LOCATION: Florida Junior
College, Downtown

PARTICIPANTS: 25 I.B.E.W.
Journeymen

PROGRAM COSTS PROVIDED BY:
Participant: 100%

PRINTED MATERIALS AVAILABLE
FROM: Institution

140. IBM CORPORATION
with
EVERGREEN VALLEY COLLEGE

MECHANICAL DESIGNER TRAINING
PROGRAM

COMPANY CONTACT:
Ed Sheldon
Professional Education
Department
IBM Corporation
5600 Cottle Road
San Jose, CA   95193
(408) 256-7731

INSTITUTIONAL CONTACT:
Andrew McFarlin
Engineering Instructor
and Coordinator
Evergreen Valley College
3095 Yerba Buena Road
San Jose, CA   95135
(408) 274-7900, X6570

PROGRAM DESCRIPTION/OBJECTIVES:
To provide a group of courses
to develop an understanding and
appreciation of a variety of
theoretical concepts necessary
in the competent execution of
mechanical design problems and
projects.

PROGRAM INITIATED: 1978

LENGTH OF STUDY FOR PARTICI-
PANT: 2 years (15 courses, 2-
4 classes offered per quarter)

LENGTH OF CONTRACT: 1 year
with annual renewal

LOCATION: IBM Corporation

PARTICIPANTS: Approximately
20 mechanical designers,
drafters and technical personnel per quarter

PROGRAM COSTS PROVIDED BY:
Company: 100%

PRINTED MATERIALS AVAILABLE
FROM: Institution and Company

141. IBM
with
HAMPTON INSTITUTE

IBM FACULTY LOAN PROGRAM

COMPANY CONTACT:
John C. Steers
Program Manager
Affirmative Action
IBM
Armonk, NY   10504
(914) 765-1900

INSTITUTIONAL CONTACT:
Dr. Willis Sheftall
Dean, School of Business
Hampton Institute
Hampton, VA   23668
(804) 727-5361

PROGRAM DESCRIPTION/OBJECTIVES:
To expose faculty and students
to interaction with business
executives.

PROGRAM INITIATED: 1970

LENGTH OF STUDY FOR PARTICI-
PANT: 1 academic year

LENGTH OF CONTRACT: Yearly,
with renewal

LOCATION: Hampton Institute

PARTICIPANTS: 1 IBM executive
is on loan to the educational
institution; fills the role of
visiting faculty

PROGRAM COSTS PROVIDED BY:
Company: 100%

PRINTED MATERIALS AVAILABLE
FROM: Not available

142. INTERNATIONAL BUSINESS
MACHINES
with
MEDGAR EVERS COLLEGE

COOPERATIVE EDUCATION

COMPANY CONTACT:
Craig Esslinger
Customer Engineering Manager
International Business
Machines
330 Madison Avenue
New York, NY   10017
(212) 972-4523

INSTITUTIONAL CONTACT:
Brenda J. Barley
Director, Student Services
Medgar Evers College
1150 Carroll Street
Brooklyn, NY   11225
(212) 735-1776

PROGRAM DESCRIPTION/OBJECTIVES:
To provide skills in customer
service through repair of company products leading to possible management training and
development.

PROGRAM INITIATED: 1981

LENGTH OF STUDY FOR PARTICI-
PANT: Alternate semesters

LENGTH OF CONTRACT: Unlimited

LOCATION: International
Business Machines

PARTICIPANTS: 15 undergraduates per semester

PROGRAM COSTS PROVIDED BY:
Institution: $6,472
Company: $53,100

PRINTED MATERIALS AVAILABLE
FROM: Institution

143. INTERNATIONAL FENCE
INDUSTRY ASSOCIATION
with
PRINCE GEORGE'S COMMUNITY
COLLEGE

LEGAL CONSIDERATIONS OF
CONSTRUCTION CONTRACTS

COMPANY CONTACT:
Paul Champion
Champion Fence Company
P.O. Box 573
Bowie, MD   20715
(301) 262-8008

INSTITUTIONAL CONTACT:
Veronica Norwood
Director, Contract Services
Prince George's Community
College
301 Largo Road
Largo, MD   20772
(301) 322-0726

PROGRAM DESCRIPTION/OBJECTIVES:
This course addresses issues re
lating to the legal ramifica-
tions of standard clauses in
construction agreements, both
general and sub-contracts.

PROGRAM INITIATED: 1982

LENGTH OF STUDY FOR PARTICI-
PANTS: 7 hours

LENGTH OF CONTRACT: 7 hours

LOCATION: Prince George's
Community College

PARTICIPANTS: 20 fence company owners and associates

PROGRAM COSTS PROVIDED BY:
Company: 75%
Other Source: 25% (state
funds)

PRINTED MATERIALS AVAILABLE
FROM: Institution

144. INTERNATIONAL MINERALS
AND CHEMICALS
with
INDIANA STATE UNIVERSITY

COOPERATIVE PROFESSIONAL
PRACTICE PROGRAM

COMPANY CONTACT:
Pete Ray
Assistant Director of
Personnel
International Minerals and
Chemicals, Inc.
1331 South First Street
Terre Haute, IN   47802
(812) 232-0121

INSTITUTIONAL CONTACT:
Jack A. Brewer
Coordinator, Cooperative
Professional Practice Program
Indiana State University
Alumni Center 247
Terre Haute, IN   47809
(812) 232-6311, X2582

PROGRAM DESCRIPTION/OBJECTIVES:
To help provide students with
research experience in chemistry at an international chemical corporation.

PROGRAM INITIATED: 1980

LENGTH OF STUDY FOR PARTICI-
PANT: Student works 20 hours
per week during the semester

LENGTH OF CONTRACT: Not
available

LOCATION: Terre Haute, IN

PARTICIPANTS: 8 junior and
senior chemistry students

PROGRAM COSTS PROVIDED BY:
Company: $5.00 per hour

PRINTED MATERIALS AVAILABLE
FROM: Institution and Company

145. ITT*
with
BREVARD COMMUNITY COLLEGE

COMMUNICATION AND ELECTRONIC
ASSEMBLERS

COMPANY CONTACT:
Al Perry
Plant Manager
HW AIA
ITT Communications Systems
Cape Canaveral, FL   32920
(305) 783-6911

INSTITUTIONAL CONTACT:
Maurice F. Buckner
Dean, Continuing Education
Brevard Community College
1519 Clearlake Road
Cocoa, FL   32922
(305) 632-1111, X360

PROGRAM DESCRIPTION/OBJECTIVES:
Technical training for unemployed individuals (40% women,
30% minorities).

PROGRAM INITIATED: 1982

LENGTH OF STUDY FOR PARTICI-
PANT: 80 hours

LENGTH OF CONTRACT: Ongoing,
on request

LOCATION: Brevard Community
College

PARTICIPANTS: 47 on-line
employees

PROGRAM COSTS PROVIDED BY:
Institution: 16%
Company: 16%
Other Source: 68% (Industrial
Services grant from Florida
Department of Education)

PRINTED MATERIALS AVAILABLE
FROM: Not available

---

*Representative entry--complete
list available from institution.

146. JEWISH HOSPITAL OF
      ST. LOUIS
          with
      WEBSTER COLLEGE

DIMENSION III

COMPANY CONTACT;
Henry Langer
Director of Education
Jewish Hospital
216 South Kingshighway
St. Louis, MO   63110
(314) 454-8663

INSTITUTIONAL CONTACT:
Chris Cogger
Corporate Based Education
Webster College
470 East Lockwood
St. Louis, MO   63119
(314) 968-6913

PROGRAM DESCRIPTION/OBJECTIVES:
Program designed to provide 12
hours of college credit in the
basic liberal arts through a
3-way approach of closed-cir-
cuit TV, weekend sessions and
a weekly class.

PROGRAM INITIATED: 1982

LENGTH OF STUDY FOR PARTICI-
PANT: 1 semester

LENGTH OF CONTRACT: Ongoing

LOCATION: Jewish Hospital

PARTICIPANTS: 24 employees
from all levels

PROGRAM COSTS PROVIDED BY:
Company: Tuition reimbursement (80% upon completion of
course, 100% upon completion
of degree)

PRINTED MATERIALS AVAILABLE
FROM: Institution

147. JOHNNY APPLESEED, INC.*
          with
      GORDON COLLEGE

COOPERATIVE EDUCATION

COMPANY CONTACT:
Russell W. Copeland
Vice President
Johnny Appleseed, Inc.
54 Dodge Street
Beverly, MA   01915
(617) 922-2040

INSTITUTIONAL CONTACT:
Mary Jane Knudson
Director, Cooperative Education
and Career Development
Gordon College
255 Grapevine Road
Wenham, MA   01984
(617) 927-2300, X327

PROGRAM DESCRIPTION/OBJECTIVES:
An educational program for
liberal arts students to explore careers and apply theory
to practice. It allows employers to examine a pool of qualified recruits as well as fill
seasonal and regular personnel
needs.

PROGRAM INITIATED: 1978

LENGTH OF STUDY FOR PARTICI-
PANT: 6 months per co-op placement; 3 placements total

LENGTH OF CONTRACT: 6 months,
ongoing

LOCATION: Various employer
sites

PARTICIPANTS: 100 liberal
arts students annually

PROGRAM COSTS PROVIDED BY:
Institution: $38,000
Company: Student salaries
Other Source: $57,000 (Title
VIII grant)

PRINTED MATERIALS AVAILABLE
FROM: Institution

---

*Representative entry--complete
list available from institution.

148. JOHNSON MEMORIAL HOSPITAL
with
UNIVERSITY OF HARTFORD

EFFECTIVE MANAGERIAL SKILLS
TRAINING

COMPANY CONTACT:
Peter McGee
Director, Human Resources
Johnson Memorial Hospital
Stafford Springs, CT   06076
(203) 684-4251

INSTITUTIONAL CONTACT:
Gilbert J. Maffeo
Program Development Consultant
Division of Adult Educational
Services
University of Hartford
200 Bloomfield Avenue
West Hartford, CT   06117
(203) 243-4350/4381

PROGRAM DESCRIPTION/OBJECTIVES:
To provide basic managerial
skills training to hospital
supervisors.

PROGRAM INITIATED: 1981

LENGTH OF STUDY FOR PARTICI-
PANT: 10-12 weeks

LENGTH OF CONTRACT: 10-12
weeks ongoing

LOCATION: Johnson Memorial
Hospital

PARTICIPANTS: 15-25 different
levels of management personnel

PROGRAM COSTS PROVIDED BY:
Company: 100%

PRINTED MATERIALS AVAILABLE
FROM: Institution and Company

149. MULTIPLE COMPANIES*
with
KANSAS CITY ART INSTITUTE

INTERNSHIP

COMPANY CONTACT:
Specific company not identified

INSTITUTIONAL CONTACT:
Ronald B. Kemnitzer
Associate Professor
Design
Kansas City Art Institute
4415 Warwick Blvd.
Kansas City, MO   64111
(816) 561-4852

PROGRAM DESCRIPTION/OBJECTIVES:
To provide practical experience
for students on various aspects
of design as it relates to
their formal classroom
education.

PROGRAM INITIATED: 1975

LENGTH OF STUDY FOR PARTICI-
PANT: · 1 semester

LENGTH OF CONTRACT: Not
available

LOCATION: Kansas City Art
Institute

PARTICIPANTS: 20 juniors and
seniors annually

PROGRAM COSTS PROVIDED BY:
Not available

PRINTED MATERIALS AVAILABLE
FROM: Institute

---

*Representative entry--complete
list available from institution.

150. KOHLER COMPANY
          with
      LAKESHORE TECHNICAL
      INSTITUTE

GEOMETRIC TOLERANCING AND TRUE
POSITION DIMENSIONING

COMPANY CONTACT:
Lloyd Everard
Training Coordinator
Kohler Company
Kohler, WI   53044
(414) 457-4441

INSTITUTIONAL CONTACT:
Steve Smith
Economic Development/
Industrial Training
Lakeshore Technical Institute
1290 North Avenue
Cleveland, WI   53015
(414) 684-4408, X247

PROGRAM DESCRIPTION/OBJECTIVES:
Designed to serve industry by
training entire employee group
in new drafting method of dimensioning.

PROGRAM INITIATED: 1982

LENGTH OF STUDY FOR PARTICI-
PANT: 30 hours

LENGTH OF CONTRACT: 3 years

LOCATION: Kohler Company

PARTICIPANTS: 300 engineers,
draftsmen, assembly supervisors
and office personnel

PROGRAM COSTS PROVIDED BY:
Company: $16.30 per parti-
cipant

PRINTED MATERIALS AVAILABLE
FROM: Institution

151. KOHLER COMPANY
          with
      LAKESHORE TECHNICAL
      INSTITUTE

KOHLER SMALL ENGINE SERVICING
SCHOOL

COMPANY CONTACT:
Lloyd Everard
Training Coordinator
Kohler Company
Kohler, WI   53044
(414) 457-4441

INSTITUTIONAL CONTACT:
Steve Smith
Economic Development/Indus-
trial Training
Lakeshore Technical Institute
1290 North Avenue
Cleveland, WI   53015
(414) 684-4408, X247

PROGRAM DESCRIPTION/OBJECTIVES:
Designed to serve industry by
providing quality education for
dealers through courses pre-
senting information on increased product knowledge and
productivity.

PROGRAM INITIATED: 1979

LENGTH OF STUDY FOR PARTICI-
PANT: 40 hours

LENGTH OF CONTRACT: 1 year

LOCATION: Lakeshore Technical
Institute

PARTICIPANTS: 200 service
representatives and dealers
(nationwide)

PROGRAM COSTS PROVIDED BY:
Company: $16.30 per
participant

PRINTED MATERIALS AVAILABLE
FROM: Institutions

152. LA CROSSE TELEPHONE
      CORPORATION
              with
      WESTERN WISCONSIN
      TECHNICAL INSTITUTE

SELLING PERSONALITY

COMPANY CONTACT:
Rebecca Faas
Division Staff Personnel
Manager
La Crosse Telephone Corporation
206 5th Avenue South
La Crosse, WI   54601
(608) 782-9980

INSTITUTIONAL CONTACT:
Harold P. Erickson
Corporate Campus Administrator
Adult and Continuing Education
Western Wisconsin Technical
Institute
Sixth and Vine Streets
La Crosse, WI   54601
(608) 785-9232

PROGRAM DESCRIPTION/OBJECTIVES:
To increase sales awareness and
awareness of profitability principles for every employee of
the Telephone Corporation.

PROGRAM INITIATED: 1982

LENGTH OF STUDY FOR PARTICI-
PANT: 1 quarter

LENGTH OF CONTRACT: Not
available

LOCATION: Western Wisconsin
Technical Institute

PARTICIPANTS: 283 Telephone
Company employees

PROGRAM COSTS PROVIDED BY:
Institution: $4,200
Company: $7,641
Other Source: State funds

PRINTED MATERIALS AVAILABLE
FROM: Not reported

153. LANDS' END YACHT
      STORES, INC.
              with
      NORTHEAST IOWA TECHNICAL
      INSTITUTE

NEW AND EXPANDING BUSINESS AND INDUSTRY TRAINING

COMPANY CONTACT:
Earl Glemp
Vice President of Manufacturing
Lands' End Yacht Stores, Inc.
116 Franklin
West Union, IA   52175
(319) 422-6051

INSTITUTIONAL CONTACT:
Ken Vande Berg
Coordinator of Community
Education
Northeast Iowa Technical
Institute
P.O. Box 400
Calmar, IA   52132
(319) 562-3263

PROGRAM DESCRIPTION/OBJECTIVES:
To develop a training plan and
specific training for industrial sewing machine operators.
To provide funding for expansion within the local industry.

PROGRAM INITIATED: 1982

LENGTH OF STUDY FOR PARTICI-
PANT: 1 quarter

LENGTH OF CONTRACT: 9 months

LOCATION: Lands' End Yacht
Stores, Inc.

PARTICIPANTS: 64 operators
annually

PROGRAM COSTS PROVIDED BY:
Institution: $500
Other Source: $23,509.70
(State of Iowa, Department
of Public Instruction)

PRINTED MATERIALS AVAILABLE
FROM: Not available

154. LEATHER INDUSTRY ANNUAL
DISPLAY AND DEMONSTRATION
with
OKLAHOMA STATE TECH

LEATHER INDUSTRY ANNUAL DISPLAY
AND DEMONSTRATION OF NEW EQUIP-
MENT AND METHODS

COMPANY CONTACT:
W.C. Gatlin
Southern Leather and Shoe
Company
706 West California
Oklahoma City, OK   73102
(405) 235-0373

INSTITUTIONAL CONTACT:
Earl Bain
Supervisor, Shoe-Boot-Saddle
Program
Small Business Trades
Department
Oklahoma State Tech
4th and Mission
Okmulgee, OK   74447
(918) 756-6211, X256

PROGRAM DESCRIPTION/OBJECTIVES:
Provides members of the industry and students with an opportunity to stay current with the
field; provides contact opportunities between students and
potential employers; provides
public awareness of programs in
shoe repair, bootmaking and
saddlemaking.

PROGRAM INITIATED: 1978

LENGTH OF STUDY FOR PARTICI-
PANT: Not reported

LENGTH OF CONTRACT: Not
reported

LOCATION: Not reported

PARTICIPANTS: 125

PROGRAM COSTS PROVIDED BY:
Institution: 33%
Company: 67%

PRINTED MATERIALS AVAILABLE
FROM: Not available

155. LIFE INSURANCE MARKETING
AND RESEARCH ASSOCIATION
with
UNIVERSITY OF HARTFORD

EFFECTIVE ORAL PRESENTATION

COMPANY CONTACT:
Peter S. Roberts
Vice President
Life Insurance Marketing and
Research Association
8 Farm Sprints
Farmington, CT   06032
(203) 677-0033

INSTITUTIONAL CONTACT:
M. Brady/G. Maffeo
Director, Continuing Education
Division of Adult Educational
Services
University of Hartford
200 Bloomfield Avenue
West Hartford, CT   06117
(203) 243-4387

PROGRAM DESCRIPTION/OBJECTIVES:
Six-week seminar on planning,
preparing and delivering oral
presentations before both large
and small audiences. Training
included didactic material as
well as speaking practicum and
feedback.

PROGRAM INITIATED: 1982

LENGTH OF STUDY FOR PARTICI-
PANT: 6 half days (24 contact
hours)

LENGTH OF CONTRACT: 1 time
(for 6 weeks)

LOCATION: Farmington, CT

PARTICIPANTS: 14 profes-
sionals

PROGRAM COSTS PROVIDED BY:
Company: 100%

PRINTED MATERIALS AVAILABLE
FROM: Institution

156. LOCKHEED MISSILES AND
SPACE CORPORATION*
with
EVERGREEN VALLEY COLLEGE

(Cont.)

156. (Cont.)

TRANSITION INTO ELECTRONICS

COMPANY CONTACT:
Carol Trammell
Lockheed Missiles and Space
Corporation
6105 Castleknoll Drive
San Jose, CA 95129
(408) 742-2080
             and
Clara Brock
Lockheed Missiles and Space
Corporation
19930 Oakmont Drive
Los Gatos, CA 95030
(408) 742-5413

INSTITUTIONAL CONTACT:
Andrew McFarlin
Engineering Instructor
and Coordinator
Evergreen Valley College
3095 Yerba Buena Road
San Jose, CA 95135
(408) 274-7900, X6570

PROGRAM DESCRIPTION/OBJECTIVES:
To provide those with no prior
understanding of technical
fields of employment in the
electronics industry with a realistic exposure to several
such fields so that intelligent
approach might be made in determining a suitable training
program.

PROGRAM INITIATED: 1980

LENGTH OF STUDY FOR PARTICI-
PANT: 10 weeks

LENGTH OF CONTRACT: Varies
with individual company personnel to teach

LOCATION: Evergreen Valley
College

PARTICIPANTS: 12-24 primarily
displaced homemakers, reentry
students per semester

PROGRAM COSTS PROVIDED BY:
Institution: 100% the following years
Other Source: 100% the first year
from Displaced Homemakers Act

PRINTED MATERIALS AVAILABLE
FROM: Institution

*Representative entry--complete
list available from institution.

157.   LUCAS CAV*
                with
        GREENVILLE TECHNICAL
        COLLEGE

TECHNICAL SCHOLARSHIP PROGRAM

COMPANY CONTACT:
Peter Elliman
Vice President and General Mgr.
Lucas CAV
P.O. Box 5755, Station B
Greenville, SC 29606
(803) 297-1700

INSTITUTIONAL CONTACT:
Marty Jensen
Director, Technical Scholarship
Program
Greenville Technical College
P.O. Box 5616, Station B
Greenville, SC 29606
(803) 242-3170

PROGRAM DESCRIPTION/OBJECTIVES:
To equip Greenville people for
jobs in area industries by providing classroom theory at Greenville TEC and on-the-job application of this theory at work.

PROGRAM INITIATED: 1979

LENGTH OF STUDY FOR PARTICI-
PANT: 6 to 11 quarters

LENGTH OF CONTRACT: No contract

LOCATION: Greenville Technical
College

PARTICIPANTS: In Fall 1981,
95 associate degree engineering
technology and business division students

PROGRAM COSTS PROVIDED BY:
Institution: $29,000
Company: $88,000
Other Source: $89,000 (Title
VIII)

PRINTED MATERIALS AVAILABLE
FROM: Institution

*Representative entry--complete
list available from institution.

158. MAIL-WELL ENVELOPE COMPANY*
with
OREGON STATE UNIVERSITY

PRODUCTIVITY BY OBJECTIVES

COMPANY CONTACT:
Pete Gartshore
Vice President
Mail-Well Envelope Company
2515 SW Mail-Well Drive
Milwaukie, OR   97222
(503) 654-3141

INSTITUTIONAL CONTACT:
Jim Riggs
Director, Oregon Productivity
Center
Head, Industrial Engineering
Department
Oregon State University
Corvallis, OR   97331
(503) 754-4645

PROGRAM DESCRIPTION/OBJECTIVES:
A total productivity program
that involves managers and workers. It is heavily oriented to
technical training and employee
involvement. Features a unique
productivity measurement system.

PROGRAM INITIATED: 1980

LENGTH OF STUDY FOR PARTICI-
PANT: 6 months - 1 year

LENGTH OF CONTRACT: 6 months
- 1 year

LOCATION: At plant site

PARTICIPANTS: 400+ employees
and managers

PROGRAM COSTS PROVIDED BY:
Variable, depends on need

PRINTED MATERIALS AVAILABLE
FROM: Institution

---

*Representative entry--complete
list available from institution.

159. MANUFACTURERS HANOVER
TRUST COMPANY
with
HERBERT H. LEHMAN COLLEGE/
CUNY

COOPERATIVE EDUCATION PROGRAM

COMPANY CONTACT:
Christine Hobrecht
Assistant Secretary
Manufacturers Hanover Trust
Company
320 Park Avenue
New York, NY   10022
(212) 350-3300

INSTITUTIONAL CONTACT:
Joseph Enright
Director of Cooperative
Education
Herbert H. Lehman College
Bronx, NY   10468
(212) 960-8366

PROGRAM DESCRIPTION/OBJECTIVES:
To provide a high quality liberal arts education by creative-
ly combining work experience
with theoretical learning. To
improve the career opportunities of students. To provide
employers with higher quality
workers and potential recruits.

PROGRAM INITIATED: 1980

LENGTH OF STUDY FOR PARTICI-
PANT: 1 semester or 1 semester
+ summer

LENGTH OF CONTRACT: 1 semester
with renewal option

LOCATION: Not reported

PARTICIPANTS: 300 sophomore,
junior and senior liberal arts
majors annually

PROGRAM COSTS PROVIDED BY:
Institution: 100%

PRINTED MATERIALS AVAILABLE
FROM: Institution

160. NOT REPORTED*
            with
     MARSHALL UNIVERSITY

COOPERATIVE EDUCATION PROGRAM
IN CHEMISTRY AND GEOLOGY

COMPANY CONTACT:
Specific company not identified

INSTITUTIONAL CONTACT:
E.S. Hanrahan
Dean, College of Science
Marshall University
Huntington, WV   28701
(304) 696-2372

PROGRAM DESCRIPTION/OBJECTIVES:
To improve maturity and employ-
ability of graduates and improve relationships with
industries.

PROGRAM INITIATED: 1971

LENGTH OF STUDY FOR PARTICI-
PANT: Not reported

LENGTH OF CONTRACT: Informal
agreement

LOCATION: Not reported

PARTICIPANTS: 6-10 interns

PROGRAM COSTS PROVIDED BY:
None

PRINTED MATERIALS AVAILABLE
FROM: Institution

----

*Representative entry--complete
list available from institution.

161. MARRIOTT'S GREAT AMERICA
            with
     COLLEGE OF LAKE COUNTY

PREVENTING RETAIL THEFT

COMPANY CONTACT:
Mike Newton
Training and Development
Manager
Marriott's Great America
Interstate 94 and Route 132
Gurnee, IL   60031
(312) 249-1776

INSTITUTIONAL CONTACT:
Keri Thiessen
Business/Industry Training
Coordinator
Open Campus
College of Lake County
Grayslake, IL   60030
(312) 223-3616

PROGRAM DESCRIPTION/OBJECTIVES:
Customized course providing
information on shoplifter methods and operation, preventive
tactics to be taken, and legal
considerations of the employee
and shoplifter.

PROGRAM INITIATED: 1981

LENGTH OF STUDY FOR PARTICI-
PANT: 1 day

LENGTH OF CONTRACT: 1 day

LOCATION: Marriott's Great
America

PARTICIPANTS: 27 managers and
security personnel

PROGRAM COSTS PROVIDED BY:
Company: $95.20

PRINTED MATERIAL AVAILABLE
FROM: Institution

162. MARTINDALE-HUBBELL, INC.
          with
      KEAN COLLEGE OF NEW JERSEY*

CENTER FOR CORPORATE EDUCATION

COMPANY CONTACT:
Suzanne Durang
Vice President
Martindale-Hubbell, Inc.
630 Central Avenue
New Providence, NJ   07974
(201) 464-6800

INSTITUTIONAL CONTACT:
Ethel J. Madsen
Director
Special Programs
Kean College of New Jersey
Morris Avenue
Union, NJ   07083
(201) 527-2163

PROGRAM DESCRIPTION/OBJECTIVES:
Advisory committee made up of
representatives from various
companies and from the college
assist in conducting needs as-
sessments, designing programs
to meet specific needs, providing instruction for credit
and non-credit courses, review
evaluations, overall planning.

PROGRAM INITIATED: 1979

LENGTH OF STUDY FOR PARTICI-
PANT: Varies

LENGTH OF CONTRACT: Varies

LOCATION: On campus and on
company sites

PARTICIPANTS: Varying number
of employees

PROGRAM COSTS PROVIDED BY:
Institution: 5%
Company: 75%
Participant: 20%

PRINTED MATERIALS AVAILABLE
FROM: Institution

---

*Representative entry--complete
list available from institution.

163. COMMONWEALTH OF MASSACHU-
      SETTS DEPARTMENT OF
      SOCIAL SERVICES
          with
      UNIVERSITY OF MASSACHU-
      SETTS

UNDERGRADUATE PROGRAM

COMPANY CONTACT:
Elaine Marks
Director of Training
Department of Social Services
150 Causeway Street
Boston, Ma   02114
(617) 727-0900

INSTITUTIONAL CONTACT:
Barbara M. Buchanan
Director of Field Education
College of Public and Community
Service
University of Massachusetts
Downtown Center
Boston, MA   02125
(617) 287-1900

PROGRAM DESCRIPTION/OBJECTIVES:
To provide a curriculum relevant to the career needs of the
Department's non-credentialed
workers; to impact positively
on service delivery through improved worker skills and knowledge; to provide access to the
BA degree.

PROGRAM INITIATED: 1981

LENGTH OF STUDY FOR PARTICI-
PANT: To completion of BA
degree, if desired

LENGTH OF CONTRACT: 12 months
with renewal

LOCATION: University of Massachusetts

PARTICIPANTS: 20-30 non-cre-
dential social service staff
each semester

PROGRAM COSTS PROVIDED BY:
Institution: 35%
Company: 55%
Participant: 10%

PRINTED MATERIALS AVAILABLE
FROM: Institution and Company

164. MASSILON CITY HOSPITAL
          with
      KENT STATE UNIVERSITY

HEALTH ASSESSMENT SKILLS

COMPANY CONTACT:
Randy Hilscher
Massilon City Hospital
875 8th Street, NE
Massilon, OH   44646

INSTITUTIONAL CONTACT:
Karen Rylander
Director, Continuing Education
Kent State University
327 Rockwell Hall
Kent, OH   44242
(216) 672-3100

PROGRAM DESCRIPTION/OBJECTIVES:
Parallels basic health assess-
ment course taught by School of
Nursing.

PROGRAM INITIATED: 1982

LENGTH OF STUDY FOR PARTICI-
PANT: 60 hours

LENGTH OF CONTRACT: 60 hours

LOCATION: Massilon City
Hospital

PARTICIPANTS: 12 registered
nurses

PROGRAM COSTS PROVIDED BY:
Company: 100%

PRINTED MATERIALS AVAILABLE
FROM: Institution

165. MATTHEW BENDER AND
      COMPANY, INC.*
          with
      SIENA COLLEGE

INTERNATIONAL STUDIES, FOREIGN
LANGUAGES AND BUSINESS PROGRAM

COMPANY CONTACT:
Paul Carter
Director
International Division
Matthew Bender and Company, Inc.
1275 Broadway
Albany, NY   12204
(518) 462-3331

INSTITUTIONAL CONTACT:
James S. Dalton
Program Director, Assistant
Dean, Arts Division
Siena College
Loudonville, NY   12211
(518) 783-2325

PROGRAM DESCRIPTION/OBJECTIVES:
To provide understanding of and
training in International Studies and business through the
study of language, culture and
business practice.

PROGRAM INITIATED: 1980

LENGTH OF STUDY FOR PARTICI-
PANT: 4 years (certificate
program)

LENGTH OF CONTRACT: Internship semester (120-150 hours
for 3 credits)

LOCATION: Various

PARTICIPANTS: 20-30 students
annually

PROGRAM COSTS PROVIDED BY:
Institution: 90%
Company: 10%

PRINTED MATERIALS AVAILABLE
FROM: Institution

---

*Representative entry--complete
list available from institution.

166. MAYVILLE METALS PRODUCTS
      COMPANY
            with
      CENTRAL ARIZONA COLLEGE

MAYVILLE METALS I

COMPANY CONTACT:
Tom Wallangk
Administrative Manager
Mayville Metals Products
Company
999 Thornton Road
P.O. Box 999
Casa Grande, AZ   85222
(602) 836-5544

INSTITUTIONAL CONTACT:
Francis E. Colgan
Occupational Dean
Technology Department
Central Arizona College
Woodruff at Overfield Road
Coolidge, AZ   85228
(602) 723-4141

PROGRAM DESCRIPTION/OBJECTIVES:
Precision measurement tools;
precision sheetmetal, frame,
blueprint; quality assurance,
safety practice and work ethic.

PROGRAM INITIATED: 1982

LENGTH OF STUDY FOR PARTICI-
PANT: 8 weeks

LENGTH OF CONTRACT: 8 weeks;
renewable

LOCATION: In-plant classroom

PARTICIPANTS: 12 per shift,
2 shifts; all production
skills

PROGRAM COSTS PROVIDED BY:
Institution: 25%
Company: 50%
Other Source: 25% (state aid)

PRINTED MATERIALS AVAILABLE
FROM: Institution

167. MERCY CATHOLIC MEDICAL
      CENTER
            with
      GWYNEDD-MERCY COLLEGE

COMPREHENSIVE HOSPITALWIDE
EDUCATION PROGRAM

COMPANY CONTACT:
Joseph Malonoski
Vice President, Personnel
Mercy Catholic Medical Center
Lansdowne Avenue and Baily Road
Darby, PA   19023
(215) 237-4000

INSTITUTIONAL CONTACT:
Margaret K. Yaure
Provost
Edmonda Campus
Gwynedd-Mercy College
Lansdowne Avenue and Baily Road
Darby, PA   19023
(215) 237-0440

PROGRAM DESCRIPTION/OBJECTIVES:
To provide staff development,
continuing education, patient
and consumer education to the
Medical Center and people of
the surrounding community.

PROGRAM INITIATED: 1979

LENGTH OF STUDY FOR PARTICI-
PANT: Ongoing

LENGTH OF CONTRACT: Ongoing

LOCATION: Gwynedd Valley, PA

PARTICIPANTS: 2,000 employees
of the Medical Center and
people from the community

PROGRAM COSTS PROVIDED BY:
Company: $350,000
Other Source: $100,000 (fed-
eral grants)

PRINTED MATERIALS AVAILABLE
FROM: Institution and Company

168. METROPOLITAN LIFE INSURANCE
COMPANY
with
COMMUNITY COLLEGE OF RHODE
ISLAND

ELEMENTARY ACCOUNTING I AND II AND BUSINESS WRITING

COMPANY CONTACT:
Joanna Dorazio
Training Director
Personnel Department
Metropolitan Insurance Company
Quaker Lane
Warwick, RI   02886
(401) 827-2723

INSTITUTIONAL CONTACT:
Robert Danilowicz
Coordinator
Missing Link Project
Off Campus Credit Programs
Community College of Rhode
Island
Flanagan Campus
Louisquisset Pike
Lincoln, RI 02865
(401) 333-7127

PROGRAM DESCRIPTION/OBJECTIVES:
Basic procedures of accounting.
Business writing includes correspondence of all business communication abstract and precise
writing and some report writing.

PROGRAM INITIATED: 1981

LENGTH OF STUDY FOR PARTICI-
PANT: Elementary Accounting I
& II (2 semesters); Business
Writing (1 semester)

LENGTH OF CONTRACT: Ongoing

LOCATION: Metropolitan Insurance Company and Community College of Rhode Island

PARTICIPANTS: Average of 15
mid-management and clerical
personnel per course

PROGRAM COSTS PROVIDED BY:
Participant: $4,754

PRINTED MATERIALS AVAILABLE
FROM: Institution and Company

169. METROPOLITAN LIFE
INSURANCE COMPANY
with
PRINCE GEORGE'S COM-
MUNITY COLLEGE

PROPERTY AND CASUALTY INSURANCE TRAINING

COMPANY CONTACT:
John Dunn
General Manager
Career Success School
Metropolitan Life Insurance
Company
Metropolitan Plaza
Tampa, FL   33607
(813) 871-3174

INSTITUTIONAL CONTACT:
Veronica S. Norwood
Director, Contract Services
Prince George's Community
College
301 Largo Road
Largo, MD   20772
(301) 322-0726

PROGRAM DESCRIPTION/OBJECTIVES:
To provide training which will
enable the participants to suc-
cessfully complete the state of
Maryland Insurance Agency
Brokers License Qualification
Examination.

PROGRAM INITIATED: 1980

LENGTH OF STUDY FOR PARTICI-
PANT: 96 hours (1 8-hour class
per week)

LENGTH OF CONTRACT: 12 weeks

LOCATION: Prince George's
Community College

PARTICIPANTS: 15 insurance
salesmen per session

PROGRAM COSTS PROVIDED BY:
Company: 32%
Other Source: 68% (state
funds)

PRINTED MATERIALS AVAILABLE
FROM: Institution

170. METROVISION, INC. AND
      STORER CABLE, INC.
           with
      PRINCE GEORGE'S COM-
      MUNITY COLLEGE

CABLE COMMUNICATION WORKSHOP

COMPANY CONTACT:
Susan Wallace
Director, Community Relations
Metrovision, Inc.
211 Perimeter Center Parkway
Suite 930
Atlanta, GA   30346
(800) 241-9271
         and
John Margieson
Assistant Manager
Storer Cable of Prince
George's County
4314 Farragut Street
Hyattsville, MD   20781
(301) 699-8881

INSTITUTIONAL CONTACT:
Jacques Dubois
Director, Special Academic
Areas
Prince George's Community
College
301 Largo Road
Largo, MD   20772
(301) 322-0785

PROGRAM DESCRIPTION/OBJECTIVES:
Communicate the potential of
cable television as a comprehensive communications resource
for business, civic, community
and education uses.

PROGRAM INITIATED: 1982

LENGTH OF STUDY FOR PARTICI-
PANT: 8 hours

LENGTH OF CONTRACT: 1 day

LOCATION: Prince George's
Community College

PARTICIPANTS: 250 business,
community, government and
education leaders.

PROGRAM COSTS PROVIDED BY:
Institution: Time and effort
Company: $1,000 each

PRINTED MATERIALS AVAILABLE
FROM: Institution

171. MICHIGAN MOLECULAR
      INSTITUTE
           with
      CENTRAL MICHIGAN
      UNIVERSITY

GRADUATE STUDIES IN MACRO-MOLECULAR SCIENCE

COMPANY CONTACT:
Hans-G. Elias
Director
Michigan Molecular Institute
1910 West St. Andrews Road
Midland, MI   48640
(517) 631-9450

INSTITUTIONAL CONTACT:
Karl R. Lindfors
Chairman
Department of Chemistry
Central Michigan University
Mt. Pleasant, MI   48859
(517) 774-3981

PROGRAM DESCRIPTION/OBJECTIVES:
Graduate training in macro-
molecular science.

PROGRAM INITIATED: 1973

LENGTH OF STUDY FOR PARTICI-
PANT: 2 years

LENGTH OF CONTRACT: 12 months
with renewal option

LOCATION: Michigan Molecular
Institute

PARTICIPANTS: 3 chemistry
graduate students per year

PROGRAM COSTS PROVIDED BY:
Company: 100%

PRINTED MATERIALS AVAILABLE
FROM: Institution and Company

172. MICHIGAN REFORMATORY
with
CENTRAL MICHIGAN UNIVERSITY

PRISON EDUCATION PROGRAM

COMPANY CONTACT:
Joseph Wittebols
Treatment Director
Michigan Reformatory
P.O. Box 500
Ionia, MI   48846
(616) 527-2500

INSTITUTIONAL CONTACT:
Lawrence R. Murphy
Director
Institute for Personal and
Career Development
Central Michigan University
Mt. Pleasant, MI   48859
(517) 774-3865

PROGRAM DESCRIPTION/OBJECTIVES:
Baccalaureate Degree completion
programs: BS in Management and
Supervision, and Community Development and on-site counseling and instruction.

PROGRAM INITIATED: Not
reported

LENGTH OF STUDY FOR PARTICI-
PANT: Approximately 3 full
years

LENGTH OF CONTRACT: Ongoing

LOCATION: Michigan Reformatory

PARTICIPANTS: Approximately
50 incarcerated individuals
with AA or equivalent

PROGRAM COSTS PROVIDED BY:
Institution: 55%
Participant: 45%

PRINTED MATERIALS AVAILABLE
FROM: Institution

173. MIDLAND GLASS COMPANY
with
OKLAHOMA STATE TECH

BASIC ELECTRICITY, INTRODUCTION
TO MOTORS AND CONTROLS, INTRO-
DUCTION TO ELECTRICAL WIRING

COMPANY CONTACT:
Jim Glynn
Personnel Director
Midland Glass Company
Henryetta, OK   74437
(918) 652-9631

INSTITUTIONAL CONTACT:
Bill J. Lyons
Department Head
Electrical-Electronics
Technology
Oklahoma State Tech
4th and Mission
Okmulgee, OK   74447
(918) 756-6211, X252

PROGRAM DESCRIPTION/OBJECTIVES:
Shorter training time for entry
level electricians, training in
areas of expertise not available at Midland Glass Company.

PROGRAM INITIATED: 1981

LENGTH OF STUDY FOR PARTICI-
PANT: Not reported

LENGTH OF CONTRACT: Not
reported

LOCATION: Not reported

PARTICIPANTS: 30 employees
annually

PROGRAM COSTS PROVIDED BY:
Company: 100%

PRINTED MATERIALS AVAILABLE
FROM: Not available

174. MIDSTATE TELEPHONE
      COMPANY
            with
      JAMESTOWN COMMUNITY
      COLLEGE

PLANNING FOR YOUR RETIREMENT

COMPANY CONTACT:
William Kelly
Director of Training
Midstate Telephone Company
525 Falconer Street
Jamestown, NY   14701
(716) 665-5220

INSTITUTIONAL CONTACT:
Rose M. Scott
Continuing Education Assistant
Jamestown Community College
525 Falconer Street
Jamestown, NY   14701
(716) 665-5220

PROGRAM DESCRIPTION/OBJECTIVES:
This program affords company
employees approximately 50
years of age and/or older, the
vehicle through which they can
take a serious look at retirement. Participants of the program will be made aware of a
wide scope of retirement interests including such matters as
the potential for future opportunities (and pitfalls), good
health, where to live, legal
security, optimum financial security, preparations for changing role and expansion of new
interests, a possible second
(or third) career, techniques
of good personal management,
and preparation for widowhood.

PROGRAM INITIATED: Not
reported

LENGTH OF STUDY FOR PARTICI-
PANT: 8 weeks

LENGTH OF CONTRACT: 12 months
- renewal option

LOCATION: Midland Telephone
Company

PARTICIPANTS: 24 personnel
ten years away from retirement or closer per class

PROGRAM COSTS PROVIDED BY:
Institution: 40%
Company: 20%
Other Source: 20%

PRINTED MATERIALS AVAILABLE
FROM: Not available

175. CITY OF MILWAUKEE*
               with
        ALVERNO COLLEGE

OFF CAMPUS EXPERIENTIAL
LEARNING

COMPANY CONTACT:
Barry Zalben
Research Coordinator
Legislative Reference Bureau
City of Milwaukee
Milwaukee, WI   53202
(414) 278-2295

INSTITUTIONAL CONTACT:
Kate Hardy
Coordinator
Off Campus Experiential
Learning Program
Alverno College
3401 S. 39 Street
Milwaukee, WI   53215
(414) 647-3999

PROGRAM DESCRIPTION/OBJECTIVES:
Both liberal arts and professional area students work in
business or service agencies.
Business mentor benefits from
student involvement; student
learns to learn in non-academic setting.

PROGRAM INITIATED: 1972

LENGTH OF STUDY FOR PARTICI-
PANT: Mentor, 3 hour orienta-
tion session; student, concur-
rent seminar

LENGTH OF CONTRACT: 1 semester each

LOCATION: Alverno College and
businesses

PARTICIPANTS: 100 students,
professionals in particular
fields

PROGRAM COSTS PROVIDED BY:
Absorbed by institution and
businesses in operating
expenses.

PRINTED MATERIALS AVAILABLE
FROM: Institution

176. MINNESOTA MINING &
        MANUFACTURING
               with
        LAKEWOOD COMMUNITY
        COLLEGE

3M-LAKEWOOD COOPERATIVE PROGRAM

COMPANY CONTACT:
Ray Haas
Director
Education & Training
Minnesota Mining &
Manufacturing
St. Paul, MN   55144
(612) 733-1110

INSTITUTIONAL CONTACT:
Monica Manning
Dean of Community Service
Lakewood Community College
3401 Century Avenue North
White Bear Lake, MN   55110
(612) 770-1331, X140

PROGRAM DESCRIPTION/OBJECTIVES:
To provide college courses, academic advising and recognition
by credit for on-the-job experience leading to an Associate of
Arts degree and transfer to a
baccalaureate institution.

PROGRAM INITIATED: 1982

LENGTH OF STUDY FOR PARTICI-
PANT: 6 months - 3 years

LENGTH OF CONTRACT: 12 months

LOCATION: 3M Center

PARTICIPANTS: Employees of information systems and data
processing

PROGRAM COSTS PROVIDED BY:
Institution: $4,000
Company: $10,000 + tuition

PRINTED MATERIALS AVAILABLE
FROM: Institution

177. MOBIL OIL CORPORATION
with
PRINCETON UNIVERSITY

TEN DAYS AT PRINCETON

COMPANY CONTACT:
Jack Ballard
Foreign Executive Development
Program
Fund for Multinational
Management Education
684 Park Avenue
New York, NY   10021
(212) 535-9386

INSTITUTIONAL CONTACT:
William H. O'Brien, Jr.
Director, Center for Visitor
and Conference Services
Prospect House
Princeton, NJ   08544
(609) 452-3371

PROGRAM DESCRIPTION/OBJECTIVES:
To provide an intensive study
of American society in a schol-
arly atmosphere which presents
a picture of American society
to assist foreign national executives obtain a better perspective on U.S. management
styles.

PROGRAM INITIATED: 1979

LENGTH OF STUDY FOR PARTICI-
PANT: 10 days

LENGTH OF CONTRACT: Not
reported

LOCATION: Princeton University

PARTICIPANTS: 40 foreign executives annually

PROGRAM COSTS PROVIDED BY:
Institution: $2,500
Participant: $2,100
Other Source: Mobil
Corporation

PRINTED MATERIALS AVAILABLE
FROM: Company

178. MONTANA DAKOTA UTILITIES
with
UNIVERSITY OF NORTH
DAKOTA

RENEWABLE ENERGY INSTITUTE

COMPANY CONTACT:
Warren Saterlee
Montana Dakota Utilities
Bismarck, ND   58501
(701) 258-0005

INSTITUTIONAL CONTACT:
Don V. Mathsen
Acting Director
Engineering Experiment Station
University of North Dakota
Box 8103, University Station
Grand Forks, ND   58202
(701) 777-3120

PROGRAM DESCRIPTION/OBJECTIVES:
To research and develop concepts on renewable energy from
the view point of the electric
utility and the consumer.

PROGRAM INITIATED: 1981

LENGTH OF STUDY FOR PARTICI-
PANT: Dependent on participant and project

LENGTH OF CONTRACT: Renewed
annually

LOCATION: University of North
Dakota

PARTICIPANTS: About 15 students and faculty in mechanical engineering

PROGRAM COSTS PROVIDED BY:
Institution: 30%
Company: 70%

PRINTED MATERIALS AVAILABLE
FROM: Institution

179. MONSANTO COMPANY
with
WASHINGTON UNIVERSITY

PRODUCTIVITY IMPROVEMENT/
PROCESS OPTIMIZATION

COMPANY CONTACT:
G.T. Kennedy
Director of Training
Corporate Training Department
Monsanto Company
800 North Lingbergh Blvd.
St. Louis, MO   63166
(314) 694-1000

INSTITUTIONAL CONTACT:
M.P. Dudukovic
Program Director
Chemical Engineering Department
Washington University
Campus Box 1198
St. Louis, MO   63130
(314) 869-6082

PROGRAM DESCRIPTION/OBJECTIVES:
This program is designed to
broaden the background of those
with previous engineering degrees, particularly chemical,
electrical and mechanical engineering and for those with
career experience in or with
the desire to enter a full-time
career in the area of process
control. Course materials are
uniquely tailored to match the
skills and knowledge required
for the chemical engineer participant, primarily emphasizing
process control, computer control, industrial electronics
and analytical instrumentation.
Emphasis for the electrical and
mechanical engineer will in addition include courses to provide the understanding of chemical process control systems.

PROGRAM INITIATED: 1977

LENGTH OF STUDY FOR PARTICI-
PANT: 1 year (93 trimesters
and a 2-week pre-course
review)

LENGTH OF CONTRACT: 1 year
renewable

LOCATION: Washington University

PARTICIPANTS: 10 senior chemi-

cal, electrical and mechanical
Monsanto engineers annually
(Program also open to employees
of other companies.)

PROGRAM COSTS PROVIDED BY:
Institution: Course design
Company: 100%

PRINTED MATERIALS AVAILABLE
FROM: Institution

180. MONTANA POWER COMPANY
with
MILES COMMUNITY COLLEGE

POWER PLANT TECHNOLOGY

COMPANY CONTACT:
Blair Ricks
Director of Employee Development
Montana Power Company
40 East Broadway
Butte, MT   59701
(406) 723-5421, X2830

INSTITUTIONAL CONTACT:
Dr. John Koch
Director of Public Services
Miles Community College
2715 Dickinson
Miles City, MT   59301
(406) 232-3031, X13

PROGRAM DESCRIPTION/OBJECTIVES:
To train entry level personnel
for coal fired electrical generation facilities (mechanic,
operator, instrumentation and
control, business administration.

PROGRAM INITIATED: 1978

LENGTH OF STUDY FOR PARTICI-
PANT: 3 years

LENGTH OF CONTRACT: Open-ended

LOCATION: Billings-Colstrip

PARTICIPANTS: 40 employees

PROGRAM COSTS PROVIDED BY:
Institution: $25,000
Company: $100,000
Other Source: $20,000

PRINTED MATERIALS AVAILABLE
FROM: Institution

181. MT. SINAI HOSPITAL
            with
      UNIVERSITY OF HARTFORD

MANAGEMENT TRAINING FOR
HOSPITAL NURSES

COMPANY CONTACT:
Ronald Waack
Director of Nursing
Mt. Sinai Hospital
Blue Hills Avenue
Hartford, CT   06112
(203) 242-4431

INSTITUTIONAL CONTACT:
M. Brady/B. Koerner
Director, Continuing Education
Division of Adult Educational
Services
University of Hartford
200 Bloomfield Avenue
West Hartford, CT   06117
(203) 243-4387

PROGRAM DESCRIPTION/OBJECTIVES:
Introduction to management principles and practices for first
line supervisors and middle managers in acute hospital nursing.

PROGRAM INITIATED: 1982

LENGTH OF STUDY FOR PARTICI-
PANT: 8 weeks with follow-up
(30 hours)

LENGTH OF CONTRACT: 1 time
(pilot) with possible renewal

LOCATION: Mt. Sinai Hospital

PARTICIPANTS: 25 professional
nurses

PROGRAM COSTS PROVIDED BY:
Company: 100%

PRINTED MATERIALS AVAILABLE
FROM: Institution

182. MT. WASHINGTON VALLEY
      CHAMBER OF COMMERCE*
            with
      UNIVERSITY OF NEW
      HAMPSHIRE

MBA ASSOCIATES

COMPANY CONTACT:
Michael Hickey
Executive Director
Mt. Washington Valley Chamber
of Commerce
North Conway, NH   03860
(603) 356-3171

INSTITUTIONAL CONTACT:
William E. Wetzel, Jr.
Professor of Business
Administration
Whittemore School of Business
& Economics
University of New Hampshire
Durham, NH   03821
(603) 862-2771

PROGRAM DESCRIPTION/OBJECTIVES:
Provide consulting and project
experience for second-year MBA
candidates, through execution
of professional quality assign-
ments with business, government
and not-for-profit organizations
Provide experience in management of a small professional
consulting organization.

PROGRAM INITIATED: 1978

LENGTH OF STUDY FOR PARTICI-
PANT: Usually 1 semester, 2
semesters maximum

LENGTH OF CONTRACT: Usually
2-3 months

LOCATION: University of New
Hampshire

PARTICIPANTS: 10-20 second-
year MBA candidates annually

PROGRAM COSTS PROVIDED BY:
Institution: Indirect overhead
Company: Approximately $5,000
Other Source: Approximately
$4,000 (Small Business
Administration)
(Cont.)

182. (Cont.)

PRINTED MATERIALS AVAILABLE
FROM: Institution

---

*Representative entry--complete
list available from institution.

183. NASA, GODDARD SPACE
FLIGHT CENTER
with
PRINCE GEORGE'S COMMUNITY
COLLEGE

BEGINNING AND INTERMEDIATE
FRENCH FOR TECHNICAL PERSONNEL

COMPANY CONTACT:
Carolyn Casey
Employee Development Specialist
NASA Goddard Space Flight
Center
Greenbelt, MD   20771
(301) 344-5086

INSTITUTIONAL CONTACT:
Veronica S. Norwood
Director, Contract Services
Prince George's Community
College
301 Largo Road
Largo, MD   20772
(301) 322-0726

PROGRAM DESCRIPTION/OBJECTIVES:
To provide beginning and intermediate French language and culture instruction for personnel
subject to foreign assignment,
to enable them to communicate
with citizens of French-speak-
ing countries.

PROGRAM INITIATED: 1978

LENGTH OF STUDY FOR PARTICI-
PANT: Beginning: 80 hours (2
1-hour classes per week); Intermediate: 40 hours (1 1-hour
class per week)

LENGTH OF CONTRACT: 40 weeks

LOCATION: Goddard Space Flight
Center

PARTICIPANTS: 10 technical
personnel per class

PROGRAM COSTS PROVIDED BY:
Company: 64%
Other Source: 36% (state funds)

PRINTED MATERIALS AVAILABLE
FROM: Institution

184. NATIONAL ASSOCIATION
OF BANK WOMEN
with
LOUISIANA STATE UNIVERSITY

LSU/NAWB DEGREE PROGRAM FOR
BANK PROFESSIONALS

COMPANY CONTACT:
Anne Bryant
Educational Director
National Association of
Bank Women
500 North Michigan Avenue
Suite 1400
Chicago, IL   60611
(312) 661-1700

INSTITUTIONAL CONTACT:
Ronald F. Bush
Director of Marketing
Louisiana State University
Baton Rouge, LA   70803
(504) 388-3202

PROGRAM DESCRIPTION/OBJECTIVES:
To provide individuals in banking with the opportunity to
complete their B.S. degree requirements in management from
LSU without significant inter-
ference with their present
banking careers.

PROGRAM INITIATED: 1979

LENGTH OF STUDY FOR PARTICI-
PANT: 4 weeks annually for 3
years

LENGTH OF CONTRACT: Varies
with individual student, usually 3-5 years

LOCATION: Baton Rouge Campus,
LSU

PARTICIPANTS: 50 officers and
non-officers in the banking
industry annually

PROGRAM COSTS PROVIDED BY:
$2,300 annually normally paid
(Cont.)

184. (Cont.)

by participant and bank

PRINTED MATERIALS AVAILABLE
FROM: Institution and Company

185. NATIONAL ASSOCIATION OF
BANK WOMEN
with
MUNDELEIN COLLEGE

NABW/MUNDELEIN COLLEGE
MANAGEMENT PROGRAM

COMPANY CONTACT:
Anne L. Bryant
Educational Director
National Association of Bank
Women
500 North Michigan Avenue
Suite 1400
Chicago, IL 60611
(312) 661-1700

INSTITUTIONAL CONTACT:
Vivian Wilson, BVM
Assistant Director, Admissions
Mundelein College
6363 North Sheridan Road
Chicago, IL 60660
(312) 262-8100, X473

PROGRAM DESCRIPTION/OBJECTIVES:
To provide management major in
a quick format for people in
banking and other financial
institutions.

PROGRAM INITIATED: 1977

LENGTH OF STUDY FOR PARTICI-
PANT: 12 weeks spread over 3
years at 2-week sessions twice
each year

LENGTH OF CONTRACT: Ongoing

LOCATION: Mundelein College

PARTICIPANTS: Between 20 and
40 promotable banking employees
per 2-week session

PROGRAM COSTS PROVIDED BY:
$1,575 per 2-week session pro-
vided by either company or
participant

PRINTED MATERIALS AVAILABLE
FROM: Institution

186. NATIONAL ASSOCIATION OF
BANK WOMEN
with
SIMMONS COLLEGE

NATIONAL ASSOCIATION OF BANK
WOMEN/SIMMONS COLLEGE
BACHELOR'S DEGREE PROGRAM

COMPANY CONTACT:
Anne Bryant
Educational Director
National Association of Bank
Women
500 North Michigan Avenue
Suite 1400
Chicago, IL 60611
(312) 661-1700

INSTITUTIONAL CONTACT:
Louise Comeau
Program Director
Continuing Education
Simmons College
300 The Fenway
Boston, MA 02115
(617) 738-2141

PROGRAM DESCRIPTION/OBJECTIVES:
To provide a high quality curri
culum in management which leads
to a Bachelor's degree for
women who are employed full-
time. Students learn on a part
time basis by attending 6
2-week institutes.

PROGRAM INITIATED: 1976

LENGTH OF STUDY FOR PARTICI-
PANT: 3-5 years

LENGTH OF CONTRACT: 3-5 years

LOCATION: Simmons College

PARTICIPANTS: 4 middle
management women

PROGRAM COSTS PROVIDED BY:
Company: Approximately $3,200
to $4,800
Participant: Partial payment
by some participants

PRINTED MATERIALS AVAILABLE
FROM: Institution

187. NATIONAL CREDIT UNION
      INSTITUTE
            with
      UNIVERSITY OF WISCONSIN
      EXTENSION

CREDIT UNION ACCOUNTING (A58)

COMPANY CONTACT:
Glenn C. Hoyle
Director
National Credit Union Institute
Credit Union National
Association, Inc.
P.O. Box 431
Madison, WI   53701
(608) 231-4051

INSTITUTIONAL CONTACT:
Phil Rowin
Program Assistant
Business and Management/
Economics
University of Wisconsin -
Extension
One South Park Street, Room 759
Madison, WI   53706
(608) 262-4876

PROGRAM DESCRIPTION/OBJECTIVES:
To provide participants with
knowledge necessary to function
at a higher level of understanding and problem-solving within
their credit union in the area
of accounting.

PROGRAM INITIATED: 1979

LENGTH OF STUDY FOR PARTICIPANT:
1 year

LENGTH OF CONTRACT: 6 months
with renewal option

LOCATION: University of Wisconsin - Extension

PARTICIPANTS: 300 credit union
employees in each course

PROGRAM COSTS PROVIDED BY:
Institution: 50%
Company: 50%

PRINTED MATERIALS AVAILABLE
FROM: Institution and Company

188. NATIONAL CREDIT UNION
      INSTITUTE
            with
      UNIVERSITY OF WISCONSIN
      - EXTENSION

CREDIT UNION MANAGEMENT (M55)

COMPANY CONTACT:
Glenn C. Hoyle
Director
National Credit Union Institute
Credit Union National
Association, Inc.
P.O. Box 431
Madison, WI   53701
(608) 231-4051

INSTITUTIONAL CONTACT:
Phil Rowin
Program Assistant
Business and Management/
Economics
University of Wisconsin -
Extension
One South Park Street, Room 759
Madison, WI   53706
(608) 262-4876

PROGRAM DESCRIPTION/OBJECTIVES:
To provide participants with
knowledge necessary to function
at a higher level of understanding and problem-solving within
their credit union in the area
of management.

PROGRAM INITIATED: 1971

LENGTH OF STUDY FOR PARTICI-
PANT: 1 year

LENGTH OF CONTRACT: 6 months
with renewal option

LOCATION: University of
Wisconsin - Extension

PARTICIPANTS: 300 credit union
employees in each course

PROGRAM COSTS PROVIDED BY:
Institution: 50%
Company: 50%

PRINTED MATERIALS AVAILABLE
FROM: Institution and Company

189.   NATIONAL MINE SAFETY AND
       HEALTH ACADEMY
              with
       MARSHALL UNIVERSITY

MASTER'S DEGREE PROGRAM IN MINE
SAFETY EDUCATION

COMPANY CONTACT:
Not reported

INSTITUTIONAL CONTACT:
James Stone
Associate Professor
Marshall University
Harris Hall
Huntington, WV   25701
(304) 696-2380

PROGRAM DESCRIPTION/OBJECTIVES:
To improve the safety record
in mines (coal, etc.).

PROGRAM INITIATED: 1979

LENGTH OF STUDY FOR PARTICI-
PANT: Not reported

LENGTH OF CONTRACT: Not
reported

LOCATION: Not reported

PARTICIPANTS: 80 full-time

PROGRAM COSTS PROVIDED BY:
Institution: $40,000

PRINTED MATERIALS AVAILABLE
FROM: Not reported

190.   NAVAL AIR STATION -
       NORTH ISLAND
              with
       SOUTHWESTERN COLLEGE

BASIC SIGN LANGUAGE (Human
Services 50)

COMPANY CONTACT:
Leonard Sharnar
Training Officer
Naval Air Station - North
Island
San Diego, CA   92135
(714) 437-7418

INSTITUTIONAL CONTACT:
Mary Wylie
Southwestern College
900 Otay Lakes Road
Chula Vista, CA   92910
(714) 265-1586

PROGRAM DESCRIPTION/OBJECTIVES:
Introduction to the system of
manual communication used by
deaf persons in the U.S.; designed for relatives, the publi
lic servant and those who wish
to work with the deaf.

PROGRAM INITIATED: 1982

LENGTH OF STUDY FOR PARTICI-
PANT: 8 weeks; 24 hours of
instruction

LENGTH OF CONTRACT: 8 weeks

LOCATION: Naval Air Station -
North Island

PARTICIPANTS: 25 base
personnel

PROGRAM COSTS PROVIDED BY:
Company: $2,779

PRINTED MATERIALS AVAILABLE
FROM: Institution

191. NCR CORPORATION
         with
      CORNELL UNIVERSITY

TRAINING AND DEVELOPMENT
PROGRAM: AN OVERVIEW

COMPANY CONTACT:

Theodore J. Settle
Program Development and
Evaluation Director
NCR Management College and
Career Development Center
NCR Corporation
101 West Schantz
Dayton, OH   45479
(513) 445-2346

INSTITUTIONAL CONTACT:
Dr. Donald Kane
Program Director
School of Industrial and
Labor Relations
Cornell University
P.O. Box 1000
Ithaca, NY   14853
(607) 256-4462

PROGRAM DESCRIPTION/OBJECTIVES:
Provide an overview and experience with the critical elements
of the course development
process.

PROGRAM INITIATED: 1981

LENGTH OF STUDY FOR PARTICI-
PANT: 4 consecutive days

LENGTH OF CONTRACT: 1 program

LOCATION: NCR Corporate Education Center, Dayton, OH

PARTICIPANTS: 20 NCR educators

PROGRAM COSTS PROVIDED BY:
Company: 100%

PRINTED MATERIALS AVAILABLE
FROM: Institution

192. NCR CORPORATION
         with
      OHIO STATE UNIVERSITY

FIELD ENGINEER EDUCATION

COMPANY CONTACT:
Theodore J. Settle
Program Development and
Evaluation Director
NCR Management College and
Career Development Center
NCR Corporation
101 West Schantz
Dayton, OH   45479
(513) 445-2346

INSTITUTIONAL CONTACT:
James Buffer
Director, Office of Research
and Development Service
College of Education
Ohio State University
1945 North High Street
Columbus, OH   43210
(614) 422-7231

PROGRAM DESCRIPTION/OBJECTIVES:
Improving systems to develop
instructional program which
prepare field engineers to become acquainted with new
products.

PROGRAM INITIATED: 1981

LENGTH OF STUDY FOR PARTICI-
PANT: Not available

LENGTH OF CONTRACT: 1 year

LOCATION: Dayton, OH

PARTICIPANTS: Not available

PROGRAM COSTS PROVIDED BY:
Company: 100%

PRINTED MATERIALS AVAILABLE
FROM: Institution

193. NCR CORPORATION
with
OHIO UNIVERSITY/EDUCA-
TIONAL TESTING SERVICE

COMPUTERIZED CAREER GUIDANCE
SYSTEM FOR ADULTS

COMPANY CONTACT:
Anne Ayres-Gerhart
Corporate Career Planning and
Development
NCR Corporation
101 West Schantz
Dayton, OH   45479
(513) 445-2376

INSTITUTIONAL CONTACT:
Betty Menson
Director, Adult Learning
Services
Ohio University
Tupper Hall 309
Athens, OH   45701
(614) 594-6569

PROGRAM DESCRIPTION/OBJECTIVES:
To develop a computerized
career guidance system for
adults which is patterned after
SIGI, a current system which is
oriented toward high school and
early college-age students.

PROGRAM INITIATED: 1982

LENGTH OF STUDY FOR PARTICI-
PANT: Not available

LENGTH OF CONTRACT: Not
available

LOCATION: Princeton, NJ

PARTICIPANTS: Not available

PROGRAM COSTS PROVIDED BY:
Other Source: 100% (ETS/Kellogg)

PRINTED MATERIALS AVAILABLE
FROM: Institution: (ETS)

194. NCR CORPORATION*
with
TRI-COUNTY TECHNICAL
COLLEGE

ELECTRONICS TECHNICIAN
(FAST TRACK)

COMPANY CONTACT:
Fred Parks
Manufacturing Engineer
NCR Corporation
1150 Anderson Drive
Liberty, SC   29657
(803) 843-2711

INSTITUTIONAL CONTACT:
Ronald N. Talley
Director, Comprehensive
Manpower Training
Tri-County Technical College
P.O. Box 587
Pendleton, SC   29670
(803) 646-8361

PROGRAM DESCRIPTION/OBJECTIVES:
To provide accelerated training
for electronics technicians.
Eligible applicants are selected from among persons who are
currently unemployed.

PROGRAM INITIATED: 1981

LENGTH OF STUDY FOR PARTICI-
PANT: 12 months

LENGTH OF CONTRACT: 12 months

LOCATION: Tri-County Technical College

PARTICIPANTS: 18 electronic
technicians annually

PROGRAM COSTS PROVIDED BY:
Institution: Indirect
Company: Indirect
Other Source: $65,131 (federal
CETA funds)

PRINTED MATERIALS AVAILABLE
FROM: Institution

---

*Representative entry--complete
list available from institution.

195. NCR CORPORATION
with
UNIVERSITY OF DAYTON

EXECUTIVE DEVELOPMENT PROGRAM

COMPANY CONTACT:
Theodore J. Settle
Program Development and
Evaluation Director
NCR Management College and
Career Development Center
NCR Corporation
101 West Schantz
Dayton, OH   45479
(513) 445-2346

INSTITUTIONAL CONTACT:
William Hoben
Dean, School of Business
Administration
University of Dayton
Dayton, OH   45469
(513) 229-3731

PROGRAM DESCRIPTION/OBJECTIVES:
To increase managers' awareness
of the legal, political, technological, social, and cultural
environments and their impact
on a multinational company.

PROGRAM INITIATED: 1980

LENGTH OF STUDY FOR PARTICI-
PANT: 8 weeks, 3 hours per
week

LENGTH OF CONTRACT: 1 program

LOCATION: University of Dayton

PARTICIPANTS: 50 high level
executives per program

PROGRAM COSTS PROVIDED BY:
Company: 100%

PRINTED MATERIALS AVAILABLE
FROM: Company

196. NCR CORPORATION
with
UNIVERSITY OF MICHIGAN

CAREER MOVEMENT OF NCR
EMPLOYEES

COMPANY CONTACT:
Theodore J. Settle
Program Development and
Evaluation Director
NCR Management College and
Career Development Center
NCR Corporation
101 West Schantz
Dayton, OH   45479
(513) 445-2346

INSTITUTIONAL CONTACT:
Andrea Foote
Institute of Labor and
Industrial Relations
University of Michigan and
Wayne State University
401 Fourth Street
Ann Arbor, MI   48103
(313) 763-1187

PROGRAM DESCRIPTION/OBJECTIVES:
A comprehensive research study
of career movement of NCR employees to identify career
paths.

PROGRAM INITIATED: 1981

LENGTH OF STUDY FOR PARTICI-
PANT: Not available

LENGTH OF CONTRACT: 12 months

LOCATION: University of
Michigan

PARTICIPANTS: Not available

PROGRAM COSTS PROVIDED BY:
Company: 100%

PRINTED MATERIALS AVAILABLE
FROM: Institution and Company

197. THE NORTH AMERICAN COAL
      CORPORATION*
          with
      MARY COLLEGE

ENERGY MANAGMENT/AREA OF EMPHASIS

COMPANY CONTACT:
Richard Espeland
Director of Personnel
The North American Coal
Corporation
Kirkwood Office Tower
Bismarck, ND   58501
(701) 258-2200

INSTITUTIONAL CONTACT:
Fran Gronberg
Coordinator, Areas of Emphasis
Mary College
Apple Creek Road
Bismarck, ND   58501
(701) 255-4681, X328

PROGRAM DESCRIPTION/OBJECTIVES:
Designed to qualify persons in
supervisory and management
roles in the energy industry.
May term courses give general
background in the energy field,
with the internships providing
guaranteed summer employment
and on-location learning experiences with a major energy
company or agency.

PROGRAM INITIATED: 1979

LENGTH OF STUDY FOR PARTICI-
PANT: 3 May terms and 3
3-month internships

LENGTH OF CONTRACT: 12 month
renewable

LOCATION: May term at Mary
College; internships at business location

PARTICIPANTS: 12 business ad-
ministration/accounting undergraduate majors annually

PROGRAM COSTS PROVIDED BY:
Institution: 50%
Company: 50%

PRINTED MATERIALS AVAILABLE
FROM: Institution

---

*Representative entry--complete
list available from institution.

198. NORTHEAST UTILITIES
          with
      UNIVERSITY OF HARTFORD

ON-SITE MBA COURSES

COMPANY CONTACT:
William Naughton
Northeast Utilities
P.O. Box 270
Hartford, CT   06101
(203) 249-5711

INSTITUTIONAL CONTACT:
William T. George
Program Development Consultant
Division of Adult Educational
Services
University of Hartford
200 Bloomfield Avenue
West Hartford, CT   06117
(203) 243-4507/4381

PROGRAM DESCRIPTION/OBJECTIVES:
8 to 10 courses from the CORE
MBA sequence.

PROGRAM INITIATED: 1981

LENGTH OF STUDY FOR PARTICI-
PANT: Self-paced

LENGTH OF CONTRACT: 2 years

LOCATION: Berlin, CT

PARTICIPANTS: Approximately
80 employees

PROGRAM COSTS PROVIDED BY:
Company: 75%
Participant: 25%

PRINTED MATERIAL AVAILABLE
FROM: Institution

199. NORTHERN STATES POWER
with
UNIVERSITY OF NORTH
DAKOTA

RENEWABLE ENERGY INSTITUTE

COMPANY CONTACT:
Conrad Aas
Northern State Power
Minneapolis, MN   55440
(612) 330-5500

INSTITUTIONAL CONTACT:
Don V. Mathsen
Acting Director
Engineering Experiment Station
University of North Dakota
Box 8103, University Station
Grand Forks, ND   58202
(701) 777-3120

PROGRAM DESCRIPTION/OBJECTIVES:
To research and develop concepts on renewable energy from
the viewpoint of the electric
utility and the consumer.

PROGRAM INITIATED: 1981

LENGTH OF STUDY FOR PARTICI-
PANT: Dependent on participant and project

LENGTH OF CONTRACT: Renewed
annually

LOCATION: University of North
Dakota

PARTICIPANTS: About 15 students and faculty in mechanical, electrical and chemical
engineering

PROGRAM COSTS PROVIDED BY:
Institution: 30%
Company: 70%

PRINTED MATERIALS AVAILABLE
FROM: Institution

200. NORTHWEST FOOD PROCESSORS
ASSOCIATION*
with
OREGON STATE UNIVERSITY

PRODUCTIVITY BY OBJECTIVES

COMPANY CONTACT:
Dave Click
Executive Director
Northwest Food Processors
Association
2828 SW Corbett
Portland, OR   97201
(503) 226-2848

INSTITUTIONAL CONTACT:
Jim Riggs
Director, Oregon Productivity
Center
Head, Industrial Engineering
Department
Oregon State University
Corvallis, OR   97331
(503) 754-4645

PROGRAM DESCRIPTION/OBJECTIVES:
Provides company with opportunity for productivity interfirm
comparisons.

PROGRAM INITIATED: 1980

LENGTH OF STUDY FOR PARTICI-
PANT: 6 months to 1 year

LENGTH OF CONTRACT: 6 months
to 1 year

LOCATION: At plant site

PARTICIPANTS: 400+ employees
and managers

PROGRAM COSTS PROVIDED BY:
Variable, depends on need

PRINTED MATERIALS AVAILABLE
FROM: Institution

---

*Representative entry--complete
list available from institution.

201. NORSK HYDRO ALUMINUM
     COMPANY*
          with
     BREVARD COMMUNITY COLLEGE

TRAINING OF ON-LINE EMPLOYEES
FOR ALUMINUM EXTRUSION COMPANY

COMPANY CONTACT:
Charles Hayes
Plant Manager
Norsk Hydro Aluminum Company
Rockledge, FL   32955
(305) 636-8147

INSTITUTIONAL CONTACT:
Maurice F. Buckner
Dean, Continuing Education
Brevard Community College
1519 Clearlake Road
Cocoa, FL   32922
(305) 632-1111, X263

PROGRAM DESCRIPTION/OBJECTIVES:
To provide specialized skills
in operation of extrusion
processes.

PROGRAM INITIATED: 1979

LENGTH OF STUDY FOR PARTICI-
PANT: 5 weeks

LENGTH OF CONTRACT: 12 months,
non-renewable

LOCATION: Brevard Community
College

PARTICIPANTS: 92 laborers to
skilled machinists

PROGRAM COSTS PROVIDED BY:
Institution: $3,000
Company: $3,000
Other Source: $12,850 (Indus-
trial Services grant from
Florida Department of Education)

PRINTED MATERIALS AVAILABLE
FROM: Institution

---

*Representative entry--complete
list available from institution.

202. NORTON COMPANY
          with
     WORCESTER STATE COLLEGE

COLLABORATIVE MANAGEMENT
DEVELOPMENT PROGRAM

COMPANY CONTACT:
John Conn
Manager, Organizational and
Employee Development
Norton Company
One New Bond Street
Worcester, MA   01606
(617) 853-1000

INSTITUTIONAL CONTACT:
William O'Neil
Dean, Division of Graduate and
Continuing Education
Worcester State College
486 Chandler Street
Worcester, MA   01602
(617) 793-8100

PROGRAM DESCRIPTION/OBJECTIVES:
To develop a new continuing education pool while meeting the
needs of local companies; to
provide practical training for
entry-level managers; career-
path development, college
credit, skill development.

PROGRAM INITIATED: 1981

LENGTH OF STUDY FOR PARTICI-
PANT: 21 credits; 2 years
average

LENGTH OF CONTRACT: Agreement
has no termination date

LOCATION: Norton Company
plant and WSC campus

PARTICIPANTS: 50-60 entry-
level and middle managers

PROGRAM COSTS PROVIDED BY:
Institution: $845 per parti-
cipant
Company: $845 per participant
Participant: $100

PRINTED MATERIALS AVAILABLE
FROM: Institution

104

203. NUTRI-SYSTEMS
with
COLLEGE OF LAKE COUNTY

THE ART OF DRAWING BLOOD

COMPANY CONTACT:
Robert Sheridan
Manager
Nutri-Systems
2424 Washington
Waukegan, IL   60085
(312) 662-0615

INSTITUTIONAL CONTACT:
Keri Thiessen
Business/Industry Training
Coordinator
Open Campus
College of Lake County
Grayslake, IL   60030
(312) 223-3616

PROGRAM DESCRIPTION/OBJECTIVES:
To provide nurses with phle-
botomy techniques to be utilized on weight reducing
clientele.

PROGRAM INITIATED: 1982

LENGTH OF STUDY FOR PARTICI-
PANT: 1 day

LENGTH OF CONTRACT: 1 day

LOCATION: Nutri-Systems

PARTICIPANTS: 6 nurses

PROGRAM COSTS PROVIDED BY:
Company: $31.00

PRINTED MATERIALS AVAILABLE
FROM: Institution

204. OAKLAND POLICE DEPARTMENT
with
MERRITT COLLEGE

JOINT POLICE ACADEMY

COMPANY CONTACT:
R. Crawford
Sergeant, Training
Oakland Police Department
455 Washington Street
Oakland, CA   94607
(415) 273-3552

INSTITUTIONAL CONTACT:
Kenneth Giles
Assistant Dean
Technical Division
Merritt College
12500 Campus Drive
Oakland, CA   94619
(415) 436-2427

PROGRAM DESCRIPTION/OBJECTIVES:
Training of police officers
with pre-police students.
Allows for students to receive
training prior to becoming a
police officer.

PROGRAM INITIATED: 1981

LENGTH OF STUDY FOR PARTICI-
PANT: 1 year

LENGTH OF CONTRACT: 1 year

LOCATION: Oakland Police
Department

PARTICIPANTS: 7 Administration of Justice students

PROGRAM COSTS PROVIDED BY:
Institution: $12,000
Company: $12,000

PRINTED MATERIALS AVAILABLE
FROM: Institution

205. OAKLAND YOUTH WORKS
with
MERRITT COLLEGE

OAKLAND YOUTH WORKS

COMPANY CONTACT:
Joan Dark
Director
Oakland Youth Works
1515 Webster Street
Oakland, CA   94612
(415) 763-9890

INSTITUTIONAL CONTACT:
Wesley Ingram
Counselor
Career Center
Merritt College
12500 Campus Drive
Oakland, CA   94619
(415) 436-2447

PROGRAM DESCRIPTION/OBJECTIVES:
Place students ages 17-21 in
part-time jobs related to their
studies. Provide screening pre-
employment and supportive services in order to give employer
a better performing employee.

PROGRAM INITIATED: 1980

LENGTH OF STUDY FOR PARTICI-
PANT: At least 1 semester

LENGTH OF CONTRACT: At least
1 semester

LOCATION: Merritt College

PARTICIPANTS: 6 business, primarily data processing and
electronics students per
semester

PROGRAM COSTS PROVIDED BY:
Institution: Staff salary
Company: Youth Works support
staff
Other Source: Placement com-
panies provide student salaries

PRINTED MATERIALS AVAILABLE
FROM: Institution and Company

206. OHIO EDISON*
with
THE UNIVERSITY OF AKRON

COOPERATIVE EDUCATION

COMPANY CONTACT:
Herb Lowelien
Director of Personnel
Ohio Edison
76 South Main Street
Akron, OH   44308
(216) 382-2607

INSTITUTIONAL CONTACT:
Ralph B. McNerney
Director, Cooperative Education
The University of Akron
212 Gardner Student Center
Akron, OH   44235
(216) 375-6723

PROGRAM DESCRIPTION/OBJECTIVES:
Alternating and parallel system
co-op programs available. Students seek co-op employment in
career related, paid work experiences. The university
seeks to place 4,000 students
between 1981 and 1986.

PROGRAM INITIATED: 1913

LENGTH OF STUDY FOR PARTICI-
PANT: 3/4 semester

LENGTH OF CONTRACT: 1 semester
with renewal option

LOCATION: Nationwide

PARTICIPANTS: 575 students
currently available from 4
colleges, in 28 major fields
annually

PROGRAM COSTS PROVIDED BY:
Institution: $67,000
Other Source: $94,000 (federal
grant)

PRINTED MATERIALS AVAILABLE
FROM: Institution

*Representative entry--complete
list available from institution

207. OKC REFINING COMPANY
with
OKLAHOMA STATE TECH

INTRODUCTION TO MOTORS AND
CONTROLS, INTERMEDIATE MOTORS
AND CONTROLS

COMPANY CONTACT:
Not available

INSTITUTIONAL CONTACT:
Bill J. Lyons
Department Head
Electrical-Electronics
Technology
Oklahoma State Tech
4th and Mission
Okmulgee, OK   74447
(918) 756-6211, X252

PROGRAM DESCRIPTION/OBJECTIVES:
To enhance the employee's competence in the regular routine
maintenance of the facilities.

PROGRAM INITIATED: 1980

LENGTH OF STUDY FOR PARTICI-
PANT: Not reported

LENGTH OF CONTRACT: Not
reported

LOCATION: Not reported

PARTICIPANTS: 24 employees
annually

PROGRAM COSTS PROVIDED BY:
Company: 100%

PRINTED MATERIALS AVAILABLE
FROM: Not available

208. OKLAHOMA ASSOCIATION OF
DRYCLEANERS
with
OKLAHOMA STATE TECH

OKLAHOMA ASSOCIATION OF DRY-
CLEANERS ANNUAL SEMINAR/
WORKSHOP

COMPANY CONTACT:
Dorothy Bennett
Executive Secretary
State Drycleaners Board
4001 North Lincoln
Oklahoma City, OK   73105
(405) 521-2395

INSTITUTIONAL CONTACT:
Lloyd Bennett
Supervisor, Drycleaning
Program
Small Business Trades
Department
Oklahoma State Tech
4th and Mission
Okmulgee, OK   74447
(918) 756-6211, X207

PROGRAM DESCRIPTION/OBJECTIVES:
To promote greater appreciation
of drycleaning procedures; provide students opportunities to
gain better understanding of industry procedures; enhance job
placement prospects for students and provide institutional
advertisement.

PROGRAM INITIATED: 1981

LENGTH OF STUDY FOR PARTICI-
PANT: Not reported

LENGTH OF CONTRACT: Not
reported

LOCATION: Not reported

PARTICIPANTS: 115 annually

PROGRAM COSTS PROVIDED BY:
Institution: 20%
Company: 100%

PRINTED MATERIALS AVAILABLE
FROM: Institution

209. OLD BEN COAL COMPANY
with
REND LAKE COLLEGE

UNDERGROUND REPAIRMAN TRAINING
PROGRAM

COMPANY CONTACT:
Jim Spiller
Director of Training
Old Ben Coal Company
Main Office
Benton, IL   62812
(618) 435-8176

INSTITUTIONAL CONTACT:
Carroll Turner
Dean, Vocational Technical
Education
Rend Lake College
RR 1
Ina, IL   62846
(618) 437-5321

PROGRAM DESCRIPTION/OBJECTIVES:
To provide skill training for
underground miners going from
laborer classification to
repairman.

PROGRAM INITIATED: 1975

LENGTH OF STUDY FOR PARTICI-
PANT: 29 weeks

LENGTH OF CONTRACT: Ongoing
with termination notice

LOCATION: Rend Lake College

PARTICIPANTS: 466 underground
repairmen over the past 6 years

PROGRAM COSTS PROVIDED BY:
Company: 25% (facilities and
equipment)
Other Source: 75% (state and
local funds)

PRINTED MATERIALS AVAILABLE
FROM: Not available

210. ORE-IDA FOODS, INC.
with
THE UNIVERSITY OF AKRON

TAKING OFF

COMPANY CONTACT:
Nancy Brannon
Safety and Personnel Director
Ore-Ida Foods, Inc.
P.O. Box 567
Massillon, OH   44646
(216) 833-4151

INSTITUTIONAL CONTACT:
Pauline Russell
Program Associate
Adult Resource Center
The University of Akron
Akron, OH   44235
(216) 275-7448

PROGRAM DESCRIPTION/OBJECTIVES:
To help participants develop
knowledge about themselves,
adult development and opportunities for growth. To develop skills in communication,
time management, decision
making and goal setting.

PROGRAM INITIATED: 1981

LENGTH OF STUDY FOR PARTICI-
PANT: 10 hours

LENGTH OF CONTRACT: 1
workshop

LOCATION: Ore-Ida Foods

PARTICIPANTS: 12 staff of
all levels

PROGRAM COSTS PROVIDED BY:
Company: 100%

PRINTED MATERIALS AVAILABLE
FROM: Not available

211. PENNSYLVANIA ELECTRIC
     COMPANY
            with
     INDIANA UNIVERSITY OF
     PENNSYLVANIA

PENELEC/IUP PERSONNEL
DEVELOPMENT TRAINING PROGRAM

COMPANY CONTACT:
Denny Strawmire
Coordinator of Training
Pennsylvania Electric Company
1001 Broad Street
CEED Building
Johnstown, PA   15907
(814) 533-8425

INSTITUTIONAL CONTACT:
Brian J. McCue
Director, Business, Industry
and Labor
School of Continuing Education
Indiana University of
Pennsylvania
Stright Hall
Indiana, PA   15705
(412) 357-2227

PROGRAM DESCRIPTION/OBJECTIVES:
CPM courses (3 courses in pur-
chasing and materials management); contract law course;
grievance resolution; water
treatment for boilers and cool-
ing towers and other training
areas.

PROGRAM INITIATED: 1976

LENGTH OF STUDY FOR PARTICI-
PANT: 8 weeks - 1 semester

LENGTH OF CONTRACT: Semester
and annual with renewal option

LOCATION: Various industrial
sites and IUP campus

PARTICIPANTS: 100+ office personnel, generation personnel,
supervisors, and middle management annually

PROGRAM COSTS PROVIDED BY:
Institution: $3,150
Company: $10,500 (course-by-
course basis determines fee
structure)

PRINTED MATERIALS AVAILABLE
FROM: Institution

212. COMMONWEALTH OF PENNSYL-
     VANIA JUVENILE COURT
     JUDGES COMMISSION
            with
     SHIPPENSBURG STATE COLLEGE

MASTER'S DEGREE-ADMINISTRATION
OF JUSTICE

COMPANY CONTACT:
Ronald Fennell
Deputy Director
Juvenile Court Judges
Commission
P.O. Box 1234
Federal Square Station
Harrisburg, PA   17108
(717) 787-6910

INSTITUTIONAL CONTACT:
Harry Bobonich
Dean of the School of Graduate
Studies
Shippensburg State College
Shippensburg, PA   17257
(717) 532-1213

PROGRAM DESCRIPTION/OBJECTIVES:
Master's degree in Administration of Justice with a special-
ization in juvenile justice designed to train probation officers to deal more effectively
with juveniles, especially in
the development of preventive
measures in order to cut down
on juvenile crime.

PROGRAM INITIATED: 1982

LENGTH OF STUDY FOR PARTICI-
PANT: 2 years

LOCATION: Weekend classes on
Shippensburg State College
campus

PARTICIPANTS: 60 chief probation officers throughout the
Commonwealth

PROGRAM COSTS PROVIDED BY:
Institution: 34%
Company: 66%

PRINTED MATERIALS AVAILABLE
FROM: Not yet available

213. PENNSYLVANIA POWER AND
      LIGHT
           with
      WILKES COLLEGE AND PENN-
      SYLVANIA STATE UNIVER-
      SITY - HAZLETON

ON-SITE COLLEGE CREDIT COURSES

COMPANY CONTACT:
James White
Supervisor
Training Support Services
Nuclear Department
Pennsylvania Power and Light
P.O. Box 467
Berwick, PA   18603
(717) 542-2149

INSTITUTIONAL CONTACT:
Larry Gingrich
Assistant Director
Continuing Education
Pennsylvania State University -
Hazleton
Highacres
Hazleton, PA   18201
(717) 454-8731

PROGRAM DESCRIPTION/OBJECTIVES:
Provide college credit courses
at a convenient location and
time.

PROGRAM INITIATED: 1981

LENGTH OF CONTRACT: Informal
agreement

LOCATION: Susquehanna Training
Center

PARTICIPANTS: Approximately
70 employees

PROGRAM COSTS PROVIDED BY:
Company: $180 per person
Participant: Books

PRINTED MATERIALS AVAILABLE
FROM: Not available

214. PFIZER, INC.
           with
      MARYMOUNT MANHATTAN
      COLLEGE

PFIZER/MARYMOUNT MANHATTAN
COLLEGE PROGRAM

COMPANY CONTACT:
Steve Shapiro
Training Department
Pfizer, Inc.
235 East 42nd Street
New York, NY   10021
(212) 573-7268

INSTITUTIONAL CONTACT:
Joyce Kaffel
Director, Corporate Education
Programs
Marymount Manhattan College
New York, NY   10021
(212) 472-3800

PROGRAM DESCRIPTION/OBJECTIVES:
To provide Pfizer employees
with an opportunity to take
courses leading to a baccalaureate degree, a Certificate in
Business Management, or specific courses deemed valuable for
career development. Courses
are offered at the company
training center at convenient
hours.

PROGRAM INITIATED: 1977

LENGTH OF STUDY FOR PARTICI-
PANT: Academic year

LENGTH OF CONTRACT: Ongoing

LOCATION: Pfizer, Inc.

PARTICIPANTS: As of 1982, 80
participants of various educational levels and backgrounds.

PROGRAM COSTS PROVIDED BY:
Company: 100% of current
tuition

PRINTED MATERIALS AVAILABLE
FROM: Institution

215. PHILIP MORRIS, U.S.A.
            with
      JOHN TYLER COMMUNITY
      COLLEGE

PHILIP MORRIS CERTIFICATE IN
MANAGEMENT STUDIES

COMPANY CONTACT:
Carson Tucker
Manager, Management Development
Philip Morris, U.S.A.
P.O. Box 26603
Richmond, VA   23261
(804) 274-3404

INSTITUTIONAL CONTACT:
Samuel L. Hancock
Director, Continuing Education
Division of Continuing
Education
John Tyler Community College
13101 Jefferson Davis Highway
Chester, VA   23831
(804) 796-4111

PROGRAM DESCRIPTION/OBJECTIVES:
To provide a core management
training program for employees
who currently are or who may
wish in the future to fill key
leadership and management positions at Philip Morris.

PROGRAM INITIATED: 1980

LENGTH OF STUDY FOR PARTICI-
PANT: 10 quarters, 1 course
each quarter

LENGTH OF CONTRACT: Ongoing

LOCATION: Richmond, VA

PARTICIPANTS: 25 company
employees

PROGRAM COSTS PROVIDED BY:
Institution: Instructors'
salaries
Company: Tuition, books and
facilities

PRINTED MATERIALS AVAILABLE
FROM: Institution

216. PHILLIPS PETROLEUM
      COMPANY
            with
      OKLAHOMA STATE TECH

BASIC INSTRUMENTATION

COMPANY CONTACT:
Rex Miller
Gas Measurement and Instrument
Superintendent
Phillips Petroleum Company
Okmulgee, OK   74447
(918) 756-4151

INSTITUTIONAL CONTACT:
Bill J. Lyons
Department Head
Electrical-Electronics
Technology
Oklahoma State Tech
4th and Mission
Okmulgee, OK   74447
(918) 756-6211, X252

PROGRAM DESCRIPTION/OBJECTIVES:
Petroleum and natural gas pump
station operators in the process and control of facilities
similar to those with which
they are presently assigned.

PROGRAM INITIATED: 1982

LENGTH OF STUDY FOR PARTICI-
PANT: Not reported

LENGTH OF CONTRACT: Not
reported

LOCATION: Not reported

PARTICIPANTS: 48 employees
annually

PROGRAM COSTS PROVIDED BY:
Company: 100%

PRINTED MATERIALS PROVIDED BY:
Not available

217. PORTAGE COUNTY CETA
with
KENT STATE UNIVERSITY

STAFF DEVELOPMENT

COMPANY CONTACT:
Maureen Frederick
Portage County CETA
449 Meridian
Ravenna, OH   44266
(216) 297-5741

INSTITUTIONAL CONTACT:
Karen Rylander
Director, Continuing Education
Kent State University
327 Rockwell Hall
Kent, OH   44242
(216) 672-3100

PROGRAM DESCRIPTION/OBJECTIVES:
Includes overviews of communication skills, motivation, problem-solving, time management,
and team building.

PROGRAM INITIATED: 1981

LENGTH OF STUDY FOR PARTICI-
PANT: 8 hours

LENGTH OF CONTRACT: 8 hours

LOCATION: Portage County CETA

PARTICIPANTS: 25 staff
members

PROGRAM COSTS PROVIDED BY:
Company: 100%

PRINTED MATERIALS AVAILABLE
FROM: Institution

218. PRATT & WHITNEY AIRCRAFT
with
MANCHESTER COMMUNITY
COLLEGE

MANCHESTER COMMUNITY COLLEGE/
PRATT & WHITNEY AIRCRAFT
COOPERATIVE PROGRAM

COMPANY CONTACT:
Robert C. Barnes
Manager, Educational Programs
Pratt & Whitney Aircraft
400 Main Street
East Hartford, CT   06108
(203) 565-7008

INSTITUTIONAL CONTACT:
R. Dianne K. McHutchison
Director, Contract and Grants
Community Services Division
Manchester Community College
MS #5, P.O. Box 1046
Manchester, CT   06040
(203) 646-5838

PROGRAM DESCRIPTION/OBJECTIVES:
Cooperative on-site instructional program providing credit
and non-credit courses to employees of Pratt & Whitney
Aircraft.

PROGRAM INITIATED: 1976

LENGTH OF STUDY FOR PARTICI-
PANT: Varies; need to complete
30 credits

LENGTH OF CONTRACT: 5 years

LOCATION: On-site at Pratt &
Whitney Aircraft

PARTICIPANTS: 350-400 graduate
apprentices, salaried employees
and non-apprentice hourly workers per semester

PROGRAM COSTS PROVIDED BY:
Not reported

PRINTED MATERIALS AVAILABLE
FROM: Institution and Company

219. PRATT & WHITNEY AIRCRAFT
with
SOUTH CENTRAL COMMUNITY
COLLEGE

OFF CAMPUS CREDIT EXTENSION
PROGRAM

COMPANY CONTACT:
Paul Parisi
Senior Personnel Manager
Pratt & Whitney Aircraft
415 Washington Avenue
North Haven, CT   06473
(203) 239-2541

INSTITUTIONAL CONTACT:
Louis S. D'Antonio
Director of Community Services
South Central Community
College
60 Sargent Drive
New Haven, CT   06511
(203) 789-7069

PROGRAM DESCRIPTION/OBJECTIVES:
To provide as Associate Degree
program in science or general
studies, on-site, to employees
of company.

PROGRAM INITIATED: 1980

LENGTH OF STUDY FOR PARTICI-
PANT: 1 semester

LENGTH OF CONTRACT: 12 months
with renewal

LOCATION: Pratt & Whitney
Aircraft

PARTICIPANTS: 200 hourly and
salary employees

PROGRAM COSTS PROVIDED BY:
Company: $61 per course
Participant: $20 per course

PRINTED MATERIALS AVAILABLE
FROM: Institution

220. PRINCE GEORGE'S COUNTY
GOVERNMENT
with
PRINCE GEORGE'S COMMUNITY
COLLEGE

STAFF DEVELOPMENT TRAINING

COMPANY CONTACT:
Betty Austin
Training and Development
Specialist
Prince George's County
Government
County Administration Building
Upper Marlboro, MD   20772
(301) 952-3750

INSTITUTIONAL CONTACT:
Veronica S. Norwood
Director, Contract Services
Prince George's Community
College
301 Largo Road
Largo, MD   20772
(301) 322-0726

PROGRAM DESCRIPTION/OBJECTIVES:
To provide staff development
training in communications, supervisory and management techniques, time management, delegation skills, business writing,
oral presentation skills, problem solving/decision making
and performance appraisal.

PROGRAM INITIATED: 1975

LENGTH OF STUDY FOR PARTICI-
PANT: 12-24 hours

LENGTH OF CONTRACT: 12 months
with renewal option

LOCATION: County Administration Building

PARTICIPANTS: 25 supervisors,
managers, and administrative
support personnel per session

PROGRAM COSTS PROVIDED BY:
Company: 53%
Other Source: 47% (state
funds)

PRINTED MATERIALS AVAILABLE
FROM: Institution

221. PRIVATE INDUSTRY COUNCIL
with
CENTRE COLLEGE OF KENTUCKY

MANAGEMENT TRAINING PROGRAM

COMPANY CONTACT:
Joseph Paterno
Executive Director
Private Industry Council
71 Wilkinson Blvd.
Frankfort, KY   40601
(502) 227-9002

INSTITUTIONAL CONTACT:
W.E. Jackson III
Lorraine Downs
Program Director
Economics Department
Centre College of Kentucky
Danville, KY   40422
(606) 236-5211, X254

PROGRAM DESCRIPTION/OBJECTIVES:
To assist in developing a pool
of well-trained personnel in
the local business community by
teaching them interpersonal and
supervisory skills.

PROGRAM INITIATED: 1982

LENGTH OF STUDY FOR PARTICI-
PANT: 1 quarter

LENGTH OF CONTRACT: 4 months
with renewal pending

LOCATION: Centre College

PARTICIPANTS: 15 pre-supervisory personnel per quarter

PROGRAM COSTS PROVIDED BY:
Institution: Not available
Company: $33,000 or est. 80%
(contributions from 3 firms
who are PIC)

PRINTED MATERIALS AVAILABLE
FROM: Not yet available

222. PROCTOR AND GAMBLE COMPANY
with
UNIVERSITY OF CINCINNATI

INTERNATIONAL TRAINING SCHOOL

COMPANY CONTACT:
Leonard Chapman
Project Coordinator
International Division
Proctor and Gamble Company
6100 Center Hill Road
Cincinnati, OH   45224
(513) 977-4559

INSTITUTIONAL CONTACT:
James H. Vondrell
Director of Extension
Division of Continuing
Education
M.L. #146
350 French Hall
Cincinnati, OH   45221
(513) 475-6836

PROGRAM DESCRIPTION/OBJECTIVES:
To provide English language and
cultural training plus American
business practices course work
to Japanese employees of Proctor and Gamble working in Japan
so that they can work in
English and understand American
business practices.

PROGRAM INITIATED: 1979

LENGTH OF STUDY FOR PARTICI-
PANT: 1 year

LENGTH OF CONTRACT: 1 year

LOCATION: University of Cincinnati campus

PARTICIPANTS: 8 mid-level
managers, sales personnel and
engineers

PROGRAM COSTS PROVIDED BY:
Institution: $5,000 (in kind)
Company: $100,000

PRINTED MATERIALS AVAILABLE
FROM: Institution and Company

223.   PROVIDENT NATIONAL BANK
with
PEIRCE JUNIOR COLLEGE

PROVIDENT/PIC/PEIRCE CLERICAL
TRAINING PROGRAM

COMPANY CONTACT:
Robert L. Schoonmaker
Vice President and Director
Training, Development and
Employee Relations
Provident National Bank
100 South Broad Street
Philadelphia, PA   19101
(215) 585-6620

INSTITUTIONAL CONTACT:
Carolyn Francesconi
Director, Peirce Center for
Training and Development
Peirce Junior College
1420 Pine Street
Philadelphia, PA   19102
(215) 545-6400

PROGRAM DESCRIPTION/OBJECTIVES:
To provide pre-employment clerical training in basic skills
(English, math,typing, etc.)
for adult trainees from disadvantaged backgrounds.

PROGRAM INITIATED: 1981

LENGTH OF STUDY FOR   PARTICI-
PANT: 12 weeks

LENGTH OF CONTRACT: 12 weeks
with renewal option

LOCATION: Peirce Junior
College

PARTICIPANTS: 12 unemployed
adults each session

PROGRAM COSTS PROVIDED BY:
Other Source: Private Industry
Council, Philadelphia, PA

PRINTED MATERIALS AVAILABLE
FROM: Institution and Private
Industry Council, 101 South
Broad Street, Philadelphia,
PA   19101

224.   PULP AND PAPER FOUNDATION
(156 paper and supplier
companies)
with
UNIVERSITY OF MAINE AT
ORONO

PULP AND PAPER FOUNDATION

COMPANY CONTACT:
Stanley N. Marshall, Jr.
Executive Director
University of Maine Pulp and
Paper Foundation
217 Jenness Hall
Orono, ME   04469
(207) 581-7559

INSTITUTIONAL CONTACT:
Stanley N. Marshall, Jr.
Executive Director
University of Maine Pulp and
Paper Foundation
217 Jenness Hall
Orono, ME   04469
(207) 581-7559

PROGRAM DESCRIPTION/OBJECTIVES:
Attract students to paper-related technical careers; provide a capable well-motivated
faculty; promote and interest
in production-management; provide financial assistance to
students and to the university.

PROGRAM INITIATED: 1952

LENGTH OF STUDY FOR PARTICI-
PANT: 4 years

LENGTH OF CONTRACT: Renewable
annually (30-year-old
foundation)

LOCATION: Orono, ME

PARTICIPANTS: 125 students
and 156 companies

PROGRAM COSTS PROVIDED BY:
Institution: $4,500
Company: $233,000
Other Source: $168,000 (in-
vestment funds)

PRINTED MATERIALS AVAILABLE
FROM: Institution

225. PURITAN LIFE INSURANCE
      COMPANY
            with
      COMMUNITY COLLEGE OF
      RHODE ISLAND

BUSINESS WRITING

COMPANY CONTACT:
Diana VandenDorpel
Training Director
Personnel Department
Puritan Life Insurance Company
Allendale Park
Johnston, RI   02916
(401) 456-6979

INSTITUTIONAL CONTACT:
Robert Danilowicz
Coordinator
Missing Link Project
Off Campus Credit Programs
Community College of
Rhode Island
Flanagan Campus
Louisquisset Pike
Lincoln, RI   02865
(401) 333-7127

PROGRAM DESCRIPTION/OBJECTIVES:
Course includes correspondence,
general policies of all business correspondence, abstract
and precise writing and some
report writing. Objective to
improve skills of company
personnel.

PROGRAM INITIATED: 1981

LENGTH OF STUDY FOR PARTICI-
PANT: 1 semester

LENGTH OF CONTRACT: 1 semester

LOCATION: Puritan Life Insurance Company

PARTICIPANTS: 20 mid-management

PROGRAM COSTS PROVIDED BY:
Company: $1,525

PRINTED MATERIALS AVAILABLE
FROM: Institution and Company

226. RAYTHEON, INC.
            with
      UNIVERSITY OF MASSACHU-
      SETTS - AMHERST

VIDEOTAPE INSTRUCTION PROGRAM
FOR ENGINEERS

COMPANY CONTACT:
Raytheon, Inc.
            through
John Gillespie, Jr.
Bay State Skills Corporation
McCormack Office Building
One Ashburton Place
Room 2110
Boston, MA   02108
(617) 727-5431

INSTITUTIONAL CONTACT:
Harvey Stone
Director, Office of Extended
Engineering Education
113 Engineering Building East
University of Massachusetts
Amherst, MA   01003
(413) 545-0063

PROGRAM DESCRIPTION/OBJECTIVES:
A videotape instructional program in engineering areas and
computer technology providing
graduate level training in CAD/
CAM, management, microwave, computer systems and computer
communications.

PROGRAM INITIATED: 1982

LENGTH OF STUDY FOR PARTICI-
PANT: Self-paced

LENGTH OF CONTRACT: 6 months

LOCATION: Raytheon, Inc.

PARTICIPANTS: 200 engineers

PROGRAM COSTS PROVIDED BY:
Company: $100,000
Other Source: $97,969 (Bay
State Skills Corporation)

PRINTED MATERIALS AVAILABLE
FROM: Company

227. RHODE ISLAND HOSPITAL
with
UNIVERSITY OF RHODE ISLAND

EMPLOYEE EDUCATIONAL OPP
OPPORTUNITIES

COMPANY CONTACT:
Barbara Parker
Manager, Employee Education
Rhode Island Hospital
Eddy Street
Providence, RI   02908
(401) 277-8353

INSTITUTIONAL CONTACT:
Hollis B. Farnum
Coordinator of Academic
Programs
College of Continuing Education
University of Rhode Island
Promenade Street
Providence, RI   02908
(401) 277-3810

PROGRAM DESCRIPTION/OBJECTIVES:
To make university credit
courses available to hospital
staff on the hospital grounds.

PROGRAM INITIATED: 1982

LENGTH OF STUDY FOR PARTICI-
PANT: 1 sem ster per course

LENGTH OF CONTRACT: Academic
year; renegotiable each academic year

LOCATION: Rhode Island
Hospital

PARTICIPANTS: 12 hospital
staff members

PROGRAM COSTS PROVIDED BY:
Participant: 100%

PRINTED MATERIALS AVAILABLE
FROM: Company

228. CITY OF RICHMOND, VIRGINIA
with
VIRGINIA COMMONWEALTH
UNIVERSITY

RICHMOND REVITALIZATION
PROGRAM

COMPANY CONTACT:
Charles Peters
Director, Planning and
Community Development
City Hall
900 East Broad Street
Richmond, VA   23219
(804) 780-4346

INSTITUTIONAL CONTACT:
Morton B. Gulak
Director, Urban Studies and
Planning
Virginia Commonwealth
University
812 West Franklin Street
Richmond, VA   23284
(804) 257-1134

PROGRAM DESCRIPTION/OBJECTIVES:
To stimulate revitalization in
the city through assessment of
selected areas in the city and
the involvement of the private
sector and the involvement of
students at the university.

PROGRAM INITIATED: 1980

LENGTH OF STUDY FOR PARTICI-
PANT: 1 year

LENGTH OF CONTRACT: 3 years,
ongoing through other sources

LOCATION: Virginia Commonwealth University

PARTICIPANTS: 70 graduate
urban planning, communication
arts, interior design, business, architecture students
annually

PROGRAM COSTS PROVIDED BY:
Institution: 10%
Company: 45%
Participant: 45%

PRINTED MATERIALS AVAILABLE
FROM: Institution

229. RICHMOND PRIVATE INDUSTRY
COUNCIL AND RICHMOND
PUBLIC SCHOOLS
with
VIRGINIA COMMONWEALTH
UNIVERSITY

NEW HORIZONS

COMPANY CONTACT:
Jona McKee
New Horizons Coordinator
Richmond Private Industry
Council
Franklin Street
Richmond, VA   23220
(804) 643-0864

INSTITUTIONAL CONTACT:
Thomas A. Hephner
Associate Professor
Educational Studies
Virginia Commonwealth
University
1015 West Main Street
Richmond, VA   23284
(804) 257-1332

PROGRAM DESCRIPTION/OBJECTIVES:
A cooperative program among the
Richmond Private Industry Council, Richmond Public Schools
and Virginia Commonwealth University to train disadvantaged
youth for entry level jobs.

PROGRAM INITIATED: 1980

LENGTH OF STUDY FOR PARTICI-
PANT: Up to 2 years

LENGTH OF CONTRACT: Year-to-
year grant

LOCATION: Richmond, VA

PARTICIPANTS: 100 high school
students

PROGRAM COSTS PROVIDED BY:
Company: 100%

PRINTED MATERIALS AVAILABLE
FROM: Institution and Company

230. RISDON CORPORATION
with
UNIVERSITY OF HARTFORD

EFFECTIVE WRITING SKILLS FOR
FINANCIAL MANAGERS (3
(3 Programs)

COMPANY CONTACT:
Kenneth Baldyga
Manager, Corporate Personnel
Risdon Corporation
1 Risdon Street
Naugatuck, CT   06770
(203) 729-8231

INSTITUTIONAL CONTACT:
Gilbert J. Maffeo
Program Development Consultant
Division of Adult Educational
Services
University of Hartford
200 Bloomfield Avenue
West Hartford, CT   06117
(203) 243-4350

PROGRAM DESCRIPTION/OBJECTIVES:
To upgrade current skills of financial managers in the areas
of acquisition, monthly reports,
yearly reports and planning
documents.

PROGRAM INITIATED: 1981

LENGTH OF STUDY FOR PARTICI-
PANTS: 2-3 days

LENGTH OF CONTRACT: Ongoing

LOCATION: On-site or at a
neutral site

PARTICIPANTS: 10-20 line
management to vice presidents

PROGRAM COSTS PROVIDED BY:
Company: 100%

PRINTED MATERIALS AVAILABLE
FROM: Institution and Company

231. A.H. ROBINS COMPANY
            with
       VIRGINIA COMMONWEALTH
       UNIVERSITY

EMPLOYEE IMPROVEMENT AND EDUCA-
TION AT A.H. ROBINS COMPANY

COMPANY CONTACT:
Bette H. Kellehay
Manager, Personnel Training
and Library Service
A.H. Robins Company
1407 Cummings Drive
Richmond, VA   23220
(804) 257-2858

INSTITUTIONAL CONTACT:
John B. Callander
Coordinator for Off-Campus
Credit
Continuing Education and
Public Service
Virginia Commonwealth University
901 West Franklin Street
Richmond, VA   23284
(804) 257-6032

PROGRAM DESCRIPTION/OBJECTIVES:
To provide training for professional research personnel in
pharmacology, computer science
and general research.

PROGRAM INITIATED: 1978

LENGTH OF STUDY FOR PARTICI-
PANT: 1 semester continuing

LENGTH OF CONTRACT: Semester
with renewal

LOCATION: A.H. Robins Company

PARTICIPANTS: Approximately
50 chemical research personnel
annually

PROGRAM COSTS PROVIDED BY:
Institution: 10%
Company: 90%

PRINTED MATERIALS AVAILABLE
FROM: Not available

232. CITY OF SAN DIEGO
            with
       MIRAMAR COLLEGE

REGIONAL BASIC FIRE ACADEMY

COMPANY CONTACT:
Donald W. Farney
Director, Personnel and
Training
San Diego Fire Department
1222 First Avenue
San Diego, CA   92101
(714) 236-6475

INSTITUTIONAL CONTACT:
Thoyd Latham
Dean of Instruction
Fire Science
Miramar College
10440 Black Mountain Road
San Diego, CA   92126
(714) 230-6512

PROGRAM DESCRIPTION/OBJECTIVES:
To provide required basic fire
fighting training to persons
seeking employment with the San
Diego Fire Department prior to
being hired.

PROGRAM INITIATED: 1981

LENGTH OF STUDY FOR PARTICI-
PANT: 10 weeks

LENGTH OF CONTRACT: 12 months
with renewal option

LOCATION: Miramar College

PARTICIPANTS: 144 entry
level firefighter I annually

PROGRAM COSTS PROVIDED BY:
Institution: $80,000 or 66%
Company: $40,000 or 33%

PRINTED MATERIALS AVAILABLE
FROM: Institution

233. ST. JOHN MEDICAL CENTER*
with
UNIVERSITY OF
STEUBENVILLE

FACULTY INTERNSHIP

COMPANY CONTACT:
Catherine Zavatsky
Director of Quality
Assurance/Education
St. John Medical Center
St. John Heights
Steubenville, OH   43952
(614) 264-8000

INSTITUTIONAL CONTACT:
Robert J. Convery
Dean of the Faculty
University of Steubenville
Franciscan Way
Steubenville, OH   43952
(614) 283-3771

PROGRAM DESCRIPTION/OBJECTIVES:
To provide non-academic experiences for faculty to broaden
their perspectives for teaching
and advising students.

PROGRAM INITIATED: 1979

LENGTH OF STUDY FOR PARTICI-
PANT: Equivalent to 1 month

LENGTH OF CONTRACT: Variable

LOCATION: Variable

PARTICIPANTS: 6 annually

PROGRAM COSTS PROVIDED BY:
Other Source: $22,000 (Title
III grant)

PRINTED MATERIALS AVAILABLE
FROM: Not reported

----

*Representative entry--complete
list available from institution.

234. ST. JOSEPH HOSPITAL
with
NATIONAL COLLEGE OF
EDUCATION

BACHELOR OF ARTS DEGREE PRO-
GRAM IN APPLIED BEHAVIORAL
SCIENCES

COMPANY CONTACT:
Tom Hounihan
Director
Training and Development
St. Joseph Hospital
2900 North Lakeshore Drive
Chicago, IL   60657
(312) 985-3190

INSTITUTIONAL CONTACT:
Edward Storke
Assistant Dean
Field Experience Program
National College of Education
2 S 361 Glen Park Road
Lombard, IL   60148
(312) 629-5320

PROGRAM DESCRIPTION/OBJECTIVES:
This program is a series of
courses and work-related projects leading to the completion
of a baccalaureate degree or a
masters degree. The emphasis
is on interpersonal and supervisory skills related to job
performance.

PROGRAM INITIATED: 1981

LENGTH OF STUDY FOR PARTICI-
PANT: 1 year

LENGTH OF CONTRACT: 1 year
(oral agreement)

LOCATION: St. Joseph Hospital

PARTICIPANTS: 26 supervisors
and head nurses

PROGRAM COSTS PROVIDED BY:
Institution: 15%
Company: 75%
Participant: 10% (Shared by
company and participant based
on the length of employment at
company. Some students also receive government assistance.)

PRINTED MATERIALS AVAILABLE
FROM: Institution

235. ST. LAWRENCE COUNTY ECO-
NOMIC DEVELOPMENT OFFICE
with
SUNY AGRICULTURAL AND
TECHNICAL COLLEGE AT
CANTON

MACHINE TRADES PROGRAM

COMPANY CONTACT:
David Williams
Director of Training
St. Lawrence County Economic
Development Office
Courthouse Building
Canton, NY   13617
(315) 379-2291

INSTITUTIONAL CONTACT:
Robert Mattice
Project Director
Office of Sponsored Research
SUNY Agricultural and Technical
College at Canton
Canton, NY   13617
(315) 386-7210

PROGRAM DESCRIPTION/OBJECTIVES:
To prepare individuals for
careers as machine operators in
local and regional industry.

PROGRAM INITIATED: 1978

LENGTH OF STUDY FOR PARTICI-
PANT: 450 hours

LENGTH OF CONTRACT: 6 months
with renewal option

LOCATION: SUNY Agricultural
and Technical College at
Canton

PARTICIPANTS: Approximately
15-18 operators annually

PROGRAM COSTS PROVIDED BY:
Company: Approximately $50,000

PRINTED MATERIALS AVAILABLE
FROM: Institution

236. ST. MICHAEL'S MEDICAL
CENTER
with
RUTGERS, THE STATE UNI-
VERSITY OF NEW JERSEY

PRIMARY AFFILIATION

COMPANY CONTACT:
Norah McCarthy
Vice President
Nursing Services
St. Michael's Medical Center
306 High Street
Newark, NJ   07102
(201) 877-5359

INSTITUTIONAL CONTACT:
Lucille Joel
Associate Dean for Clinical
Affairs
College of Nursing
Rutgers, The State University
of New Jersey
University Avenue
Newark, NJ   07102
(201) 648-5298

PROGRAM DESCRIPTION/OBJECTIVES:
Manpower sharing; student
placement.

PROGRAM INITIATED: 1982

LENGTH OF STUDY FOR PARTICI-
PANT: Academic year

LENGTH OF CONTRACT: 10 months

LOCATION: St. Michael's
Medical Center and Rutgers

PARTICIPANTS: 2

PROGRAM COSTS PROVIDED BY:
Shared equally by exchange of
time between company and
institution

PRINTED MATERIALS AVAILABLE
FROM: Institution

237. SCHENECTADY EMPLOYMENT AND
TRAINING ADMINISTRATION
with
SCHENECTADY COUNTY COM-
MUNITY COLLEGE

CAREER DEVELOPMENT NETWORK

COMPANY CONTACT:
Anthony Insogna
Assistant to County Manager
for SETA
Schenectady Employment and
Training Administration
240 Broadway
Schenectady, NY   12306
(518) 382-3567

INSTITUTIONAL CONTACT:
Sanford E. Lake
Director, Career Life Skills
Center
Schenectady County Community
College
78 Washington Avenue
Schenectady, NY   12305
(518) 346-6211, X205

PROGRAM DESCRIPTION/OBJECTIVES:
To measurably improve "employa-
bility" of participants through
counseling and training in self-
assessment skills, interviewing
techniques, resume writing, and
general socio-behavioral skills
areas as well as in occupation-
al-specific areas of instruction.

PROGRAM INITIATED: 1980

LENGTH OF STUDY FOR PARTICI-
PANT: Varies (6-26 weeks)

LENGTH OF CONTRACT: Varies

LOCATION: Schenectady County
Community College

PARTICIPANTS: Maximum 15 un-
skilled generalists, clerical,
retailing, nurses' aides, culi-
nary arts individuals per program group

PROGRAM COSTS PROVIDED BY:
Company: CETA 70%; Schenec-
tady ETA 20%
Other Source: Pell Grants 5%,
Schenectady 5%

PRINTED MATERIALS AVAILABLE
FROM: Not reported

238. SCHNELLER AND ASSOCIATES
with
KENT STATE UNIVERSITY

EFFECTIVE BUSINESS WRITING

COMPANY CONTACT:
Donald Strange
Schneller and Associates
P.O. Box 670
Kent, OH   44240
(216) 673-1400

INSTITUTIONAL CONTACT:
Karen Rylander
Director, Continuing Education
Kent State University
327 Rockwell Hall
Kent, OH   44242
(216) 672-3100

PROGRAM DESCRIPTION/OBJECTIVES:
Provides a practical review of
the fundamentals of written communication for professionals in
business and industry. It emphasizes the application of successful strategies for writing
persuasive and efficient prose
in the various business forms.

PROGRAM INITIATED: 1981

LENGTH OF STUDY FOR PARTICI-
PANT: 10 hours + 1 hour individual follow-up

LENGTH OF CONTRACT: 10 hours
+ 1 hour individual follow-up

LOCATION: Schneller and
Associates

PARTICIPANTS: 12 sales
representatives

PROGRAM COSTS PROVIDED BY:
Company: 100%

PRINTED MATERIALS AVAILABLE
FROM: Institution

239. SEATT CORP
        with
     COLLEGE OF DUPAGE

SEATT TRAINING

COMPANY CONTACT:
James Reilly
Vice President of
Manufacturing
Seatt Corporation
Downers Grove, IL   60515
(312) 963-1550

INSTITUTIONAL CONTACT:
Joan Bevelacqua
Director
Business and Professional
Institute
Open College
College of DuPage
Glen Ellyn, IL   60137
(312) 858-6870

PROGRAM DESCRIPTION/OBJECTIVES:
To provide training for 61 new
employees. (Jobs created by an
expansion.) The training is on
the job and classroom. It is
designed to prepare the employee to be productive on the job.

PROGRAM INITIATED: 1979

LENGTH OF STUDY FOR PARTICI-
PANT: 2-3 months

LENGTH OF CONTRACT: 1 year

LOCATION: In plant

PARTICIPANTS: 61 entry level
electronic manufacturing personnel, office staff and data
processing staff

PROGRAM COSTS PROVIDED BY:
Other Source: $150,000 (Illi-
nois Board of Higher Education
High Impact Training Grant)

PRINTED MATERIALS AVAILABLE
FROM: Institution

240. SMITHERS-OASIS
        with
     KENT STATE UNIVERSITY

BASIC SUPERVISORY TRAINING

COMPANY CONTACT:
David Otto
Smithers-Oasis
P.O. Box 118
Kent, OH   44240
(216) 673-5831

INSTITUTIONAL CONTACT:
Karen Rylander
Director, Continuing Education
Kent State University
327 Rockwell Hall
Kent, OH   44242
(216) 672-3100

PROGRAM DESCRIPTION/OBJECTIVES:
Includes an overview of communication skills, motivation, problem-solving, time-management,
and team building.

PROGRAM INITIATED: 1980

LENGTH OF STUDY FOR PARTICI-
PANT: 28 hours

LENGTH OF CONTRACT: 28 hours

LOCATION: Smithers-Oasis

PARTICIPANTS: 20 first-line
supervisors

PROGRAM COSTS PROVIDED BY:
Company: 100%

PRINTED MATERIALS AVAILABLE
FROM: Institution

241. SOCIAL SECURITY
      ADMINISTRATION*
         with
      BOWLING GREEN STATE
      UNIVERSITY

COOPERATIVE EDUCATION

COMPANY CONTACT:
Lloyd Borer
Manager
Social Security Administration
Bowling Green, OH   43403
(419) 352-8481

INSTITUTIONAL CONTACT:
Bruce W. Smith
Acting Director
Cooperative Education Program
Bowling Green State University
Bowling Green, OH   43403
(419) 372-2451

PROGRAM DESCRIPTION/OBJECTIVES:
To place college students in
cooperative education assign-
ments in the public and private sectors.

PROGRAM INITIATED: 1978

LENGTH OF STUDY FOR PARTICI-
PANT: Multiple semesters

LENGTH OF CONTRACT: Ongoing

LOCATION: Bowling Green, OH

PARTICIPANTS: 740 college
students annually

PROGRAM COSTS PROVIDED BY:
Institution: 63%
Company: Student salaries
Other Source: 37% (federal
grant)

PRINTED MATERIALS AVAILABLE
FROM: Institution

---

*Representative entry--complete
list available from institution.

242. SOCIETY OF DIE CAST
      ENGINEERS
         with
      TRITON COLLEGE

TRITON COLLEGE/SOCIETY OF DIE
CAST ENGINEERS PARTNERSHIP

COMPANY CONTACT:
James Cannon
Executive Director
Society of Die Cast Engineers
2000 Fifth Avenue
River Grove, IL   60171
(312) 452-0700

INSTITUTIONAL CONTACT:
David Kozlowski
Associate Vice President
Triton College
2000 Fifth Avenue
River Grove, IL   60171
(312) 456-0300, X538

PROGRAM DESCRIPTION/OBJECTIVES:
Triton built and leased back to
the SDCE a facility to their
specifications. Triton uses
facility to conduct die casting
classes and seminars at no cost.
SDCE uses college staff and
support services.

PROGRAM INITIATED: 1982

LENGTH OF STUDY FOR PARTICI-
PANT: 2 years, seminars are 1
to 5 days

LENGTH OF CONTRACT: 10 years
with reopener for second 10
years

LOCATION: Triton College

PARTICIPANTS: Not available

PROGRAM COSTS PROVIDED BY:
Institution: Building loan
Company: $43,200 per year
lease

PRINTED MATERIALS AVAILABLE
FROM: Institution

243. STANDARD OIL COMPANY*
         with
      INTERNATIONAL FOUNDATION
      OF EMPLOYEE BENEFIT PLANS

I.F. INTERNS

COMPANY CONTACT:
C.E. Webb
Manager, Benefits Administra-
tion and Payroll Accounting
Standard Oil Company
200 East Randolph Street
P.O. Box 5738
Chicago, IL   60680
(312) 856-6355

INSTITUTIONAL CONTACT:
Robert D. Cooper
Director, Research
International Foundation of
Employee Benefit Plans
18700 West Bluemound Road
Brookfield, WI   53005
(414) 786-6700

PROGRAM DESCRIPTION/OBJECTIVES:
Pilot project in Chicago with
expansion to Milwaukee, 1983
and New York City, 1984. Professional development program
that recruits high quality students from several universities
and prepares them for careers
in benefits administration and
counseling through education
and on-the-job training.

PROGRAM INITIATED: 1981

LENGTH OF STUDY FOR PARTICI-
PANT: 2 years (part-time) including 2 full-time summer
experiences

LENGTH OF CONTRACT: Not
available

LOCATION: Principally Chicago

PARTICIPANTS: 30+ college
juniors and seniors

PROGRAM COSTS PROVIDED BY:
Institution: $75,000
Company: $4,500 per year,
per student

PRINTED MATERIALS AVAILABLE
FROM: Institution

*Representative entry--complete
list available from institution.

244. THE STANLEY WORKS
         with
      UNIVERSITY OF HARTFORD

ASSOCIATE DEGREE IN ARTS AND
SCIENCES ON-SITE

COMPANY CONTACT:
Thomas Jones
The Stanley Works
480 Myrtle Steeet
New Britain, CT   06050
(203) 223-9968

INSTITUTIONAL CONTACT:
William T. George
Program Development Consultant
Division of Adult Educational
Services
University of Hartford
200 Bloomfield Avenue
West Hartford CT   06117
(203) 243-4507/4381

PROGRAM DESCRIPTION/OBJECTIVES:
Associate Degree in Arts and
Sciences on-site.

PROGRAM INITIATED: 1979

LENGTH OF STUDY FOR PARTICI-
PANT: 60 semester hours

LENGTH OF CONTRACT: Ongoing

LOCATION: On-site

PARTICIPANTS: 100 qualified
employees

PROGRAM COSTS PROVIDED BY:
Company: 75%
Participant: 25%

PRINTED MATERIALS AVAILABLE
FROM: Institution

125

245. STOCKHAM VALVES AND
       FITTING*
            with
       BIRMINGHAM-SOUTHERN
       COLLEGE

CONTRACT LEARNING CENTER

COMPANY CONTACT:
Pat Swofford
Personnel Department
Stockham Valves and Fitting
P.O. Box 10325
Birmingham, AL   35202
(205) 592-6361

INSTITUTIONAL CONTACT:
Nancy Poynor
Coordinator Experiential
Learning
Office of the President
Birmingham Southern College
Birmingham, AL   35254
(205) 328-5250, X394

PROGRAM DESCRIPTION/OBJECTIVES:
Designed to administer internships for Birmingham-Southern
College students in local business and industry.

PROGRAM INITIATED: 1979

LENGTH OF STUDY FOR PARTICI-
PANT: May be taken on a semes-
ter-by-semester basis or these
may be taken in conjunction
with fulfilling a contract
during interim, a 4-week term
between semesters.

LENGTH OF CONTRACT: Ongoing

LOCATION: Business site

PARTICIPANTS: 192 for Spring
1982

PROGRAM COSTS PROVIDED BY:
Participant: Included in
admissions fee

PRINTED MATERIALS AVAILABLE
FROM: Institution

---

*Representative entry--complete
list available from institution.

246. STOUFFER FOODS
            with
       KENT STATE UNIVERSITY

PROFIT MANAGEMENT

COMPANY CONTACT:
John Shoupe
Stouffer Foods
29800 Bainbridge Road
Solon, OH   44139
(216) 248-3600

INSTITUTIONAL CONTACT:
Karen Rylander
Director, Continuing Education
Kent State University
327 Rockwell Hall
Kent, OH   44242
(216) 672-3100

PROGRAM DESCRIPTION/OBJECTIVES:
Designed to introduce first and
second level supervisors to concepts of performance objectives,
profit planning and control,
and the employees' role in
achieving profit objectives.
Program to be implemented by
Stouffer trainers.

PROGRAM INITIATED: 1982

LENGTH OF STUDY FOR PARTICI-
PANT: Program content and
material development

LENGTH OF CONTRACT: Not
reported

LOCATION: Stouffer Foods

PARTICIPANTS: Unknown number
of supervisors

PROGRAM COSTS PROVIDED BY:
Company: 100%

PRINTED MATERIALS AVAILABLE
FROM: Institution

247. SUMTER POLICE DEPARTMENT
      AND NCR CORPORATION
              with
      SUMTER AREA TECHNICAL
      COLLEGE

COMPUTERIZING CRIME INFORMATION:
IS THERE AN ANALYST IN THE HOUSE?

COMPANY CONTACT:
L.W. Griffin
Chief of Police
Sumter Police Department
107 East Hampton
Sumter, SC   29150
(803) 773-1561

INSTITUTIONAL CONTACT:
Gus Becker
Dean, Continuing Education
Sumter Area Technical College
506 North Guignard Drive
Sumter, SC   29150
(803) 773-9371

PROGRAM DESCRIPTION/OBJECTIVES:
To develop a seminar for law enforcement administrators to
achieve hands-on familiarity
with a cost-effective computerized crime reporting/information
system. Provides NCR sales representatives with real-life
product evaluation.

PROGRAM INITIATED: 1981

LENGTH OF STUDY FOR PARTICI-
PANT: 1-day seminar

LENGTH OF CONTRACT: Informal
agreement

LOCATION: Sumter Area Community
College

PARTICIPANTS: 35 financial
managers, law enforcement and
NCR personnel

PROGRAM COSTS PROVIDED BY:
Institution: 20%
Company: 20%
Participant: 60%

PRINTED MATERIALS AVAILABLE
FROM: Institution

248. SUNBURST SYSTEMS, INC.*
              with
      SOUTHEASTERN MASSACHU-
      SETTS UNIVERSITY

ENERGY MARKETING AND SALES

COMPANY CONTACT:
Rico Correia
President
Sunburst Systems, Inc.
751 Kempton Street
New Bedford, MA   02740

INSTITUTIONAL CONTACT:
Southeastern Massachusetts
University (North Dartmouth)
           through
John Gillespie, Jr.
Bay State Skills Corporation
McCormick Office Building
One Ashburton Place
Room 2110
Boston, MA   02108
(617) 727-5431

PROGRAM DESCRIPTION/OBJECTIVES:
To train individuals in energy
sales and marketing and to provide an opportunity to observe
energy retrofitting and instal-
lations.

PROGRAM INITIATED: 1982

LENGTH OF STUDY FOR PARTICI-
PANT: 25 weeks (35 hours per
week)

LENGTH OF CONTRACT: 6 months

LOCATION: Southeastern Massachusetts University and on-the-
job training

PARTICIPANTS: 30 unemployed
individuals

PROGRAM COSTS PROVIDED BY:
Institution: $15,100
Company: $51,148
Other Source: $42,739 (Bay
State Skills Corporation grant)

PRINTED MATERIALS AVAILABLE
FROM: Institution

_____

*Representative entry--complete
list available from institution.

249. THE TAUBMAN COMPANY*
            with
      HENRY FORD COMMUNITY
      COLLEGE

SUNRISE SEMINARS

COMPANY CONTACT:
Lin Berry
Director of Special Promotions
The Taubman Company
3270 West Big Beaver Road
Suite 300
P.O. Box 3270
Troy, MI   48099
(313) 649-5000

INSTITUTIONAL CONTACT:
Robert J. Kopecky
Director, Center for New
Directions
Henry Ford Community College
Dearborn, MI   48128
(313) 271-2750, X330

PROGRAM DESCRIPTION/OBJECTIVES:
On-site continuing education
for retailers in shopping malls
to develop positive attitudes,
insightful solutions of business problems, effective tenant-
management relationships, and
long range commitments toward
increasing shopping center profits and reducing costs.

PROGRAM INITIATED: 1980

LENGTH OF STUDY FOR PARTICI-
PANT: 4 weeks

LENGTH OF CONTRACT: 4 weeks

LOCATION: Shopping center
restaurant

PARTICIPANTS: 30 managers and
assistant managers in mall
stores per seminar

PROGRAM COSTS PROVIDED BY:
Company: $1,200 per series

PRINTED MATERIALS AVAILABLE
FROM: Institution

_____

*Representative entry--complete
list available from institution.

250. TERRE HAUTE AREA CHAMBER
      OF COMMERCE
            with
      INDIANA STATE UNIVERSITY

COMMUNITY-WIDE WORKFORCE
DEVELOPMENT PROJECT

COMPANY CONTACT:
Ross Hedges
President
Terre Haute Area Chamber of
Commerce
P.O. Box 689
Terre Haute, IN   47808
(812) 232-2391

INSTITUTIONAL CONTACT:
E.R. Pettebone
Director, Cooperative
Professional Practice
Indiana State University
Terre Haute, IN   47809
(812) 232-6311, X2582

PROGRAM DESCRIPTION/OBJECTIVES:
Project involves creation of a
mechanism capable of meeting
the long term quantitative and
qualitative workforce needs of
the employing community through
mutual cooperative effort.

PROGRAM INITIATED: Project in
formative stage

LENGTH OF STUDY FOR PARTICI-
PANT: Variable

LENGTH OF CONTRACT: Not
available

LOCATION: Vigo County, IN

PARTICIPANTS: Not available

PROGRAM COSTS PROVIDED BY:
Not yet determined

PRINTED MATERIALS AVAILABLE
FROM: Not yet available

251. TEXAS GULF SULPHUR
         with
     WHARTON COUNTY JUNIOR
     COLLEGE

INDUSTRIAL TRAINING FIELD
DEPARTMENT TEXAS GULF SULPHUR

COMPANY CONTACT:
Mr. Edgar Roades
Training Supervisor
Texas Gulf Sulphur
New Gulf, TX   77462
(713) 657-4481, X240

INSTITUTIONAL CONTACT:
Dr. John E. Brooks
Dean, Continuing Education
Wharton County Junior College
911 Boling Highway
Wharton, TX   77488
(713) 532-4560, X237

PROGRAM DESCRIPTION/OBJECTIVES:
To develop a training module
for personnel to be employed in
the pipeline department. The
module uses visual, oral and
written techniques of instruction. It is individualized and
programmed for individual or
group presentation. It allows
for open-entry and exit.

PROGRAM INITIATED: 1981

LENGT OF STUDY FOR PARTICI-
PANT: Not available

LENGTH OF CONTRACT: Open-
ended

LOCATION: New Gulf, TX

PARTICIPANTS: 70-100 field
maintenance and pipelining
of sulphur personnel

PROGRAM COSTS PROVIDED BY:
Institution: Undetermined at
this time
Company: Open

PRINTED MATERIALS AVAILABLE
FROM: Institution

252. TEXAS INSTRUMENTS, INC.
         with
     NORTH LAKE COLLEGE OF
     THE DALLAS COUNTY COMMU-
     NITY COLLEGE DISTRICT

PRECISION OPTICS TECHNOLOGY

COMPANY CONTACT:
John H. Pulliam
Manager
Optics Manufacturing
and Materials
Texas Instruments, Inc.
P.O. Box 226015
Dallas, TX   75266
(214) 995-2011

INSTITUTIONAL CONTACT:
Clif Weaver
Associate Dean
Technology/Occupation Programs
North Lake College
5001 MacArthur Boulevard
Irving, TX   75062
(214) 659-5233

PROGRAM DESCRIPTION/OBJECTIVES:
Graduate of this program will
be able to perform the basic,
entry-level skills of precision
optics technicans including:
the manufacturing of precision
optics lenses, and assisting in
engineering tasks related to
lens manufacture.

PROGRAM INITIATED: 1981

LENGTH OF STUDY FOR PARTICI-
PANT: 4 semesters

LENGTH OF CONTRACT: 12 months
with renewal option

LOCATION: North Lake College

PARTICIPANTS: 20 to 25 entry-
level employees annually

PROGRAM COSTS PROVIDED BY:
Institution: 40%
Company: 60%

PRINTED MATERIALS AVAILABLE
FROM: Institution

253. THE TIMKEN COMPANY
            with
      KENT STATE UNIVERSITY

EFFECTIVE BUSINESS WRITING

COMPANY CONTACT:
Gerry Woltman
The Timken Company
1835 Duebar Avenue, SW
Canton, OH   44706
(216) 438-3487

INSTITUTIONAL CONTACT:
Karen Rylander
Director, Continuing Education
Kent State University
327 Rockwell Hall
Kent, OH   44242
(216) 672-3100

PROGRAM DESCRIPTION/OBJECTIVES:
The Effective Business Writing
Seminar provides a practical review of the fundamentals of
written communication for professionals in business and industry. It emphasizes the application of successful strategies for writing persuasive and
efficient prose in the various
business forms.

PROGRAM INITIATED: 1980

LENGTH OF STUDY FOR PARTICI-
PANT: 10 hours + 1 hour individual follow-up

LENGTH OF CONTRACT: 10 hours
+ 1 hour individual follow-up

LOCATION: The Timken Company

PARTICIPANTS: 81 management
employees

PROGRAM COSTS PROVIDED BY:
Company: 100%

PRINTED MATERIALS AVAILABLE
FROM: Institution

254. TIMKEN MERCY
            with
      THE UNIVERSITY OF AKRON

MATCHING INDIVIDUAL AND
ORGANIZATIONAL NEEDS

COMPANY CONTACT:
Shirley Hayes, R.N.
Faculty Development Training
Timken Mercy
1320 Timken Mercy Drive, NW
Canton, OH   44708
(216) 489-1142 or 489-1140

INSTITUTIONAL CONTACT:
Kathryn Vegso
Associate Dean
Continuing Education and
Public Services
Adult Resource Center
The University of Akron
Akron, OH   44325
(216) 375-7448

PROGRAM DESCRIPTION/OBJECTIVES:
To provide career/life planning
to training personnel.

PROGRAM INITIATED: 1982

LENGTH OF STUDY FOR PARTICI-
PANT: 1/2 day sessions

LENGTH OF CONTRACT: 3 sessions
with 3 different staffs

LOCATION: Business site

PARTICIPANTS: 150 training
personnel and support staff

PROGRAM COSTS PROVIDED BY:
Company: 100%

PRINTED MATERIALS AVAILABLE
FROM: Institution

255. TOSCO CORPORATION*
            with
      CALIFORNIA STATE COLLEGE -
      BAKERSFIELD

MANAGEMENT INTERNSHIP PROGRAM

COMPANY CONTACT:
Jan Leavitt
Personnel Administrator
Tosco Corporation
5121 Stockdale Highway
Bakersfield, CA   93309
(805) 397-2220

INSTITUTIONAL CONTACT:
Marcia Homme
Coordinator, Center for
Business and Economic Research
California State College -
Bakersfield
9001 Stockdale Highway
Bakersfield, CA   93309
(805) 833-2151

PROGRAM DESCRIPTION/OBJECTIVES:
Provide opportunity for students to gain relevant, career-
related experience. Interns
gain experience in the working
world and have an exceptional
opportunity to personally participate in career and management-
related positions.

PROGRAM INITIATED: 1979

LENGTH OF STUDY FOR PARTICI-
PANT: 3 quarters

LENGTH OF CONTRACT: 12 months
with grant renewal option

LOCATION: California State
College - Bakersfield

PARTICIPANTS: 20 juniors,
seniors and graduates

PROGRAM COSTS PROVIDED BY:
Other Source: Federal grant
monies

PRINTED MATERIALS AVAILABLE
FROM: Institution

———————

*Representative entry--complete
list available from institution.

256. TRADEWELL*
            with
      GREEN RIVER COMMUNITY
      COLLEGE

DYNAMIC SUPERVISION
MANAGEMENT

COMPANY CONTACT:
Dan McIalwain
Training Director
Tradewell
7890 South 188th
Kent, WA   98031
(206) 251-8300

INSTITUTIONAL CONTACT:
Margaret Kaus
Associate Dean
Continuing Education
Green River Community College
12401 SE 320th Street
Auburn, WA   98002
(206) 833-9111, X231

PROGRAM DESCRIPTION/OBJECTIVES:
Present custom tailored supervisory communications education
for employees. Addresses specific needs of personnel in food
processing/grocery industry.

PROGRAM INITIATED: 1979

LENGTH OF STUDY FOR PARTICI-
PANT: 10 weeks

LENGTH OF CONTRACT: 10 weeks

LOCATION: Tradewell Training
Center

PARTICIPANTS: 24 office
personnel

PROGRAM COSTS PROVIDED BY:
Company: $1,376 (including
texts)

PRINTED MATERIALS AVAILABLE
FROM: Institution book store

———————

*Representative entry--complete
list available from institution.

131

257.   THE TREATY COMPANY
            with
       EDISON STATE COMMUNITY
       COLLEGE

SUPERVISION: THE ART OF
MANAGEMENT

COMPANY CONTACT:
Jack Oliver
Vice President
Personnel Department
The Treaty Company
Gray Avenue
Greenville, OH   45331
(513) 548-2181

INSTITUTIONAL CONTACT:
Gary W. Wilson
Assistant Dean for
Continuing Education
Edison State Community College
1973 Edison Drive
Piqua, OH   45356
(513) 778-8600

PROGRAM DESCRIPTION/OBJECTIVES:
Comprehensive training experience for supervisory staff
which will serve as a means of
improving the varied levels of
supervisory experience.

PROGRAM INITIATED: 1981

LENGTH OF STUDY FOR PARTICI-
PANT: 40 hours

LENGTH OF CONTRACT: 5 weeks

LOCATION: Edison State
Community College

PARTICIPANTS: 20 first-line
supervisors

PROGRAM COSTS PROVIDED BY:
Institution: $2,453.64
Company: $3,036.50
Other Source: $210.00

PRINTED MATERIALS AVAILABLE
FROM: Institution

258.   TULSA PORT OF CATOOSA
            with
       CLAREMORE COLLEGE

CLAREMORE COLLEGE TRAINING
CENTER AT THE TULSA PORT OF
CATOOSA

COMPANY CONTACT:
Bill Thomas
Director of Administration
Port Authority
Tulsa Port of Catoosa
5350 Cimarron Road
Catoosa, OK   74015
(918) 266-2291

INSTITUTIONAL CONTACT:
Kathy Callaham
Director of Community Services
Claremore College
College Hill
Claremore, OK   74017
(918) 341-7510

PROGRAM DESCRIPTION/OBJECTIVES:
To provide college courses,
credit and non-credit at a convenient location and time for
port personnel.

PROGRAM INITIATED: 1982

LENGTH OF STUDY FOR PARTICI-
PANT: Not available

LENGTH OF CONTRACT: Ongoing

LOCATION: Tulsa Port of
Catoosa

PARTICIPANTS: Not reported

PROGRAM COSTS PROVIDED BY:
Company: 100%

PRINTED MATERIALS AVAILABLE
FROM: Institution

259. SEVERAL COMPANIES*
with
TURABO UNIVERSITY

GRADUATE PROGRAM IN BUSINESS
ADMINISTRATION

COMPANY CONTACT:
Specific company not identified

INSTITUTIONAL CONTACT:
Josue Guzman
Program Director
Graduate Program in Business
Administration
Turabo University
P.O. Box 1091
Caguas, Puerto Rico   00625
(809) 744-8792

PROGRAM DESCRIPTION/OBJECTIVES:
Graduate Program in Business
Administration to offer high
level education of quality in
Puerto Rico.

PROGRAM INITIATED: 1981

LENGTH OF STUDY FOR PARTICI-
PANT: 3 years (part-time)

LENGTH OF CONTRACT: 3 years

LOCATION: Turabo University

PARTICIPANTS: 75 junior executives, technicians, engineers,
etc.

PROGRAM COSTS PROVIDED BY:
Company: 60%
Participant: 40%

PRINTED MATERIALS AVAILABLE
FROM: Institution

---

*Representative entry--complete
list available from institution.

260. UC INDUSTRIES
with
KENT STATE UNIVERSITY

FIRST LINE SUPERVISION

COMPANY CONTACT:
Michael Weisenberg
UC Industries
P.O. Box 37
Tallmadge, OH   44278
(216) 633-5848

INSTITUTIONAL CONTACT:
Karen Rylander
Director, Continuing Education
Kent State University
327 Rockwell Hall
Kent, OH   44242
(216) 672-3100

PROGRAM DESCRIPTION/OBJECTIVES:
This "how to" approach to supervisory training covers motiva-
tions, communication, decision
making, problem solving, time
management, delegation and
people skills.

PROGRAM INITIATED: 1981

LENGTH OF STUDY FOR PARTICI-
PANT: 14 hours

LENGTH OF CONTRACT: 14 hours

LOCATION: UC Industries

PARTICIPANTS: 10 first-line
supervisors

PROGRAM COSTS PROVIDED BY:
Company: 100%

PRINTED MATERIALS AVAILABLE
FROM: Institution

261. UNITED AIR LINES
         with
      COLLEGE OF SAN MATEO

MANAGEMENT CERTIFICATE PROGRAM

COMPANY CONTACT:
Karen Kobrosky
Training Officer
United Air Lines
San Francisco International
Airport
San Francisco, CA   94101
(415) 876-5517

INSTITUTIONAL CONTACT:
Michael Kimball
Director of Instructional
Services
College of San Mateo
1700 West Hillsdale Blvd.
San Mateo, CA   94402
(415) 574-6544

PROGRAM DESCRIPTION/OBJECTIVES:
12-course program leading to a
certificate in the area of management training.

PROGRAM INITIATED: 1981

LENGTH OF STUDY FOR PARTICI-
PANT: 1-6 semesters

LENGTH OF CONTRACT: Informal,
ongoing agreement

LOCATION: United Air Lines

PARTICIPANTS: Approximately
80 primarily United Airlines
employees

PROGRAM COSTS PROVIDED BY:
Institution: 50%
Company: 50%

PRINTED MATERIALS AVAILABLE
FROM: Company

262. UNITED AUTO WORKERS
         with
      CENTRAL MICHIGAN
      UNIVERSITY

UAW STAFF COUNCIL PROGRAM

COMPANY CONTACT:
Bruce Kingery
United Auto Workers
International Headquarters
8000 East Jefferson Avenue
Detroit, MI   48214
(313) 886-7437

INSTITUTIONAL CONTACT:
Lawrence R. Murphy
Director
Institute for Personal and
Career Development
Central Michigan University
Mt. Pleasant, MI   48859
(517) 774-3865

PROGRAM DESCRIPTION/OBJECTIVES:
Provide undergraduate training
in Labor Studies leading to a
BS degree for labor organization leaders.

PROGRAM INITIATED: Not
reported

LENGTH OF STUDY FOR PARTICI-
PANT: 1-3 years

LENGTH OF CONTRACT: Ongoing

LOCATION: Dave Miller Retirement Center

PARTICIPANTS: 20-50 Staff
Council members and union
leaders

PROGRAM COSTS PROVIDED BY:
Company: 85%
Participant: 15%

PRINTED MATERIALS AVAILABLE
FROM: Institution

263. UNITED HOSPITALS MEDICAL
CENTER
with
RUTGERS, THE STATE UNI-
VERSITY OF NEW JERSEY

PRIMARY AFFILIATION

COMPANY CONTACT:
Delores Henderson
Administrator
Nursing Services
United Hospitals Medical
Center
15 South Ninth Street
Newark, NJ   07107
(201) 268-8767

INSTITUTIONAL CONTACT:
Lucille Joel
Associate Dean for Clinical
Affairs
College of Nursing
Rutgers, The State University
of New Jersey
University Avenue
Newark, NJ   07102
(201) 648-5298

PROGRAM DESCRIPTION/OBJECTIVES:
Manpower sharing; student
placement.

PROGRAM INITIATED: 1981

LENGTH OF STUDY FOR PARTICI-
PANT: Academic year

LENGTH OF CONTRACT: 10 months

LOCATION: United Hospitals
Medical Center and Rutgers

PARTICIPANTS: 2

PROGRAM COSTS PROVIDED BY:
Shared equally by exchange of
time between company and
institution.

PRINTED MATERIALS AVAILABLE
FROM: Institution

264. UNITED PARCEL SERVICE*
with
MERRITT COLLEGE

JOB PLACEMENT

COMPANY CONTACT:
Glenn Leydecker
Personnel
United Parcel Service
579 McCormick Avenue
San Leandro, CA   94501
(415) 635-6227

INSTITUTIONAL CONTACT:
George Ito
Placement Officer
Career Center
Merritt College
12500 Campus Drive
Oakland, CA   94619
(415) 436-2449

PROGRAM DESCRIPTION/OBJECTIVES:
Match student job applicants to
job opportunities. Particular
interest in matching skills
gained in Merritt training with
needs of employers.

PROGRAM INITIATED: 1968

LENGTH OF STUDY FOR PARTICI-
PANT: At least 1 semester

LENGTH OF CONTRACT: Ongoing

LOCATION: Merritt College

PARTICIPANTS: Approximately
1,000 current student and
graduate student applicants
per semester

PROGRAM COSTS PROVIDED BY:
Institution: $30,000
Other Source: $10,000

PRINTED MATERIALS AVAILABLE
FROM: Institution

*Representative entry--complete
list available from institution.

135

265. UNITED NUCLEAR CORPORATION
with
QUINEBAUG VALLEY COMMUNI-
TY COLLEGE

ON-SITE EDUCATION

COMPANY CONTACT:
Ed Pailes
College Program Coordinator
United Nuclear
67 Sandy Desert Road
Uncasville, CT   06382
(203) 848-1511

INSTITUTIONAL CONTACT:
Frank Aleman
Director
Division of Business Adminis-
tration and Mathematics
Quinebaug Valley Community
College
24 School Street
Danielson, CT   06239
(203) 774-1130

PROGRAM DESCRIPTION/OBJECTIVES:
To make college courses conveniently available to company
employees interested in the
college's Industrial Supervision Program.

PROGRAM INITIATED: 1979

LENGTH OF STUDY FOR PARTICI-
PANT: 1 semester per course

LENGTH OF CONTRACT: Semester
by semester

LOCATION: United Nuclear

PARTICIPANTS: Varies, approximately 36 current and aspiring
supervisors per semester

PROGRAM COSTS PROVIDED BY:
Institution: Some overhead
Company: $850 per course
Participant: Unknown

PRINTED MATERIALS AVAILABLE
FROM: Not reported

266. UNITED NUCLEAR CORPORATION
with
UNIVERSITY OF HARTFORD

IMPROVING INTERPERSONAL
EFFECTIVENESS FOR MANAGERS

COMPANY CONTACT:
John C. Parker
Manager, Human Resources
United Nuclear Corporation
67 Sandy Desert Road
Uncasville, CT   06382
(203) 848-1511

INSTITUTIONAL CONTACT:
M. Brady/G. Maffeo
Director, Continuing Education
Division of Adult Educational
Services
University of Hartford
200 Bloomfield Avenue
West Hartford, CT   06117
(203) 243-4387

PROGRAM DESCRIPTION/OBJECTIVES:
Intensive 1-day seminar designed to teach managers and
supervisors how to interact
more effectively with subordinates, peers and superiors.

PROGRAM INITIATED: 1981

LENGTH OF STUDY FOR PARTICI-
PANT: 1 training day (7 contact hours)

LENGTH OF CONTRACT: 1 time-
pilot with possibility of
renewal

LOCATION: Uncasville, CT

PARTICIPANTS: 25 technical
personnel, engineers, etc.

PROGRAM COSTS PROVIDED BY:
Company: 100%

PRINTED MATERIALS AVAILABLE
FROM: Institution

267. U.S. DEPARTMENT OF HEALTH
     AND HUMAN SERVICES
              with
     PRINCE GEORGE'S COMMUNI-
     TY COLLEGE

CERTIFIED PROFESSIONAL
SECRETARIAL PROGRAM

COMPANY CONTACT:
Elaine Lazaroff
EEO Specialist
Health Resources
Administration
U.S. Department of Health and
Human Services
3700 East-West Highway
Hyattsville, MD   20782
(301) 436-7210

INSTITUTIONAL CONTACT:
Veronica S. Norwood
Director, Contract Services
Prince George's Community
College
301 Largo Road
Largo, MD   20772
(301) 322-0726

PROGRAM DESCRIPTION/OBJECTIVES:
To prepare participants to successfully complete the Certified Professional Secretary Examination and to enhance present skills and abilities, leading to positions of greater
responsibility.

PROGRAM INITIATED: 1979

LENGTH OF STUDY FOR PARTICI-
PANT: 5 1-semester credit
classes and 3 18-30 hour non-
credit classes offered over a
24-month period

LENGTH OF CONTRACT: Renewable
each semester

LOCATION: Health Resources
Administration

PARTICIPANTS: 16 secretaries
and clerk-typists

PROGRAM COSTS PROVIDED BY:
Company: 50%
Other Source: 50% (state
funds)

PRINTED MATERIALS AVAILABLE
FROM: Institution

268. U.S. DEPARTMENT OF JUSTICE
              with
     PRINCE GEORGE'S COMMU-
     NITY COLLEGE

CAREER PLANNING

COMPANY CONTACT:
Allison Howell
Office of Justice Assistance
and Research
U.S. Department of Justice
633 Indiana Avenue
Washington, DC   20531
(202) 724-3154

INSTITUTIONAL CONTACT:
Veronica Norwood
Director, Contract Services
Prince George's Community
College
301 Largo Road
Largo, MD   20772
(301) 322-0726

PROGRAM DESCRIPTION/OBJECTIVES:
To familiarize participants
with a career-life planning and
decision-making model which can
be effectively utilized in a
career change situation.

PROGRAM INITIATED: 1982

LENGTH OF STUDY FOR PARTICI-
PANT: 4 days, 8 hours each
day

LENGTH OF CONTRACT: 24 hours

LOCATION: Office of Justice
Assistance and Research

PARTICIPANTS: 25 employees
undergoing RIF per session

PROGRAM COSTS PROVIDED BY:
Company: 50%
Other Source: 50% (state
funds)

PRINTED MATERIALS AVAILABLE
FROM: Institution

269. U.S. POSTAL SERVICE
with
UNIVERSITY OF VIRGINIA

ADVANCED MANAGEMENT PROGRAM

COMPANY CONTACT:
Norman Buehler
General Manager
Career Development Division
HQ U.S. Postal Service
475 L'Enfant Plaza
Washington, DC   20260
(202) 245-4696

INSTITUTIONAL CONTACT:
Robert Fair
Assistant Dean
Graduate Business
Administration
University of Virginia
Charlottesville, VA   22904
(804) 924-7195

PROGRAM DESCRIPTION/OBJECTIVES:
Opportunity for selected employees to pursue college
coursework to improve managerial skills at an executive
level.

PROGRAM INITIATED: 1978

LENGTH OF STUDY FOR PARTICI-
PANT: 1 semester-1 year

LOCATION: Campus

PARTICIPANTS: 12 selected
professionals, executives and
candidates

PROGRAM COSTS PROVIDED BY:
Company: 100%

PRINTED MATERIALS AVAILABLE
FROM: Institution

270. U.S. POSTAL SERVICE
with
INSTITUTIONS THROUGHOUT
THE U.S.*

TUITION ASSISTANCE

COMPANY CONTACT:
Norman Buehler
General Manager
Career Development Division
HQ U.S. Postal Service
475 L'Enfant Plaza
Washington, DC   20260
(202) 245-4696

INSTITUTIONAL CONTACT:
Not available

PROGRAM DESCRIPTION/OBJECTIVES:
To provide tuition assistance
for executives and candidates
to provide educational development and skills for improved
performance at executive and
managerial levels.

PROGRAM INITIATED: 1978

LENGTH OF STUDY FOR PARTICI-
PANT: 1 semester-1 year

LENGTH OF CONTRACT: 1 semes-
ter-1 year

LOCATION: Varied at institutions

PARTICIPANTS: 30 Postal Service employees

PROGRAM COSTS PROVIDED BY:
Company: 100%

PRINTED MATERIALS AVAILABLE
FROM: Institution and Company ,

----

*Representative entry--complete
list available from institution.

138

271. 20 OR MORE COMPANIES*
                with
      UNIVERSITY OF ILLINOIS
      - CHICAGO CIRCLE

COOPERATIVE INTERN PROGRAM

COMPANY CONTACT:
Specific company not identified

INSTITUTIONAL CONTACT:
Dr. Fred McLinmore
Associate Dean for External
Affairs
University of Illinois -
Chicago Circle
Chicago, IL   60680
(312) 996-0529

PROGRAM DESCRIPTION/OBJECTIVES:
To provide students with a management related experience and
job contact.

PROGRAM INITIATED: 1977

LENGTH OF STUDY FOR PARTICI-
PANT: 3 quarters

LENGTH OF CONTRACT: Not
reported

LOCATION: U.S. and Europe

PARTICIPANTS: 25 MBA and undergraduate business students

PROGRAM COSTS PROVIDED BY:
Company: Student salary

PRINTED MATERIALS AVAILABLE
FROM: Institution

---

*Representative entry--complete
list available from institution.

272. VIRGINIA NATIONAL BANK
                with
      OLD DOMINION UNIVERSITY

RESEARCH ON DATA PROCESSING
PROFESSIONAL'S PRODUCTIVITY

COMPANY CONTACT:
Truman Hester
Department Chief
Data Processing
Virginia National Bank
1 Commercial Plaza
Norfolk, VA   23510
(804) 441-4000

INSTITUTIONAL CONTACT:
Mark Chadwin
Director
Bureau of Business and
Economic Research
Old Dominion University
Norfolk, VA   23508
(804) 440-4598

PROGRAM DESCRIPTION/OBJECTIVES:
Analyze determinants of pro-
grammer performance.

PROGRAM INITIATED: Not
reported

LENGTH OF STUDY FOR PARTICI-
PANT: Not available

LENGTH OF CONTRACT: 2 months
with renewal option

LOCATION: Norfolk

PARTICIPANTS: Various numbers
of data processing management,
staff, programmers and systems
analysts

PROGRAM COSTS PROVIDED BY:
Institution: Overhead
Company: $5,000

PRINTED MATERIALS AVAILABLE
FROM: Not yet available

273. WALTER REED ARMY MEDICAL
      CENTER
            with
      CENTRAL MICHIGAN
      UNIVERSITY

WALTER REED ARMY MEDICAL
CENTER PROGRAM

COMPANY CONTACT:
Michael Burnam
Education Director
Education Center
Walter Reed Army Medical Center
Washington, DC   20044
(202) 545-6700

INSTITUTIONAL CONTACT:
Dr. Lawrence R. Murphy
Director
Institute for Personal and
Career Development
Central Michigan University
Mt. Pleasant, MI   48859
(517) 774-3865

PROGRAM DESCRIPTION/OBJECTIVES:
Provide professional training
in Management and Supervision
with a health care emphasis;
leads to a MA degree.

PROGRAM INITIATED: Not
reported

LENGTH OF STUDY FOR PARTICI-
PANT: 1-3 years

LENGTH OF CONTRACT: Ongoing

LOCATION: Walter Reed Army
Medical Center

PARTICIPANTS: Military and
civilian employees of local
hospitals

PROGRAM COSTS PROVIDED BY:
Participant: 100%

PRINTED MATERIALS AVAILABLE
FROM: Institution

274. WASHINGTON SUBURBAN
      SANITARY COMMISSION
            with
      PRINCE GEORGE'S
      COMMUNITY COLLEGE

SANITARY WASTEWATER TECHNOLOGY

COMPANY CONTACT:
Mona Chase
Coordinator, Training
Washington Suburban Sanitary
Commission
4017 Hamilton Street
Hyattsville, MD   20781
(301) 699-4518

INSTITUTIONAL CONTACT:
Margaretta Bir
Program Assistant
Community Services
Prince George's Community
College
301 Largo Road
Largo, MD   20772
(301) 322-0793

PROGRAM DESCRIPTION/OBJECTIVES:
Improve performance and assist
in obtaining state license required of plant superintendents.

PROGRAM INITIATED: 1982

LENGTH OF STUDY FOR PARTICI-
PANT: 1 semester (45 ho rs)

LENGTH OF CONTRACT: 1 semester
and renewable as required

LOCATION: Prince George's
Community College

PARTICIPANTS: 12 plant superintendents and technical
personnel

PROGRAM COSTS PROVIDED BY:
Company: $90 per student
Other Source: $89 per student
(state funds)

PRINTED MATERIALS AVAILABLE
FROM: Institution

275. WEBER KNAPP
with
JAMESTOWN COMMUNITY COLLEGE

SHOP MATH

COMPANY CONTACT:
Thomas Madison
Personnel Assistant
Personnel Department
Weber Knapp
441 Changler Street
Jamestown, NY   14701
(716) 484-9135

INSTITUTIONAL CONTACT:
Rose M. Scott
Cottinuing Education Assistant
Jamestown Community College
525 Falconer Street
Jamestown, NY   14701
(716) 665-5220

PROGRAM DESCRIPTION/OBJECTIVES:
To provide a basic understanding of mathematical principles
for presently employed machinists in order to maintain
skills needed to keep pace with
changing technology.

PROGRAM INITIATED: Not
reported

LENGTH OF STUDY FOR PARTICI-
PANT: 8 weeks

LENGTH OF CONTRACT: 12 months
with option to renew

LOCATION: Weber Knapp

PARTICIPANTS: 35 machinists
per class

PROGRAM COSTS PROVIDED BY:
Institution: 40%
Company: 20%
Other Source: 20%

PRINTED MATERIALS AVAILABLE
FROM: Not available

276. WELLS FARGO BANK
with
COGSWELL COLLEGE

BUILDING SAFETY/FIRE
PREPLANNING

COMPANY CONTACT:
C. Paul Bernard
AVP and Manager
Safety Department
Wells Fargo Bank
343 Sansome Street
San Francisco, CA   94163
(415) 396-5923

INSTITUTIONAL CONTACT:
Philip Alan Cecchettini
Dean
Continuing Education
Cogswell College
600 Stockton Street
San Francisco, CA   94108
(415) 433-5550

PROGRAM DESCRIPTION/OBJECTIVES:
To provide instruction in the
basics of building safety and
fire preplanning techniques in
compliance with Titles 19 and
24 created by the State Fire
Marshall of California.

PROGRAM INITIATED: 1981

LENGTH OF CONTRACT: 6 months

LOCATION: Cogswell College
and Wells Fargo

PARTICIPANTS: 100 of a variety of designated management
personnel from bank buildings
annually

PROGRAM COSTS PROVIDED BY:
Institution: 10%
Company: 90%

PRINTED MATERIALS AVAILABLE
FROM: Institution

277. VARIOUS INDUSTRIES AND
      STATE AGENCIES*
              with
      WESLEY COLLEGE

ENVIRONMENTAL SCIENCES
INTERNSHIP

COMPANY CONTACT:
Specific company not identified

INSTITUTIONAL CONTACT:
Terrance L. Higgins
Director, Environmental
Sciences Program
Wesley College
Dover, DE   19901
(302) 736-2477

PROGRAM DESCRIPTION/OBJECTIVES:
Internship in one of a variety
of positions with private industry or governmental agency.
Each internship position will
be structured so as to provide
the student with a set of realistic learning experiences in a
professional environment.

PROGRAM INITIATED: 1981

LENGTH OF STUDY FOR PARTICI-
PANT: Minimum 15 weeks

LENGTH OF CONTRACT: Minimum
15 weeks

LOCATION: Depends upon internship site

PARTICIPANTS: 8 graduate
students

PROGRAM COSTS PROVIDED BY:
Participant: $40 per credit

PRINTED MATERIALS AVAILABLE
FROM: Institution and Company

---

*Representative entry--complete
list available from institution.

278. WEST VIRGINIA STATE
      POLICE
              with
      MARSHALL UNIVERSITY

WEST VIRGINIA STATE POLICE

COMPANY CONTACT:
John Buckalew
West Virginia State Police
Department of Public Safety
Charleston, WV   25301
(304) 348-6370

INSTITUTIONAL CONTACT:
Paul D. Hines
Vice President/Dean
Community College
Marshall University
16th Street and Hal Greer Blvd.
Huntington, WV   25701
(304) 696-3646

PROGRAM DESCRIPTION/OBJECTIVES:
To improve state police training standards.

PROGRAM INITIATED: 1977

LENGTH OF STUDY FOR PARTICI-
PANT: 20 or 36 weeks

LENGTH OF CONTRACT: Ongoing

LOCATION: Marshall University

PARTICIPANTS: 400 cadets or
full-time West Virginia State
Police

PROGRAM COSTS PROVIDED BY:
Shared depending on the year

PRINTED MATERIALS AVAILABLE
FROM: Institution

279. WESTERN ELECTRIC COMPANY
with
FRANKLIN UNIVERSITY

COMPUTER TECHNOLOGY PROGRAM

COMPANY CONTACT:
Lynn Davis
Department Chief
Training and Development
Western Electric Company
6200 East Broad
Columbus, OH   43213
(614) 860-3991

INSTITUTIONAL CONTACT:
Peg Thomas
Director of Continuing and
Management Education
Franklin University
201 South Grant Avenue
Columbus, OH   43215
(614) 224-6388

PROGRAM DESCRIPTION/OBJECTIVES:
Several courses from the computer technology area were
chosen by Western Electric managers to be offered on-site.
The objective is to involve interested employees in the new
technology and help them begin
a degree.

PROGRAM INITIATED: 1978

LENGTH OF STUDY FOR PARTICI-
PANT: 1-3 years

LENGTH OF CONTRACT: Ongoing

LOCATION: Western Electric

PARTICIPANTS: 65 company
employees

PROGRAM COSTS PROVIDED BY:
Company: 100% tuition, fees

PRINTED MATERIALS AVAILABLE
FROM: Not available

280. WESTERN PUBLISHING COMPANY
with
UNIVERSITY OF WISCONSIN -
PARKSIDE

BUSINESS/INDUSTRY LIAISON
PROGRAM

COMPANY CONTACT:
Judy Merkle
Western Publishing Company
1220 Mound Avenue
Racine, WI   53404
(414) 631-5029

INSTITUTIONAL CONTACT:
Wendi Schneider
Counselor, Community Student
Services
University of Wisconsin -
Parkside
Box 2000
Kenosha, WI   53141
(414) 553-2496

PROGRAM DESCRIPTION/OBJECTIVES:
Increase the number of adults
attending University of Wisconsin - Parkside by providing
more information about available programs and simplified
registration procedures to members of the local business community. 650 businesses are on
the mailing list, receive
visits with 15 on-site regis-
trations.

PROGRAM INITIATED: 1977

LENGTH OF STUDY FOR PARTICI-
PANT: Varies

LENGTH OF CONTRACT: Not
available

LOCATION: University of
Wisconsin - Parkside

PARTICIPANTS: 40% of the student body is over 23 years old

PROGRAM COSTS PROVIDED BY:
Institution: 100%

PRINTED MATERIALS AVAILABLE
FROM: Institution

281. WESTMINSTER BUSINESS
     SYSTEMS, INC.
              with
     COLLEGE OF LAKE COUNTY

INFORMATION PROCESSING EQUIP-
MENT SERVICE TECHNICIANS OJT

COMPANY CONTACT:
Karl Lichtenberger
President
Westminster Business
Systems, Inc.
999 Sherwood Drive
Lake Bluff, IL   60044
(312) 234-0506

INSTITUTIONAL CONTACT:
Keri Thiessen
Business/Industry Training
Coordinator
Open Campus
College of Lake County
Grayslake, IL   60030
(312) 223-3616

PROGRAM DESCRIPTION/OBJECTIVES:
High Impact Training Service
(HITS) grant which provided
funds for OJT of service technicians. Westminster Business
Systems, Inc. employees served
as instructors in the servicing
of high technology information
processing equipment.

PROGRAM INITIATED: 1982

LENGTH OF STUDY FOR PARTICI-
PANT: 6 months

LENGTH OF CONTRACT: 6 months

LOCATION: Westminster Business
Systems

PARTICIPANTS: Service
technicians

PROGRAM COSTS PROVIDED BY:
Other Source: $8,000 (state
funds)

PRINTED MATERIALS AVAILABLE
FROM: Company

282. WHIRLPOOL COMPANY
             with
     CENTRAL MICHIGAN
     UNIVERSITY

WHIRLPOOL/CMU PROGRAM

COMPANY CONTACT:
Louis Mineweaser
Corporate Personnel Manager
Whirlpool Company
Research and Engineering Center
Monte Road
Benton Harbor, MI   49022
(616) 926-5000

INSTITUTIONAL CONTACT:
Lawrence R. Murphy
Director
Institute for Personal and
Career Development
Central Michigan University
Mt. Pleasant, MI   48859
(517) 774-3865

PROGRAM DESCRIPTION/OBJECTIVES:
To provide an opportunity for
employees of the Whirlpool Research Division with high level
of technical training for complete bachelor's degrees.

PROGRAM INITIATED: Not
reported

LENGTH OF STUDY FOR PARTICI-
PANT: 27 months average

LENGTH OF CONTRACT: Ongoing

LOCATION: Whirlpool plant

PARTICIPANTS: 20 technicians

PROGRAM COSTS PROVIDED BY:
Company: 100%

PRINTED MATERIALS AVAILABLE
FROM: Institution

283. ANONYMOUS INDUSTRIAL DONOR
with
WILMINGTON COLLEGE

COOPERATIVE EDUCATION

COMPANY CONTACT:
Anonymous

INSTITUTIONAL CONTACT:
Campbell Graf
Director, Career Center
Wilmington College
Pyle Center #1306
Wilmington, OH   45177
(513) 382-6661, X344

PROGRAM DESCRIPTION/OBJECTIVES:
An alternative process for ac-
quiring baccalaureate level com-
petency for careers in agricul-
ture, business and industry by
students alternating periods of
study with periods of work
(with progressive learning).

PROGRAM INITIATED: 1981

LENGTH OF STUDY FOR PARTICI-
PANT: Typical student will re-
quire 4 years

LENGTH OF CONTRACT: 3-5 years

LOCATION: Wilmington College

PARTICIPANTS: Average of 15
undergraduate students annually

PROGRAM COSTS PROVIDED BY:
Company: $40,000

PRINTED MATERIALS AVAILABLE
FROM: Institution

284. TOWN OF WINDSOR
with
UNIVERSITY OF HARTFORD

EFFECTIVE SUPERVISORY TRAINING

COMPANY CONTACT:
Albert Ilg
City Manager
Town of Windsor
Windsor, CT   06095
(203) 688-3675

INSTITUTIONAL CONTACT:
Gilbert J. Maffeo
Program Development Consultant
Division of Adult Educational
Services
University of Hartford
200 Bloomfield Avenue
West Hartford, CT   06117
(203) 243-4350/4381

PROGRAM DESCRIPTION/OBJECTIVES:
To provide effective supervisory skills training to members of administrative staff.
To upgrade managerial skills of
department heads and assistants.

PROGRAM INITIATED: 1981

LENGTH OF STUDY FOR PARTICI-
PANT: 10-15 weeks

LENGTH OF CONTRACT: 10-15 weeks/
ongoing

LOCATION: On-site at town of
Windsor

PARTICIPANTS: 10-15 varying
level of management, homogene-
ously grouped personnel

PROGRAM COSTS PROVIDED BY:
Company: 100%

PRINTED MATERIALS AVAILABLE
FROM: Institution and Company

285. TOWN OF WINDSOR
          with
      UNIVERSITY OF HARTFORD

PROMOTION ASSESSMENT PROGRAM

COMPANY CONTACT:
Maxwell Patterson
Chief of Police
Town of Windsor
Windsor, CT   06095
(213) 688-5273

INSTITUTIONAL CONTACT:
Gilbert J. Maffeo
Program Development Consultant
Division of Adult Educational
Services
University of Hartford
200 Bloomfield Avenue
West Hartford, CT   06117
(203) 243-4350/4381

PROGRAM DESCRIPTION/OBJECTIVES:
To provide personnel assessment
skills to the town of Windsor.

PROGRAM INITIATED: 1980

LENGTH OF STUDY FOR PARTICI-
PANT: 3-6 days

LENGTH OF CONTRACT: 3-6 days

LOCATION: On campus

PARTICIPANTS: 25 town
employees

PROGRAM COSTS PROVIDED BY:
Company: 100%

PRINTED MATERIALS AVAILABLE
FROM: Institution and Company

286. WISCONSIN TELEPHONE*
          with
      ALVERNO COLLEGE

VOLUNTEER ASSESSOR PROGRAM

COMPANY CONTACT:
Harold Steen
Division Staff Manager
Wisconsin Telephone
324 East Wisconsin Avenue
Milwaukee, WI   53202
(414) 678-3375

INSTITUTIONAL CONTACT:
Patricia Jensen
Faculty Liaison
Assessment Center
Alverno College
3401 South 39th Street
Milwaukee, WI   53215
(414) 647-3896

PROGRAM DESCRIPTION/OBJECTIVES:
To provide assessors to evaluate students' achievement (e.g.,
group problem-solving skills)
who are professional, non-academic personnel; to enable assessors to remain updated on assessment art and practice.

PROGRAM INITIATED: 1973

LENGTH OF STUDY FOR PARTICI-
PANT: Training and retraining
sessions for assessors are 1/2
day. Taught by faculty.

LENGTH OF CONTRACT: 1 year;
renewable

LOCATION: Alverno College

PARTICIPANTS: Approximately
100 professional people in business and service area

PROGRAM COSTS PROVIDED BY:
Institution: Operating costs
of Assessment Center
Company: Assessor time volun-
teered by companies

PRINTED MATERIALS AVAILABLE
FROM: Institution

---

*Representative entry--complete
list available from institution.

287. WPRI-TV
        with
     COMMUNITY COLLEGE OF
     RHODE ISLAND

INTRODUCTION TO MICROCOMPUTERS

COMPANY CONTACT:
Edward Passarelli
Business Manager
WPRI-TV
25 Catamore Boulevard
East Providence, RI   02914
(401) 438-7200

INSTITUTIONAL CONTACT:
Robert Danilowicz
Coordinator
Missing Link Project
Off Campus Credit Programs
Community College of
Rhode Island
Flanagan Campus
Louisquisset Pike
Lincoln, RI   02865
(401) 333-7127

PROGRAM DESCRIPTION/OBJECTIVES:
Course was designed to familiarize students with methodology
and application of microcomputers system, number systems,
logic functions.

PROGRAM INITIATED: 1981

LENGTH OF STUDY FOR PARTICI-
PANT: 8 weeks

LENGTH OF CONTRACT: 1
semester

LOCATION: WPRI-TV

PARTICIPANTS: 20 mid-
management

PROGRAM COSTS PROVIDED BY:
Company: $200
Participant: $800

PRINTED MATERIALS AVAILABLE
FROM: Institution

288. WYANDOTTE GENERAL
     HOSPITAL
        with
     CENTRAL MICHIGAN
     UNIVERSITY

WYANDOTTE GENERAL PROGRAM

COMPANY CONTACT:
Roger Griswold
Personnel Director
Wyandotte General Hospital
2333 Biddle Avenue
Wyandotte, MI   48192
(313) 284-2400

INSTITUTIONAL CONTACT:
Lawrence R. Murphy
Director
Institute for Personal and
Career Development
Central Michigan University
Mt. Pleasant, MI   48859
(517) 774-3865

PROGRAM DESCRIPTION/OBJECTIVES:
To provide an opportunity for
area health care professionals
to obtain master's level preparation for middle management position in the health care
industry.

PROGRAM INITIATED: Not
reported

LENGTH OF STUDY FOR PARTICI-
PANT: 22 months average

LENGTH OF CONTRACT: Ongoing

LOCATION: Wyandotte General
Hospital

PARTICIPANTS: Not reported

PROGRAM COSTS PROVIDED BY:
Participant: 100%

PRINTED MATERIALS AVAILABLE
FROM: Institution

289. WYMAN-GORDAN COMPANY
with
WORCESTER STATE COLLEGE

ENTRY-LEVEL MANAGEMENT PROGRAM

COMPANY CONTACT:
Jane Gallagher
Director, Human Resources
Wyman-Gordon Company
244 Worcester Street
North Grafton, MA   01536
(617) 839-4441

INSTITUTIONAL CONTACT:
William O'Neil
Dean, Division of Graduate and
Continuing Education
Worcester State College
486 Chandler Street
Worcester, MA   01602
(617) 793-8100

PROGRAM DESCRIPTION/OBJECTIVES:
To develop a new continuing education pool while meeting the
needs of local companies; to
provide practical training for
entry-level managers; career-
path development, college
credit, skill development.

PROGRAM INITIATED: 1982

LENGTH OF STUDY FOR PARTICI-
PANT: 21 credits; 2 year
average

LENGTH OF CONTRACT: Agreement
has no termination date

LOCATION: Wyman-Gordon plant
and WSC campus

PARTICIPANTS: 40-60 entry-
level and middle managers
annually

PROGRAM COSTS PROVIDED BY:
Institution: $900 per parti-
cipant
Company: $900 per participant

PRINTED MATERIALS AVAILABLE
FROM: Institution

290. XEROX CORPORATION*
with
UNIVERSITY OF THE STATE
OF NEW YORK

NEW YORK REGENTS AND XEROX COR-
PORATION COOPERATE TO AWARD
DEGREES

COMPANY CONTACT:
Von Haney
Manager of Operational Training
Xerox Corporation
Xerox Square
Rochester, NY   14644
(716) 423-4541

INSTITUTIONAL CONTACT:
Carrie Getty
Liaison for Employers
Office of Independent Study
Regents External Degree Program
of the University of the State
of New York
Cultural Education Center
Albany, NY   12230
(518) 474-3703

PROGRAM DESCRIPTION/OBJECTIVES:
To make non-residential college
degree opportunities available
to employees nationwide who are
unable to attend conventional
college for reasons of work re-
sponsibilities, travel, frequent
transfers, while allowing participant to upgrade level of education and credentials.

PROGRAM INITIATED: 1980

LENGTH OF STUDY FOR PARTICI-
PANT: Self-paced

LENGTH OF CONTRACT: Informal
agreement

LOCATION: Varies

PARTICIPANTS: 70 annually

PROGRAM COSTS PROVIDED BY:
Institution: 15%
Company: 25%
Participant: 60%

PRINTED MATERIALS AVAILABLE
FROM: Institution

---

*Representative entry--complete
list available from institution.

CASE STUDIES

CASE STUDIES

The objective of this section is to provide the reader with a bit more insight to the actual development and operation of some very successful programs.

The following case studies represent a variety of ventures which are presently underway around the country. As reflected by these entries, linkages are occurring in all types of institutions and in almost every conceivable subject area. Some ventures are research-oriented while others provide internship experiences. In all cases, the contact individuals provided in the following examples are enthusiastic and willing to share their experiences with others seeking to develop a joint venture.

Anita Ann Lee
Center for Higher Education
University of Virginia

PARTNERS IN PROGRESS

The Participants:

Bethune-Cookman College - A private liberal arts college in Daytona Beach, Florida, with a predominantly minority student enrollment of 1,747 students.

R.G. "Dick" Mulligan - A management systems director with the National Aeronautics and Space Administration who served as a visiting professor of management.

Area Businesses - Numerous private and governmental agencies in the Daytona Beach area including American Can, Honeywell, General Electric, IBM, the Chamber of Commerce, and the Kennedy Space Center.

The Contact:

The Vice President for Academic Affairs initiated the request for Dick Mulligan to serve as a visiting professor in the Business Division through the provisions of the Intergovernmental Personnel Act which allows professional governmental employees to be "loaned" to minority institutions.

The Venture:

The goals of Partners in Progress was to establish closer ties with the local business community by providing services to that group which would better acquaint them with the capabilities of Bethune-Cookman College and its students. To achieve that goal, a four-part plan was implemented:

(1) Symposia - a program in which national experts and consultants were invited by the institution to provide specialized sessions in areas such as human resource management for the local business community.

(2) Seminars and Training - specific programs presented by the campus faculty in response to needs indicated by local businesses in areas like inventory control, salesmanship, business math, or production control.

(3) Special Studies - analyses and surveys conducted by Bethune-Cookman faculty and students on various business issues for area businesses.

(4) Job Bank - designed to provide a pool of well-qualified students for part-time and full-time positions, with an emphasis on career-related work experience, in the Daytona Beach area.

The Costs:

NASA continued to pay Mulligan's salary for the year while the institution covered the basic administrative costs incurred in the presentation of the seminars. Area businessmen were usually invited to attend the seminars at little or no cost to them.

The Response:

According to Mulligan and Sister Holzer, Chairman of the Business Division at Bethune-Cookman, the venture was very successful. The number of internship opportunities for students expanded from two to 22 and the number of part-time jobs during the semester increased greatly. Although operated through the Business Division, students from various fields benefited from the contacts which were established.

Bethune-Cookman plans to further develop those contacts made during the initial year by requesting a second visiting faculty member through the IPA.

Advice and Elements of Success:

According to Mulligan, the actual program depends more on the attitude and willingness of the individual faculty member involved rather than on the amount of funding provided. The faculty member must be enthusiastic about the business community and find a means of showing the school's capabilities and its student body in a very positive and productive manner.

The program could be replicated in almost any situation if there is someone on the staff willing to invest the necessary time to develop the contacts within the community. It is also critical for the institution to carefully assess the needs of area businesses before designing any symposia or training sessions. One factor which remains constant throughout all the programs offered to the business community by the institution is the involvement of the students.

Contact Individuals:

R.G. Mulligan
NASA Headquarters
Code NS
Washington, DC   20546
(202) 755-3140

Shirley Lee
Director of Planning and
Development
Bethune-Cookman College
640 2nd Avenue
Daytona Beach, FL
(904) 255-1401, X355

Lonnie Brown
Director
Social Security Administration
115 North Ridgewood Avenue
Daytona Beach, FL
(904) 255-7543

Dale Daniels
Director, Employee Management
General Electric
1800 Volusia Avenue
Daytona Beach, FL
(904) 258-2511

TRANSITION INTO ELECTRONICS

The Participants:

Evergreen Valley College - A community college located in San Jose, California with a student enrollment of approximately 6,800.

Andrew Y. McFarlin - An engineering instructor and coordinator of various projects within the institution.

Lockheed, Memorex, IBM, Hewlett-Packard, and others - Area companies which have been supportive of this venture in such ways as release time for certain employees serving as instructors and the use of plant facilities for class tours.

The Contact:

Through informal discussions with members of the business community, Dr. McFarlin determined a program was needed which would acquaint people with the career possibilities in the field of electronics. He formalized that concern by submitting a proposal for funding within the guidelines established by the Displaced Homemakers Act. After receiving the funds, Dr. McFarlin organized an Advisory Committee to help in the actual development of the course content. Most of the Advisory Committee members were from the corporate departments of Training, Personnel, Manufacturing, or Engineering. At no time has there been an agreement established between Evergreen Valley College or any of the businesses from an executive level.

The Venture:

This 10-week program, begun in 1980, was designed to provide individuals with a realistic view of the career possibilities within the field of electronics. The participants, primarily displaced homemakers, were given the opportunity to explore the areas of computer technology, drafting, and electrical applications. Job tasks, actual working conditions, and opportunities for career advancement were examined through classroom lectures and laboratory exercises at the Evergreen campus and supplemented by the plant tours.

The Costs:

The first year the entire program was funded through the Displaced Homemakers Act. Subsequently, the program has primarily been funded by the institution although some monies have been made available through the Vocational Education Act for personal counseling and administrative expenses. Course participants pay a small fee required by the college of all students and a partial fee for course materials.

The Response:

Approximately 70-80 individuals have participated in this program
during the four times it has been offered. According to Dr. McFarlin,
the students have considered the course a positive experience and one
which has provided them with some direction in their lives. The majority of students have continued their training by enrolling in specific courses or a two-year degree program. Some few students have
chosen to go directly into the job market and have attributed their
successful employment to their class experiences. The businesses
have experienced an enlarged pool of better qualified applicants,
while the college's technical programs have become a more attractive
option to this group.

Advice and Elements of Success:

This particular program has been a success because a need existed for
additional trained personnel and a spirit of willingness and cooperation developed between the institutions and the businesses according
to Dr. McFarlin.

A careful assessment of future employment needs within a geographic
area is the most critical factor to consider before establishing a
program of this nature. In Dr. McFarlin's opinion, the program could
be easily replicated in other situations by first examining the local
needs and then developing a good rapport with the individuals who
would be involved in the actual training.

Contact Individuals:

Andrew U. McFarlin
Engineering Instructor and
Coordinator
Evergreen Valley College
3095 Yerba Buena Road
San Jose, CA   95135
(408) 274-7900, X6570

Clara Brock
Advisory Committee Member
Lockheed
19930 Oakmont Drive
Los Gatos, CA
(408) 742-5413

UNIVERSITY OF MAINE PULP AND PAPER FOUNDATION

The Participants:

University of Maine - A public institution with an enrollment of approximately 11,300 students.

Stanley N. Marshall, Jr. - The Executive Director of the University
of Maine Pulp and Paper Foundation who serves the interest of both
the institution and the corporations through this administrative
position.

156 Corporations - Firms which are involved in various aspects of the
paper industry such as chemical and equipment suppliers, consultants,
or production companies from throughout the country.

152 Students - Undergraduates and graduate students from the College
of Engineering and Science who are preparing for a paper-related
technical career.

The Contact:

During the late 1940's, the president of the University of Maine did not feel the institution was doing all that was possible to serve the needs of the state. At the same time, several alumni from the Pulp and Paper Program had assumed roles within the industry and were very interested in doing something to promote their former program, the first of its kind in the country. In 1949 a meeting was held between 17 alumni and 8 university administrators, including the president, to discuss a plan of action. By February of 1950, the Pulp and Paper Foundation was established to meet the growing needs of industry while also providing more opportunities for the influx of post-War students. It was loosely modeled after the foundation established by the textile industry at North Carolina State at Raleigh.

The Venture:

The Foundation is designed to promote the following objectives:

(1) To interest students in preparing for and advancing in engineering and forestry careers in pulp and paper-related industries.

(2) To provide financial assistance in the form of loans, scholarships and grants to students in the field.

(3) To assist and advise the University in developing a curriculum of undergraduate and advanced study and continuing education to meet the needs of the industry.

(4) To inform promising students about the career alternatives within the pulp and paper industry, particularly in the areas of operational management.

(5) To obtain well-motivated staff members of the highest quality for the program.

(6) To advance fundamental and applied research for pulp and paper-related industries.

The Costs:

The annual expense to the institution is $4,500, a portion of the Executive Director's salary, and $233,000 to the corporations. The Foundation has five different categories of membership opportunities for participants based on the amount of monetary support contributed or the dollar value of equipment donations. Active membership, which provides voting privileges, requires a minimum annual contribution of $1,300 or an equipment donation of $2,000. Approximately 50% is obtained from paper companies. The Foundation is also fortunate to have a substantial endowment income.

The Response:

The Foundation has continued to grow through increased corporated membership, its total operating budget, and the number of services which it offers. While scholarships are still provided to students throughout the College of Engineering and Science, the support for faculty research and teaching has increased and is concentrated in the Department of Chemical Engineering. Interest in the field of

155

pulp and paper has increased and number of students has remained constant. This program has served as a model for six other foundations in the pulp and paper industry of various campuses.

Advice and Elements of Success:

The partnership receives its vitality as a result of 13 committees which range from fund raising to curriculum and research. These committees report to the Executive Committee, all CEO's and a strong Board of 15 Directors-at-large, according to Stanley Marshall. The fact that corporate support comes from the vice presidential level or above has been critical to this venture. The Foundation is recognized as a vital part of the university and has the support and respect from campus administrators. Also, the unique role which Marshall assumes as a liaison is an important element in the smooth operation of this program.

Marshall feels this format could be easily replicated by other industries if the support of upper-level administrators in both the educational and business sectors is present.

Contact Individual:

Stanley N. Marshall, Jr.
Executive Director
University of Maine Pulp and
Paper Foundation
Orono, ME   04469
(207) 581-7559

ENERGY MANAGEMENT

The Participants:

Mary College - A Catholic liberal arts institution which is located in Bismarck, North Dakota, and has an enrollment of approximately 980 students.

Energy Companies - Montana Dakota Utilities Company, North American Coal Corporation, Basin Electric Power Cooperative, North Dakota Association of Rural Electric Cooperatives, and the North Dakota Office of Energy Management and Conservation.

The Contact:

Mary College has a dual administrative system with the President of the College handling academic matters while the Chairman of the Board is more involved with public affairs issues. Initially, the Chairman of the Board approached the Chief Executive Officers of the energy companies with which the college hopes to establish this program. Several of those Chief Executive Officers were serving on the Board of Mary College and had informally expressed their concern that a need existed in the area of energy management. A positive attitude existed for both sectors and after six to eight months in the planning stages, the program was launched in August 1979.

156

The Venture:

This venture not only represents a traditional liberal arts college
exploring some technical alternatives, but it also serves as an in-
teresting cooperative effort among the energy-related corporations
in the area. The program is designed to meet the needs of the
rapidly growing industry in the North Dakota region.

The Area of Emphasis in Energy Management requires 24 hours of specific energy-related courses in addition to the coursework for the
Business Administration degree. Course offerings have included such
things as "Energy Economics," "Energy: Government Regulations and
Public Concerns," and "Research." One of the strengths of the program is the opportunity for students to gain practical experience
through paid internship placements each summer during their academic
programs.

Students may apply for admission to the Energy Management Emphasis
during their freshman year. Applicants for the program are selected
by a committee comprised of members from the cooperative energy companies and faculty from the Division of Business Administration.
After the students are screened by the committee, they are interviewed and selected by one of the sponsoring firms with considera-
tion given to the individual's particular interest in the industry
and the openings available with the respective firm.

Although there is a coordinator for the Energy Management Emphasis
from the Division of Business Administration, the teaching is done
by individuals from the energy companies.

The Costs:

The expenses for this program are shared evenly between the institution and the cooperating businesses. Mary College covers the
costs related to teaching and administrative details and the businesses absorb the internship expenses.

The Response:

Student interest in the program appears to be very strong since 35-
40 individuals usually apply for the approximately twelve positions
available each year. Placement for the students who have enrolled
in a portion of the program has been good thus far; however, the
first group of students to complete the entire program, as structured,
has not yet graduated.

Other programs of a similar nature exist at Mary College in the areas
of Banking, Hotel/Motel Management, and two in the Health Care field
including Health Education which emphasizes the Wellness Concept
and Emergency Care.

Advice and Elements of Success:

"A strong commitment from the very top" is essential to the success
of a venture, according to Fran Gronberg, the Coordinator for the
Areas of Emphasis programs at Mary College. She stresses the Chief
Executive Officer must view the project as something he or she believes in and will actively encourage the cooperation of the entire
staff of the corporation.

Secondly, Gronberg said educators must be willing to learn from industry in these ventures. It is important for the students to receive training in the skills that will be most useful to them. Therefore, a spirit of willingness to adapt must be present for educators and business representatives when developing the curriculum or internship experiences.

The format of such a program can obviously be duplicated in other areas as Mary College has done, if the necessary commitment exists from all parties.

Contact Individuals:

Fran Gronberg
Coordinator, Areas of Emphasis
Mary College
Apple Creek Road
Bismarck, ND   58501
(701) 255-4681, X328

Richard Espeland
Director of Personnel
The North American Coal
Corporation
Kirkwood Office Tower
Bismarck, ND   58501
(701) 258-2200

OREGON PRODUCTIVITY CENTER

The Participants:

Oregon State University - A public institution located in Corvallis with a student enrollment of approximately 17,700. The Oregon Productivity Center is associated with the School of Engineering.

Dr. Jim Riggs - Director of the Oregon Productivity Center and Head of the Industrial Engineering Department at OSU. Riggs has been associated with the university since 1962, served as chairman of the World Confederation of Productivity Science, and authored over 14 books.

Pacific Northwest Firms - Over 200 firms and agencies in the Pacific Northwest including Mail-Well Envelope Company and the Northwest Food Processors Association. Requests for information are made by firms throughout the world although actual contact work is restricted to the Northwest region.

The Contact:

Dr. Riggs has been in the Corvallis area for a number of years and has developed numerous contacts with the business community through his experience. He recognized that the projects being conducted by the Oregon Productivity Center would be directly beneficial to industry in the area. He contacted various businesses and explained the programs which were available to them and what services the Center could perform. Through some television and newspaper coverage and stories in weekly industrial publications, word spread about the Center. The contacts are now generated through general communication and as a result of the Center's reputation.

The Venture:

The following examples are some of the mechanisms used to disseminate or implement research findings of the Center:

(1) Productivity Primer - A monthly newsletter available to firms in the Pacific Northwest, at no cost, which updates new developments and available services.

(2) "Sack Lunch Special" - A one-session course lasting three hours which is usually presented at community colleges and is designed to benefit a small company. These programs are conducted by the Center staff and are offered frequently throughout the area.

(3) Seminars - Two day sessions, presented by the Center staff, designed to deal with specific issues in a firm regarding its productivity. Seminars have been conducted for such diverse groups as high school principals or vice presidents of construction companies.

(4) Research - The Center strives to develop new things which can be implemented by practitioners. Developments have included innovative computer programs and the interfirm measurement system for productivity.

(5) Interfirm Comparison - Technique employed to present an extensive review for a corporation which provides a comparison with its competitors in a confidential manner through a system of ratios and measurements.

(6) Training for Supervisors or Employees - A practical, tool-oriented approach presented by the Center staff which is designed to increase productivity and innovation among the workforce.

(7) Facilitator Training - Sessions designed for companies which have implemented approaches such as quality circles and that are seeking to further improve communications among the employees.

(8) Total Involvement Program - A minimum one-year contract with a firm in which all areas - training, communications, measurement systems, and productivity coordinators - are examined. A system of Productivity by Objectives (PBO) is introduced.

(9) PBO - A new book, to be published in early 1983, which is based on the work done by the Center on productivity in the workplace.

The Costs:

The first year, the Center received a $100,000 grant from the Economic Development Administration of the Commerce Department which covered 100% of the program costs. Recently, the Center has been awarded a $15,000 grant from Pacific Northwestern Bell. The Center hopes to obtain future funds from other corporations through similar awards. Corporations that receive services are charged accordingly; however, guidelines have been established that provide free assistance to firms with less than 100 employees.

The Response:

The Center's activity has increased tremendously over the past two years as indicated by the growth of its 1,650-name mailing list.

159

Currently, the Center is handling as much work as possible according to Riggs. He added that 10 to 12 requests per month for assistance have to be refused because they are located outside the Northwest region. Riggs would prefer to see the Center remain its present size so it can continue to work towards new developments rather than serving primarily as a consulting firm. Interest in the activities of the Center by various groups keeps Riggs busy with speaking engagements.

Advice and Elements of Success:

It is essential for an institution to determine what the people in the field actually want if a joint venture is to be successful Riggs said. He added that it is also important for educators to be willing to "get out of theory and into practice." Riggs firmly believes if an institution offers services to meet the needs of corporations, it will have no trouble making a venture work.

Contact Individuals:

Dr. Jim Riggs
Director, Oregon Productivity
Center
Oregon State University
Corvallis, OR   97331
(503) 754-4645

Peter Gartshore
Vice President
Mail-Well Envelope Company
2515 SW Mail-Well Drive
Milwaukie, OR
(503) 654-3141

Dave Clike
Executive Director
Northwest Food Processors
Association
2828 SW Corbett
Portland, OR   97201
(503) 226-2848

SUNRISE SEMINARS

The Participants:

Henry Ford Community College - a public institution of approximately 16,200 students which is located near the Fairlane Town Center Complex at Dearborn, Michigan. The Center for New Directions, established in 1976, is responsible for services to the non-traditional students including senior citizens; child care facilities; the women's resource center; community services; and continuing education.

Taubman Company - Management firm for the Fairlane Town Center, the shopping facility at which the original Sunrise Seminars were conducted, and 21 other mall complexes around the country.

The Contact:

Dr. Robert Kopecky, Director of the Center for New Directions, realized there should be numerous programs which could be beneficial to both his institution and the shopping facility with 190 businesses which was conveniently located across the street. He spoke with the local mall management as well as the tenants. The obvious

160

need seemed to be getting the mall managers together with their tenants in a positive, productive environment. The first series of Sunrise Seminars were so well received that additional series followed at other malls in Dearborn in addition to the Fairlane Complex. The national management of the Taubman Company became interessted in the program. Dr. Kopecky made a presentation before one of the companies' vice presidents. As a result of that meeting, the Sunrise Seminars are now being conducted in the 21 shopping malls managed by the Taubman Company.

The Venture:

The following description was provided by the Center for New Directions:

These seminars were developed primarily for store managers who are invited, by formal invitation, to attend the series by the center's management staff. Sunrise Seminars are held in the center prior to opening, once a week for two hours, over four consecutive weeks. Seminars are held in restaurants before they open for daily business. Both tenants and center management personnel sit together and participate as a team; consequently, the seminar series encourages teamwork.

In addition, all participants complete a "problems questionnaire" in which they list their problems in such categories as: employee problems, customer problems, career problems, and business problems. Information from this questionnaire is utilized during the seminar series and all tenant problems are addressed.

Current topics include: "Effective Retail Management--Increasing Profits, Reducing Costs," "Retail Motivation--Improving Employee Performance and Sales," and "Stress Reduction for Retailers."

The role of the local college is that of a "neutral presenter" that guides the participants through the seminar series. Open discussion among the store managers, center personnel, and college is encouraged. A professional development certificate is awarded to all managers completing the program.

The Costs:

Each seminar series costs $1,200 and is paid for by the local mall management.

The Response:

The Sunrise Seminars have been an extremely successful venture. According to Dr. Kopecky, the end result of this program is better tenant-center management relationships, increased profits and a reduction of costs, increased interaction of store managers with each other, and community involvement through the local college. Although most of the seminars have involved a local community college, the University of Nevada-Reno has successfully conducted the program. The Center for New Directions has worked with other institutions sponsoring these programs.

In addition to the complexes managed by the Taubman Company, other mall management firms have requested the program.

The Center is presently developing a new series for mall employees with an emphasis on salesmanship through communication skills; understanding and improving attitudes; and new electronic equipment training. This program will be designed for present employees and those seeking a position within the mall.

Management will pay the cost for employees while the participant seeking a position will assume his/her own expenses.

Advice and Elements of Success:

Dr. Kopecky emphasized the importance of "tailor-making" a program for a business. The institution must be willing to alter and adapt its programs to the clients'specific needs. Secondly, he urges educators to "stop and listen to what the business is saying." Finally, if an institution has not been successful with a joint venture, or has not yet attempted one, the school should not hesitate to contact someone in the field who can serve as a consultant. A strong network of educators is developing who have had positive experiences with these projects.

Contact Individuals:

Dr. Robert J. Kopecky
Director
Center for New Directions
Henry Ford Community College
Dearborn, MI   48128
(313) 271-2854

Ms. Lin Berry
Director of Special Programs
The Taubman Company
3270 West Big Beaver Road
Suite 300
P.O. Box 3270
Troy, MI   48099
(313) 649-5000

INDEXES

STATE INDEX

Alabama, 6, 7, 35, 36, 37, 38,
    39, 40, 51, 104, 245
Alaska, 32
Arizona, 42, 166

California, 1, 19, 22, 44, 67,
    69, 94, 105, 111, 112, 130,
    131, 132, 134, 140, 156, 190,
    204, 205, 232, 255, 261, 264,
    276
Colorado, 74, 108
Connecticut, 54, 72, 123, 127,
    128, 136, 148, 155, 181, 198,
    218, 219, 230, 244, 265, 266,
    284, 285

Delaware, 91, 95, 277
District of Columbia, 10, 14,
    44, 63, 81, 109, 135, 268,
    269, 270, 273

Florida, 41, 81, 138, 139, 145,
    169, 201

Georgia, 104, 115, 116, 117,
    170,

Illinois, 10, 18, 25, 31, 52,
    82, 106, 161, 184, 185, 186,
    203, 209, 234, 239, 242, 243,
    271, 281
Indiana, 11, 76, 144, 250
Iowa, 50, 153

Kansas, 45
Kentucky, 24, 221

Louisiana, 184

Maine, 224
Maryland, 14, 34, 69, 88, 91,
    103, 109, 110, 118, 119, 143,
    169, 170, 183, 220, 267, 268,
    274
Massachusetts, 2, 26, 48, 70,
    78, 126, 133, 147, 163, 186,
    202, 226, 248, 289
Michigan, 12, 23, 25, 33, 47,
    49, 58, 60, 63, 83, 99, 113,
    171, 172, 196, 249, 262, 273,
    282, 288
Minnesota, 176, 199
Mississippi, 7, 85
Missouri, 125, 146, 149, 179
Montana, 180

Nebraska, 164
New Hampshire, 182

New Jersey, 16, 55, 64, 68, 86,
    101, 102, 162, 177, 236, 263
New York, 15, 20, 43, 56, 59,
    65, 71, 96, 100, 141, 142,
    159, 165, 174, 177, 191, 214,
    235, 237, 275, 290
North Carolina, 89, 90
North Dakota, 178, 197, 199

Ohio, 4, 5, 17, 28, 29, 30, 61,
    62, 75, 79, 80, 98, 121, 122,
    164, 191, 192, 193, 195, 196,
    206, 210, 217, 222, 233, 238,
    240, 241, 246, 253, 254, 257,
    260, 279, 283
Oklahoma, 17, 18, 27, 43, 73,
    114, 154, 173, 207, 208, 216,
    258
Oregon, 158, 200

Pennsylvania, 95, 97, 107, 136,
    137, 167, 211, 212, 213, 223

Rhode Island, 168, 225, 227,
    287

South Carolina, 46, 66, 120,
    157, 194, 247

Tennessee, 8, 106, 124
Texas, 9, 12, 57, 93, 251, 252

Utah, 129

Vermont, 87
Virginia, 69, 77, 83, 92, 141,
    215, 228, 229, 231, 269, 272

Washington, 3, 256
West Virginia, 13, 24, 160, 189,
    278
Wisconsin, 21, 53, 150, 151,
    152, 175, 187, 188, 243, 280,
    286

Canada, 47
Panama, 84
Puerto Rico, 259

Louisiana State University, 184

Macomb Community College, 113
Manchester Community College,
  218
Manhattan College, 96
Marshall University, 13, 24,
  160, 189, 278
Mary College, 197
Marymount Manhattan College,
  214
Maryville,College, 8
Medgar Evers College, 142
Meridian Junior College, 85
Merritt College, 67, 94, 131,
  204, 205, 264
Michigan Technological Univer-
  sity, 25, 60
Middlesex County College, 16
Miles Community College, 180
Miramar College, 232
Mississippi State University,
  7
Montgomery College, 110
Montgomery College, Takoma
  Park, 14
Mt. Wachusett Community College,
  26
Mundelein College, 185

National College of Education,
  234
North Lake College, 252
Northeast Iowa Technical Insti-
  tute, 153
Northland Pioneer College, 42
Northwest Community College, 32

Ohio State University, 182, 200
Ohio University, 193
Oklahoma State Tech, 17, 18, 27,
  43, 73, 114, 154, 173, 207,
  208, 216
Old Dominion University, 272
Oregon State University, 158

Palomar Community College, 132
Panama Canal College, 84
Patrick Henry Community College,
  92
Peabody College, 106
Peirce Junior College, 223
Pennsylvania State University,
  136
Pennsylvania State University,
  Hazleton, 213
Pioneer Community College, 125
Prince George's Community College,
  88, 109, 118, 119, 143, 169,
  170, 183, 220, 267, 274
Princeton University, 177
Prochnow Graduate School of Bank-
  ing, 53

Quinebaug Valley Community
  College, 265

Regis College, 133
Rend Lake College, 209
Rutgers, The State University
  of New Jersey, 55, 64, 68,
  236, 263

St. Clair College, 47
San Diego Community College,
  134
Schenectady County Community
  College, 237
Seattle Community College Dis-
  trict, 3
Shippensburg State College,
  212
Siena College, 165
Simmons College, 126, 186
South Central Community College,
  219
Southeastern Massachusetts Uni-
  versity, 248
Southwestern College, 190
Spartanburg Technical College,
  120
State University College, Buf-
  falo, 56, 100
State University of New York
  Agricultural and Technical
  College, Canton, 235
Sumter Area Technical College,
  247

Texas State Technical Institute,
  9
Tri-County Technical College,
  46, 194
Triton College, 242
Tufts University, 2
Turabo University, 259
Tusculum College, 124

University of Akron, 206, 210,
  254
University of Cincinnati, 222
University of Dayton, 195
University of Evansville, 76
University of Hartford, 72,
  123, 127, 128, 136, 148, 155,
  181, 198, 230, 244, 266, 284,
  285
University of Illinois, 10
University of Illinois, Chicago
  Circle, 271
University of Maine, Orono, 224
University of Maryland, Balti-
  more County, 91
University of Maryland, College
  Park, 103
University of Massachusetts,

ORGANIZATION INDEX

Information for <u>Directory of Campus-Business Linkages</u>, 2nd edition.

Please answer every question as completely as possible. Type/print for purposes of clarity since the entry will be published as reported.

PROGRAM TITLE:

COMPANY:
    with
INSTITUTION:

COMPANY CONTACT:
  Name:
  Title:
  Department:
  Company:
  Address:
  Telephone:

INSTITUTIONAL CONTACT:
  Name:
  Title:
  Department:
  Institution:
  Address:
  Telephone:

PROGRAM DESCRIPTION/OBJECTIVES:

PROGRAM INITIATED:

LENGTH OF STUDY FOR PARTICIPANT:

LENGTH OF CONTRACT:

LOCATION:

PARTICIPANTS:
  Number:
  Type:

PROGRAM COSTS PROVIDED BY:
  Institution:
  Company:
  Participant:
  Other Source:

PRINTED MATERIALS AVAILABLE FROM:
Institution:_____   Company:_____   Both:_____

Individual completing this form accepts responsibility for information provided.

                              Name:
                              Title:

Return to: Campus-Business Linkages, American Council on Education,
Room 1B 20, One Dupont Circle, Washington, DC   20036.

NOTES